WORD AND OBJECT IN HUSSERL, FREGE, AND RUSSELL

Word and Object in Husserl, Frege, and Russell

The Roots of Twentieth-Century Philosophy

By Claire Ortiz Hill

Ohio University Press
Athens

© copyright 1991 by Claire Ortiz Hill
Printed in the United States of America
All rights reserved

Ohio University Press books are printed on acid-free paper. ∞

First U.S. paperback edition 2001 by Ohio University Press.

Library of Congress Cataloging-in-Publication Data

Hill, Claire Ortiz.
  Word and object in Husserl, Frege, and Russell : the roots
twentieth-century philosophy / by Claire Ortiz Hill.
      p.   cm. — (Series in continental thought : 17)
  Includes bibliographical references and index.
  ISBN 0-8214-1412-7
  1. Husserl, Edmund, 1859–1938. 2. Frege, Gottlob, 1848–1925.
3. Russell, Bertrand, 1872–1970. 4. Philosophy, Modern—20th
century. I. Title. II. Series.
B3279.H94H54   1991
142'.7—dc20   91-3291
                                                            CIP

A mis abuelos:
FRANK AND MARGARET MARY ORTIZ AND
THE LATE HERBERT AND LORENA HILL

One of the things I realized in 1918 was that I had not paid enough attention to "meaning" and to linguistic problems generally. It was then that I began to be aware of the many problems concerned with the relation between words and things.

BERTRAND RUSSELL, *My Philosophical Development*

Contents

PART TWO
CONCEPTUAL CLARITY

ABBREVIATIONS

In order to facilitate reference to different editions and translations I have cited chapter and section numbers rather than page numbers whenever possible.

FREGE'S WORKS

BL   *The Basic Laws of Arithmetic.* trans., M. Furth. Berkeley: University of California Press, 1964. Originally published as *Grundgesetze der Arithmetik* (Jena: Pohle, 1893).

BS   *Begriffsschrift, a formula language, modeled upon that of arithmetic, for pure thought* in *From Frege to Gödel*, ed. Jean van Heijenoort, Cambridge, Mass: Harvard University Press, 1967. Originally published as *Begriffsschrift: eine der arithmetischen nachgebildete Formelsprache des reines Denkens* (Halle: Nebert, 1879).

FA   *The Foundations of Arithmetic,* ed. and trans. J. L. Austin, Oxford: Blackwell, 1986 (2d ed. rev.). Originally published as *Die Grundlagen der Arithmetik* (Breslau: Marcus, 1884).

FR   "Review of Dr. E. Husserl's *Philosophy of Arithmetic,*" trans. by E. W. Kluge, *Mind* 81, no. 323, (July 1972): 321–37. Originally published as "Rezension von E. Husserl: Philosophie der Arithmetik, *Zeitschrift für Philosophie und philosophische Kritik* 103 (1894): 313-32.

GB   *Translations from the Philosophical Writings of Gottlob Frege,* eds. P. Geach and M. Black, Oxford: Blackwell, 1980 (3rd. ed.).

PMC   *Philosophical and Mathematical Correspondence.* Oxford: Blackwell, 1980.

PW   *Posthumous Writings.* Oxford: Blackwell, 1979.

HUSSERL'S WORKS

OCN   *On the Concept of Number: Psychological Analyses,* trans. D. Willard. *Philosophica Mathematica* 9 (Summer

1972): 44–51; 10 (Summer 1973): 37–87. Also in *Husserl: Shorter Works,* ed. McCormick and Elliston, Notre Dame: Notre Dame University Press, 1981, pp. 92–119. Originally published as *Über den Begriff der Zahl: Psychologische Analysen,* Halle: Heynemansche Buchdruckerei, 1887. I cite vol. 12 of Husserliana (The Hague: M. Nijhoff, 1970), pp. 289–338.

PA   *Philosophie der Arithmetik.* Halle: Pfeffer, 1891. Also in vol. 12 of Husserliana as cited above.

RS   "Review of Ernst Schröder's *Vorlesungen über die Algebra der Logik,*" trans. D. Willard. *The Personalist* 59 (April 1978): 115–43. Originally published in the *Göttingische gelehrte Anzeigen* (1891): 243–78. Also in Husserl's *Early Writings*: 52–91.

LI   *Logical Investigations,* trans. J. N. Findlay. 2 vols. New York: Humanities, 1970. Originally published as *Logische Untersuchungen* (Halle: Niemeyer, 1900–1901).

ILI   *Introduction to the Logical Investigations: A Draft of a Preface to the Logical Investigations (1913),* ed. E. Fink. The Hague: M. Nijhoff, 1975. First published posthumously in *Tijdschrift voor Philosophie* (Louvain) 1 (1939): 106–33, 319–39.

ID   *Ideas: General Introduction to Pure Phenomenology,* trans. W. R. Boyce Gibson. New York: Colliers, 1962 (1931). Originally published as *Ideen zu einer reinen Phänomenologie und Philosophie* in *Jahrbuch für Philosophie und phänomenologische Forschung* vol. 1 (Halle: Niemeyer, 1913).

CM   *Cartesian Meditations: An Introduction to Phenomenology.* The Hague: M. Nijhoff, 1973. Originally published as *Cartesianische Meditationen.*

RUSSELL'S WORKS

LK   *Logic and Knowledge.* London: Allen and Unwin, 1956.

ML   *Mysticism and Logic.* London: Allen and Unwin, 1950.

MPD   *My Philosophical Development.* London: Allen and Unwin, 1959.

PM   *Principia Mathematica,* vol. 1. Cambridge: Cambridge University Press, 1927–28.

PofM   *Principles of Mathematics.* London: Norton, 1903.

Preliminary
Terminological Comments

EDMUND HUSSERL and Gottlob Frege wrote at a time marked by conceptual and logical confusion. A look at the logical writings of their contemporaries makes this clear. The manner in which Husserl and Frege confronted and dealt with these confusions served as prototypes to future generations of philosophers, so both in some measure owe their success as philosophers to having been able to forge conceptual routes in a conceptual wilderness.

Both philosophers wrote in German, and the lack of sympathy between analytic philosophers and phenomenologists has meant that many pivotal philosophical terms that both Husserl and Frege used were translated into English in very different ways. This has mixed ill with the conceptual obscurity that reigned in their lifetimes. Moreover, many of the translations are bad.

In addition, when Bertrand Russell, Rudolf Carnap, and others transmitted Frege's thought to the English-speaking world, they modified his terminological innovations in a way that never harmonized with Husserl's decision to ignore them, so that (with a few notable exceptions) communication, when attempted, between the two schools of thought has been muddled. All this has had the effect of making Husserl's writings seem confused or tantalizing or maddening to readers of English sharing interests common to Russell and Frege. It is an irony that Husserl's and Frege's respective attempts and successes in redressing the philosophical ills of their time have actually obscured for later generations the origins of their thought and the nature of the exchange of ideas that took place between them.

Still, Husserl and Frege communicated, and, though they differed, each one knew what the other was talking about. It is one of the principal goals of this work to recover the terms of their exchange so as to better understand and redress the situation described above. This situation must be sorted out on the terminological and conceptual level if there is ever to be any correct understanding of the intellectual exchanges that went into the making of twentieth-century Western philosophy.

The glossary lists terms central to Husserl's and Frege's thought. Each philosopher used these terms variously to his own ends. They are far from being philosophically neutral. In general, it is well to keep in mind that Frege used different words that had basically the same meaning in everyday discourse to mark off the distinct ontological categories his distinctions were meant to trace. Husserl knew Frege's terminological innovations and did not adopt any of them. In fact, he made a point of refusing the most important ones in print, a fact I will discuss later in depth. Husserl intended to remain closer to ordinary usage and chose to continue to use synonymous terms as synonyms. For example, he did not assign special meanings to words like "sense," "meaning," "characteristic," "property," "presentation," "thought," "proper name," "common noun." He used other ways of indicating the originality of his insights.*

The following list represents an initial attempt on my part to account for the differences I describe. So that the reader can follow my argumentation clearly, I propose to use these problematic, but pivotal terms consistently as designated in the glossary, unless otherwise indicated. My choices are well reasoned, and I explain them more fully in the sections of this work that deal specifically with conceptual clarity. In order to maintain the requisite terminological consistency I have had to modify any translations that are not my own.

The reader will notice that I have translated Frege's *"Bedeutung"* by "Meaning," rather than "reference," "denotation," or any of the other words that have been tried. My choice is imperfect, but I believe it is the best way to begin to untangle the issues and to acknowledge the tradition within which Frege worked.

---

*See for example Richard Dedekind: ". . . one must not be put off by his [Frege's] somewhat inconvenient terminology." Dedekind to Keferstein, p. 101 of *From Frege to Gödel,* ed. van Heijenoort, (Cambridge, Mass.: Harvard University Press, 1967). Husserl biographer Andrew Osborn comments: "In light of the misunderstandings of the *Logical Investigations* he began to develop a terminology of his own that he hoped would be unambiguous . . . .", *The Philosophy of Husserl in Its Development.* Ph. D diss., Columbia University, 1934, p. 109. Philip Jourdain, "The Development of the Theories of Mathematical Logic and the Principles of Mathematics," *The Quarterly of Pure and Applied Mathematics* 43 (1912): 255: "Finally, Peano remarked that certain distinctions are difficult to grasp, since often two German terms, between which Frege distinguished, correspond in the dictionary to the same Italian term. These words indicated the series of subtle distinctions whose introduction into logic formed a great part of Frege's work subsequent to the Begriffsschrift." See also P. Nidditch, "Peano and the Recognition of Frege," *Mind* 72 (1963): 107.

GLOSSARY

SINN	sense
BEDEUTUNG	Meaning for Frege; meaning for Husserl because he rejected Frege's terminological innovation.
MERKMAL	characteristic
EIGENSCHAFT	property
VORSTELLUNG	subjective presentation for Frege; presentation for Husserl because he did not adopt Frege's special usage.
GEDANKE	thought
IDEE	idea
SATZ	proposition
INHALT (of a concept)	intension
INHALT (of a judgment, expression, presentation)	content
GEHALT	content (Gehalt)
INHALTSLOGIK	intensional logic
UMFANGSLOGIK	extensional logic
BEGRIFF	concept
GLEICHHEIT	equality
GLEICH	equal

In conformity with the accepted practice in analytic philosophy I place expressions standing for names, signs, words or sentences in between quotation marks so as to distinguish these linguistic phenomena from what they otherwise denote, refer to, or designate. A tree has leaves; "tree" has four letters.

ACKNOWLEDGMENTS

I HAVE MANY people to thank. I must begin by thanking J. N. Mohanty, who many years ago took an interest in my master's thesis on this subject. Though we have only managed to meet twice, briefly, during the eleven years we have been in touch, he has always been generous with his support, encouragement, and advice.

Barry Smith's keen critical insights helped me greatly improve the final product. I am grateful for his skill and support.

A very special thank you goes to Ruth Barcan Marcus for her very kind encouragement over the past years, her extremely insightful bibliographical suggestions, her interest in the final manuscript, and for the quality of her own philosophical work.

My correspondence with Allan Casebier helped me develop certain important ideas in an informal way. I am grateful to him for this opportunity.

In addition I must thank Keith Carne and Martin Hyland of the mathematics department of King's College, Cambridge, as well as Dagfinn Føllesdal, Gustav Hensel, Juan Miguel Palacios, a Madrid specialist in Kant's logic, and Siegfried Gottwald and Lothar Kreiser, logicians at Karl Marx University in Leipzig for the opportunity to discuss this work at length with them.

Because I accomplished most of the work for this book abroad, I am especially grateful to those who helped keep me informed by sending me copies of their publications and their work in progress. David W. Smith, Richard Routley Sylvan, Dallas Willard, Juan Palacios, Siegfried Gottwald, and Arthur Szylewicz sent me entire book-length works. In addition to the people I have already named, all of whom helped in this way, Tyler Burge, David Kaplan, Richard Tieszen, Jan Sebestik, Barry Stroud, David Bell, and Ivor Grattan-Guinness supplied me with articles and bibliographical references. Siegfried Gottwald kindly sent me several German articles I could not find in the West. Sheila Turcon of the Russell Archives, Samuel IJsseling, Director of the Husserl Archives in Leuven, and Herbert Spiegelberg provided me with detailed answers to my questions.

The author is particularly grateful to Jacqueline Wegmann for giving her the opportunity to use her artwork to increase the attractiveness of this book; to the sellers of rare, out of print and antiquarian books of Le Chemin des Philosophes, 1 rue des Feuillantines, Paris 75005, France for their technical assistance; and to Dr. Judy A. Miles for her photographic work.

Many years ago Bernd Magnus gave this work its initial orientation. I am grateful for the interest Guido Küng showed in my work then and for the opportunity to attend the meetings of the seminar for Austro-German philosophy organized by Barry Smith, Kevin Mulligan, and Peter Simons in those days.

I also want to thank my teacher Maurice Clavelin of the Sorbonne, whose personal integrity outshines even his intellectual integrity; I had the great happiness of working with an honorable person. I also had the pleasure of having Jacques Bouveresse as a teacher and have greatly benefited from his erudition. As my earliest mentors tutored me beyond the call of duty, I must also thank Frank and Harriet Blume, Roger and Ann Schmidt, and Edith and Steve Erickson.

Due to the constant generosity and goodness of the Benedictines of Vanves, I was able to complete most of the work for this book under ideal conditions. I am also profoundly grateful to Fathers Russman, Révillon, Diot, de Soos, and Sommet, to Sister Elizabeth Premo, to Mme Gilberte Beaux and to my friends, for their fidelity.

Finally, I want to thank the residents of Washington D.C. inner city for the support and friendship during the years in which the ideas contained within these pages were maturing. When I was a stranger you welcomed me and I will never forget it.

CLAIRE ORTIZ HILL

INTRODUCTION

IN THE FINAL MONTHS of the nineteenth century and the first months of the twentieth century Bertrand Russell experienced an intellectual honeymoon unlike any he had ever known or would ever have again. Each day he understood something he had not understood the day before. This was the period in which he was discovering Gottlob Frege's logic, which, in a confused way, he was identifying with his own. Russell's idyll ended abruptly when, studying the work of Georg Cantor, he ran across the famous paradox that bears his name (MPD, pp. 72–76; PofM, §100, 344, 500; PMC, pp. 133, 147).

It is the logical territory that Russell sighted during this honeymoon that I seek to chart here. By reconstructing the Husserl-Frege exchange and systematically filling important gaps in the scholarship on the period I seek a better understanding of how and why Frege's logical ideas lead to the troublesome paradoxes (listed in LK, pp. 59–63; PM, pp. 60–65) and how Russell managed to displace but not remove the problems.

That logical territory was quite Continental. It has been argued that Ludwig Wittgenstein's thought was permeated with Austro-German philosophical considerations.[1] That is part of the story. His teacher Russell knew German and the Austro-German intellectual scene well enough to find the isolated mathematician Frege, to correspond at length with him in German, and to uncover the fatal flaw in his logic (PMC, pp. 130–70).

Like Edmund Husserl (and unlike Frege), Russell was influenced by the realist strain in Austrian thought. He studied Franz Brentano's ideas (MPD, p. 134), and over the course of eight years he published seven articles on the work of Brentano's student Alexius Meinong.[2] Although Husserl, another Brentano student, has been credited with having brought Bernard Bolzano's work out of obscurity,[3] Russell was already citing the *Paradoxes of the Infinite* in his 1903 *Principles of Mathematics* (§ 71, 189, 285, 339), a book Husserl owned and studied.[4]

1

Russell once wrote to Husserl that for many years he had followed Husserl's work with interest and sympathy.[5] Russell in fact owned a copy of Husserl's *Philosophy of Arithmetic* and signed and dated it June 1898.[6] Russell knew the work of Hermann Lotze (PofM, §§424–31), a man whose work directly influenced both Husserl and Frege.[7] Russell's second book was on Leibniz.[8]

And Husserl was more conversant with the ideas that went into the making of analytic philosophy than has generally been suspected. Like Frege and Russell, he worked on the foundations of mathematics, and his interest in logic was bound up with his interest in mathematics. He studied under Karl Weierstrass in Berlin and was his assistant from 1883–84 (ILI, p. 37 n.) At the decisive point in his career Husserl, like Frege and Russell, was resolute in his desire to put an end to psychologism. He owned several of Russell's books on philosophy,[9] and thoroughly studied many of Frege's main writings when Russell was still in his teens. Husserl's major works contain discussions of the thought of the British empiricists. Like Russell and Frege, Husserl studied Ernst Schröder's work on symbolic logic and found it lacking (PofM, p. 26; GB, pp. 86–106; RS). Husserl freely acknowledged his debts to Gottfried Leibniz, Bolzano, and Hermann Lotze (LI, pp. 212–24; ILI, §6). He even deemed it necessary at one point to defend himself against charges that he had been unduly influenced by the latter two (ILI, §§7, 8). Husserl, however, objected to having his ideas associated with those of Meinong, which he called "confused and often contradictory" (ILI, §7), an opinion Russell came to share (LK, pp. 42 and 45).

Russell said that he first saw how Frege's logic leads to contradictions while studying the work of Cantor, one of Frege's earliest critics.[10] Cantor (who had been promoting Bolzano's *Paradoxes of the Infinite* since the 1880s)[11] was Husserl's colleague and close friend at Halle (ILI, p. 37 n. 33) while Husserl was preparing the study of Frege's logic that appears in the *Philosophy of Arithmetic*. Adolf Fränkel, in fact, thought one could see Husserl's influence on Cantor's *Contributions to the Founding of the Theory of Transfinite Numbers* published in 1897.[12] Ernst Zermelo found the paradoxes independently from Russell and in 1902 communicated with Husserl[13] concerning a similar contradiction Husserl had discussed in his 1891 review of Schröder's *Vorlesungen über die*

Algebra der Logik (RS). Husserl had in his possession and had commented upon copies of the otherwise lost correspondence between David Hilbert and Frege. [14] Husserl was Hilbert's colleague at Göttingen (PMC, p. 60) at the time Hilbert (PMC, p. 51), Russell, and Zermelo were working to find a way out of the paradoxes, [15] which were then a subject of frequent discussion between Husserl's group and the mathematicians[16]. The only thing we know now about Husserl's 1906–7 letters to Frege is what is revealed by the tantalizing remarks of Heinrich Scholz, in whose care they had been. Apparently, they concerned Bolzano and the paradox. [17] Scholz speculated that Husserl was alluding to Russell's paradox (PMC, p. 70). In 1912 and 1920 Husserl, in fact, wrote over a hundred still unpublished pages on the paradoxes of set theory in which he tried to resolve Russell's paradox. [18] Kurt Gödel [19] and Rudolf Carnap [20] studied Husserl's thought.

As a book by the founder of phenomenology that examines Frege's ideas from Brentano's empirical standpoint, Husserl's *Philosophy of Arithmetic* is both an early work of phenomenology and of logical empiricism. In it Husserl predicted the failure of Frege's attempt to logicize arithmetic and to mathematize logic two years before the publication of the *Basic Laws of Arithmetic* in 1893. I hope to show that Husserl did so in terms that would prefigure both the account Frege would give of his error after Russell encountered the paradoxes ten years later and the discussions of *Principia Mathematica*. Moreover, in locating the source of Frege's difficulties in the ambiguous theory of identity, meaning, and denotation that forms the basis of Frege's logical project and generates Russell's contradictions, Husserl's discussions indicate that these contradictions may have as serious consequences for twentieth century philosophy of language as they have had for the philosophy of mathematics.

This book is about these Austro-German roots of twentieth-century philosophy. It is mainly about the origins of analytic philosophy, about the transmission of Frege's thought to the English speaking world, and about the relevance of Husserl's early criticism of Frege's *Foundations of Arithmetic* to some contemporary issues in philosophy. It is more about Husserl the philosopher of logic and mathematics than it is about Husserl the phenomenologist, and it is principally addressed to those members of the philosophical community who, via Russell, have been affected by Frege's logic.

This makes it very different from work on Husserl and Frege that has focused on the importance of Frege's criticism of Husserl's *Philosophy of Arithmetic* and attendant issues. The goal of this book is quite the opposite. It studies the shortcomings in Frege's thought that Husserl flagged and Russell endeavored to overcome. One possible sequel to this book would be a thorough study of Husserl's successes and failures in remedying the philosophical ills he perceived all about him, but that goes beyond the scope of this work, which follows the issues discussed into the work of Russell and his successors.

In the late seventies I worked on the relationship between Husserl's theory of noema and horizons as it related to questions raised by modal logic. Early in the eighties I began wondering *why* the issues surrounding the brief hundred-year-old exchange between Husserl and Frege seemed so contemporary. There was the connection Dagfinn Føllesdal had made between Husserl and Frege's theories of meaning, Ronald McIntyre and David Smith's work on Husserl's theories and possible world semantics, and Jaakko Hintikka's work on intensionality and intentionality. There was Husserl and Frege's correspondence on sense and reference (PMC, pp. 61–70) and their talk of intensionality and extensionality (PW, pp. 123–24; PA, pp. 104–5, 134–35). I was not satisfied with the answers that were being given and felt that the issues must go deeper.

Then there were other questions. *Why* did Frege finally blame his views on identity and extensionality for the failure of his philosophical project? And were his reasons connected to recent work on identity, intensionality, and reference? Is it a mere coincidence that identity and extensionality had been the focus of Husserl's attack on Frege's theories? For a generation of philosophers reared on Quine's reservations concerning analyticity there was Husserl's intriguing comment that for years his "efforts were directed towards working out the proper concept of the analytical as opposed to the obscure Kantian one" (ILI, p. 43). Then there was the connection Frege had made between analyticity and identity. How did Russell handle Frege's problems with identity in *Principia*? Why did identity problems recur in intensional logic? What was the present king of France doing in *Principia*? *Why* was Russell's theory of definite descriptions so instrumental in showing him a way out of Frege's difficulties — the main one of which was the paradoxes? What was the connection between Frege's Basic Law V and Russell's paradox? Did the paradoxes have a message for philosophers of language? Why was Russell's encounter with Brentano's psychologism considered laudable, and Husserl's damnable? Those are some of the questions I try to answer here.

One very good reason that these questions remain is that, although more and more is coming to light about philosophy at the turn of the century, there are still big gaps in what is known about the beginnings of twentieth-century philosophy. Though good work has now been done on connections between Husserl and Frege and on the connection between Russell and Frege, the third side of the triangle, the side connecting Russell and Husserl, is virtually missing.[21] Many philosophical, linguistic, and historical factors, not to mention pride and prejudice, have conspired to mask Husserl's skill in handling the concepts that went into the making of analytic philosophy. By accident or intent, or some combination of the two, the issues have become scrambled so that today many philosophers massively treat the symptoms of a malady whose causes are buried in history. Here I try to lend clarity to some current issues in philosophy by showing *how* the problems are rooted within the basic concepts that went into the making of twentieth-century philosophy.

To do this, a way of getting back to the issues themselves had to be found. Previous appraisals of the relationship between Husserl's and Frege's thought needed to be reviewed and revised. Frege's criticism of Husserl's *Philosophy of Arithmetic* had to undergo new scrutiny. The issues surrounding Husserl's criticisms of Frege's *Foundations* had to be opened to discussion and their relevance to analytic philosophy demonstrated. Husserl's credibility as a philosopher of mathematics and logic had to be established. Frege's virulent attack on the *Philosophy of Arithmetic* is one reason why Husserl's book has been underrated, but phenomenologists have also disregarded Husserl's early work — which, for the philosophical reasons I spell out in this book, is in significant ways more relevant to the sort of philosophy usually associated with the work of Russell and the early Wittgenstein than it is to phenomenology. These are the problems I tackle in part one.

Not only are there gaping holes in the accounts of what went on in philosophy and logic at the turn of the century, the route is blocked by daunting linguistic obstacles. Although the problem has been acknowledged, additional work needed to be done to bring the point home and a practicable way of overcoming the obstacles proposed. Unraveling the linguistic issues meant painstaking analyses of what exactly Husserl, Frege, and Russell meant by words like "presentation," "idea," "intension," "content," "extension," "sense," "meaning," "concept," "object," "proposition," "thought," "empiricism," "psychologism," "sign," "signified," "analyticity," "things-in-themselves," "function," "subjectivity," and "objectivity."

That meant plunging headlong into the confusion that bedeviled turn-of-the-century logic and that had made analytic philosophy's appeal for clarity so attractive in the first place. But the prospect of what might be found on the other side remained a tantalizing one.

And then there was the problem of the English translations of the key works. How had they been done? How should they have been done? It was not just a matter of looking at how Austro-German logical considerations had been rendered into English, but also of how they could now be properly rendered in a contemporary idiom and still do justice to the insights they expressed. When Husserl made the transcendental turn, and Frege and Russell made the linguistic turn, they so fundamentally altered the way in which Western philosophy was done that philosophers persuaded of the value of Husserl's insights and the linguistically minded have not generally been able to discuss philosophy with each other in any meaningful way ever since. Analytic philosophy and phenomenology not only differ in content, but also in vocabulary and style. A book can treat two antithetical schools of thought, but it can only be written in the idiom of one of those perspectives. I have tried to write this book using the perspective of the philosophical school that has dominated in English-speaking countries in this century.

Since it was the question of Frege's influence on Husserl that opened the field to further inquiry, this book begins with the work already done on the encounter between Husserl and Frege.

Part One

Logic, Realism, and the Foundations of Arithmetic

THE ARGUMENT THAT FREGE INFLUENCED HUSSERL

DAGFINN FØLLESDAL'S 1969 article on Husserl and Frege, "Husserl's Notion of Noema," suggested new horizons in research in twentieth-century philosophy.[1] By establishing the historical link between Husserl and Frege and by showing similarities in their thought, Føllesdal's work pointed to an area of genuine exchange between the two utterly disparate schools of philosophy that have dominated Western philosophy in this century. As an increasing number of texts became available and were translated the 1970s saw a renewal of interest in the period of the exchange between the two philosophers. This occurred at a propitious moment in the evolution of analytic philosophy, for philosophers in that tradition were once again, but in a different intellectual climate, scrutinizing the very questions that had animated the exchange between Husserl and Frege.

Before Føllesdal's paper, the fact that at a decisive point in his philosophical career Husserl had read and evaluated Frege's writings had attracted little attention. It had long been known that Frege's highly critical review of Husserl's *Philosophy of Arithmetic* was published at the time Husserl was revising his opinion of the psychologism he had advocated in that book, and that Husserl's views had changed substantially by the time he published his next major philosophical work, the *Logical Investigations*. But these facts had aroused little interest.[2] In recent years, however, numerous writers have taken up the question,[3] and the subject has aroused the interest of philosophers in both traditions of philosophy.[4]

Much of the early work on the subject sought rapprochement between the two authors, emphasized superficial similarities, and argued that Frege had played a decisive role in the formation of

Husserl's mature philosophy and that certain basic elements in Husserl's thought actually derived from Frege.[5] Despite a good body of literature that presents the rather considerable evidence to the contrary,[6] that view was popular for some time.

In his 1981 book, *The Interpretation of Frege's Philosophy,* the influential Frege scholar Michael Dummett provided a good statement of the view that Frege had a decisive, positive influence in shaping Husserl's philosophy. In his essay "Idealism" he discusses the role Frege played in the shift in perspective in Anglo-American philosophy and he writes of phenomenology:

> It may be suggested that phenomenology involves a similar shift of perspective. If so, Frege deserves a large share of the credit for that, too, since it was surely the power of his attack on the psychologism of Husserl's *Philosophie der Arithmetik* of 1891 that induced Husserl to reject psychologism and, in his *Logische Untersuchungen* of 1900–1, to make his rejection of it a fundamental thesis of his philosophy.[7]

In this work Dummett also picks up the thesis that Husserl integrated Frege's insights into his mature thought "by generalizing Frege's distinctions between sense and reference to all mental acts."[8]

Authors who, like Dummett, have drawn such connections between the work of the two philosophers have most frequently turned to some combination of the following facts:

1. Husserl and Frege exchanged letters in 1891 and 1906. Each time it was Husserl who initiated the correspondence by sending Frege copies of his writings. Frege replied in kind, sending Husserl *Begriffsschrift,* Über formalen Theorien der Arithmetik," "Über den Zweck der Begriffsschrift," and "Funktion und Begriff," among other writings (PMC, pp. 60–70).

2. In addition, Husserl had copies of all Frege's writings published before 1894. There is a sharp break here. Of the eleven or so writings Frege published *after* 1894 only the *Grundlagen der Geometrie* (1903) was found in Husserl's library at the time of his death. This has been interpreted by some as a sign that Frege's criticism had some impact on Husserl's willingness to remain in dialogue with him (PMC, p. 60).[9]

3. Husserl read and appreciated Frege's writings.

a. He took serious note of the *Foundations of Arithmetic* in his *Philosophy of Arithmetic* (he in fact discusses Frege's work more thoroughly than that of any other author cited) and this was one of the rare times that it was taken seriously in print during Frege's lifetime. Frege himself attested to this writing: "Thank you especially for your *Philosophy of Arithmetic* in which you take notice of my own similar endeavors, perhaps more thoroughly than has been done up to now" (PMC, p. 63).

b. The works by Frege found in Husserl's library show signs of careful study. Husserl frequently underlined passages and wrote in the margins.[10]

c. Even when criticizing Frege's theories, Husserl recognized the integrity of his work and referred to his work in highest terms.

-1. In his July 18, 1891 letter to Frege he wrote:

> First of all, allow me to acknowledge the large amount of stimulation and encouragement I derived from your *Foundations*. Of all the many writings that I had before me when I worked on my book, I could not name another which I studied with nearly as much enjoyment as yours. Although I could not on the whole agree with your theories, I derived constant pleasure from the originality of mind, clarity and I should almost like to say, honesty of your investigations. . . . [PMC, pp. 64-65]

-2. In 1903 he described "Function and Concept" as a work which unfortunately had not received the attention it deserved from professional logicians.[11]

4. Husserl abandoned the psychologistic stance of *Philosophy of Arithmetic* between the time he wrote it and 1896.

a. In *Philosophy of Arithmetic* he had severely criticized Frege's antipsychologism. He called Frege's goal chimerical and charged that Frege's work "wanders off into sterile hypersubtilities and concludes without positive result." He said that all the work that he (Husserl) had done up to this point had but presented arguments to refute Frege's point of view (PA, pp. 130-31).

Those comments are found in the three pages of the *Philosophy of Arithmetic* that Husserl retracted in the *Logical Investigations* (LI, p. 179).

b. Husserl never published the planned second volume of *Philosophy of Arithmetic,* but in 1894 he was still referring to a second volume to which he had given the title *Investigations on the Logic of the Deductive Sciences.*[12]

c. Husserl wrote concerning his lengthy refutation of psychologism in the *Prolegomena to Pure Logic,* published with the *Logical Investigations* in 1900, that it was "in its essential content, a mere reworking of two complementary series of lectures given at Halle in summer and autumn of 1896" (LI, p. 47).

5. Frege published his highly critical "Rezension von Husserl: *Philosophie der Arithmetik*" in 1894.

6. In *Logical Investigations* Husserl refers the reader "in relation to all the discussions of the *Prolegomena*" to the preface of Frege's 1893 *Basic Laws* (LI, p. 179). In this preface Frege uses many of the same arguments and examples he was to use in his condemnation of the *Philosophy of Arithmetic* the next year.

7. W. R. Boyce Gibson has reported that in a conversation of June 24, 1928 Husserl told him that his *Philosophy of Arithmetic* met with strong opposition only from Frege and that "Frege's criticism was the only one he [Husserl] was really grateful for. It hit the nail on the head."[13]

8. Føllesdal reports that Ingarden told him that Husserl told him that Frege's critique had been decisive.[14]

9. There are certain similarities between the semantical notions Frege outlines in his famous 1892 article "On Sense and Meaning" and certain distinctions Husserl makes in the *Logical Investigations* that become central to his phenomenology.[15]

Reviewing these facts, scholars have frequently adopted positions in line with Michael Dummett's statements cited earlier. These facts though, as persuasive as they may seem, are not conclusive, as I hope to demonstrate.

The thesis that Frege influenced Husserl in a decisive way is a thesis about Husserl's intellectual development, and it has largely been Husserl scholars and those knowledgeable about philosophy on the Continent at the turn of the century that have tried to show the contrary.[16] Frege and Husserl each managed to open new eras in philosophical inquiry, and perhaps it has been difficult for their intellectual heirs to put themselves back into the intellectual climate of the late nineteenth century to determine how much each one owed to their common milieu.

Husserl and Frege shared a great deal in terms of training, background, and interests. They were both mathematicians by training who combined this training with interests in philosophy in Germany at the close of the nineteenth century. Frege was a student of Lotze, and Husserl was the student of a student of Lotze, Carl Stumpf.[17] Husserl and Frege both worked on the foundations of arithmetic in the 1880s. Their mature work would reveal a kinship to Bolzano,[18] and they both later took up problems concerning the foundations of geometry.[19] Both authors felt at odds with their contemporaries. These points of genuine and unquestionable similarity, along with those outlined in the introduction, I believe, explain both the interest each philosopher showed in the other's work and the apparent similarities in their thought. Rather than revealing Frege's influence on Husserl, though, I claim, this genuine kinship helped confuse the issues by thinly disguising key areas of divergence — for, though both Husserl and Frege worked to untie the philosophical knots that stymied their contemporaries and though they exchanged ideas and respected each other's work, they ultimately opted for distinctly different solutions to the problems that preoccupied them, and their choices determined the further course of their thought as well as that of their successors.

In the next four chapters, then, I want to argue that the body of what can be unearthed on the Husserl-Frege connection counters rather than confirms the view that Frege's work played a decisive role in the evolution of Husserl's thought. I use the results of these inquiries to piece together a picture of the development of Husserl's early thought as it relates to his contact with Frege's logic, and I hope thereby to throw present scholarship on the subject into perspective and further shed light on the intellectual endeavors that brought philosophy into the twentieth century. The first three chapters are intended to serve as an introduction to the arguments of the later chapters. Although there is quite a bit of new material in these initial chapters, J. N. Mohanty, Barry Smith, Dallas Willard, Dagfinn Føllesdal, Michael Dummett, Baker and Hacker, Ignacio Angelelli, Hans Sluga, Ronald McIntyre, David W. Smith and others have already worked that ground pretty thoroughly. Chapter 2 is complemented by chapter 7; chapter 6 complements chapter 3. Chapter 4 probably needs to be reread in light of the discussions of the second part of the book.

2

HUSSERL, FREGE, AND PSYCHOLOGISM

IN HIS WRITINGS, and in his review of *Philosophy of Arithmetic* in particular, Frege railed against an extreme form of psychologistic thinking that is akin to subjective idealism, or even solipsism. This is the view that the external world is somehow a product of the human mind, that there is no objective reality existing outside the individual human consciousness (FR, p. 336). Frege's psychologistic thinker watches the becoming and changing of subjective presentations in his "psychological peepshow" (GB, p. 127), where he considers mental images rather than the things themselves (GB, p. 126). He "changes the moon as he likes, or produces it by psychological means" (FR, p. 325). "Concepts sprout in his mind like leaves on a tree, and he thinks to discover their nature by studying their birth, defining them psychologically in terms of the human mind" (FA, p. vii). If he pays less attention to a property, it disappears. If he disregards the colors of a cat, the cat becomes colorless (FR, p. 324). "Physical and mental objects enter into his state of consciousness and become constituents of this state" (FR, p. 324). He cannot distinguish Berlin from Dresden (FR, p. 328). In the psychologistic account, Frege complains, everything is subjective. One does away with truth (FA, p. vii).

Husserl never held this view. Even in his earliest writings he affirmed the existence of things and phenomena existing outside space, time, and subjectivity (OCN, pp. 298–99; PA, pp. 16–17; LI, p. 338), of things existing in themselves whether perceived or not (OCN, p. 317; PA, pp. 45–46). In the 1880s Husserl was already arguing that certain mathematical and logical facts were unaffected by human machinations (OCN, p. 309; PA, pp. 28–29, 201–12). In *Philosophy of Arithmetic* he maintained that a number and the

experience of a number were entirely different things (PA, p. 30),
that two apples were two apples whether one was near or far, to
the left or to the right (PA, p. 35), that minds do not *make* relations (PA, p. 42). I examine these points and Frege's complaints
in depth in chapters 5 and 7, where I quote and translate most
of the Husserl texts cited in this paragraph.

Though Husserl never held the view Frege opposed so vehe-
mently, it is easy to find places in Husserl's writings that give the
impression that he did. Throughout his career he made startling
statements that, taken out of context, are damning and invite the
kinds of criticisms Frege made. For instance in *On the Concept
of Number* (his first work published in 1887) Husserl wrote:
"Numbers are mental creations" (OCN, p. 317), but then he con-
tinued saying that to call numbers pure mental creations is an exag-
geration and distortion of the real situation because our minds
do not produce numbers (ibid.; see also PA, pp. 45–46). Even in
Husserl's refutation of psychologism in the *Prolegomena to Pure
Logic,* with which he begins the *Logical Investigations* (LI, pp.
53–247), there are such statements as: "All knowledge 'begins with
experience,'" but, he qualifies his statement writing that "it does
not therefore 'arise' from experience" (LI, p. 109). There he talks
of the number five "swimming into our consciousness" (LI, p. 180).
He also says that he accepts "as obvious that logical concepts have
a psychological origin" (LI, p. 181), and he says that he does "not
doubt that logic is to a large extent concerned with our mental
states," that science "must take full cognizance of the nature of the
mental states in which research and proof take their course" (LI,
p. 181). But then he emphatically denies that *pure* logic has any
concern with mental facts or psychological laws (ibid.). The *Prolegomena* is considered to be the most antipsychologistic of
Husserl's writings and the one most directly influenced by Frege's
attack on the *Philosophy of Arithmetic.*

§1. THE INFLUENCE OF FREGE'S REVIEW

The thesis that Frege's 1894 review of the *Philosophy of Arithmetic* was the determining factor in turning Husserl away from
psychologism was first thoroughly studied by Føllesdal in his 1958

Norwegian master's thesis: "Husserl and Frege: A Contribution to Elucidating the Origins of Phenomenological Philosophy." There he concluded that Frege's critique appeared at a time when Husserl's work was entering a new phase and that it was a valuable stimulus to him just at the time when the decisive shift in his thought took place.[1]

Analyses like Føllesdal's have led many scholars to conclude that Frege's criticism dealt the decisive blow to Husserl's psychologism and that other similarities found in the writings of these two authors could be explained by the impact Frege had on Husserl's thought.[2] In his well-known book *Frege: Philosophy of Language* Michael Dummett writes of *Philosophy of Arithmetic:*

> Frege trounced the book seeing it as a classic example of 'psychologism'—the importation of psychological considerations into logic—and of abstractionism (the faulty theory of concept formation due to the British empiricists). Husserl, to his credit, accepted Frege's criticisms, and in his *Logische Untersuchungen* (1900), which contains a generous reference to Frege, made anti-psychologism one of the principal planks of his platform.[3]

The editor of Frege's posthumous writings acknowledges the popularity of this view when he writes:

> Some recent authors have tried to clear up the relationship between them. There is now general agreement that Frege's critique of the basic psychologistic attitude in *Philosophy of Arithmetic* prepared the way for Husserl's rejection of psychologism and may have even occasioned it. Some even regard Frege as the true author of the refutation of psychologism. [PMC, p. 60]

Nevertheless, those who would defend this view must tangle with the fact that Husserl only mentions Frege twice in the lengthy *Logical Investigations* (pp. 179, 292; both mentions are brief and one is negative), while giving ample credit to Lotze and Bolzano as the decisive figures in his turn from psychologism. Husserl went even so far as to write concerning his correspondence with Frege:

> I never got to know Frege personally and I no longer remember the occasion for our correspondence. At the time he was

generally considered as an outsider who had a sharp mind but produced little or nothing, whether in mathematics or in philosophy. [PMC, p. 61]

Husserl, himself, in fact, provided a more plausible account of how he came to reject psychologism and to whom he owed his intellectual debts that conflicts with this assessment.

§2. THE QUESTION OF DATES

First, we need to take a closer look at the dates involved. Most scholars have placed Husserl's break with psychologism somewhere between 1891, the year *Philosophy of Arithmetic* was published, and 1896, the year Husserl cites for the writing of the *Prolegomena,* where he fights his earlier psychologism.[4] As late as 1982 Føllesdal was arguing that the change took place between 1894 and 1896.[5] These dates need to be pushed back.

First of all, Husserl's *Philosophy of Arithmetic* was published in 1891, but it was not written in 1891. It is the reworking and expansion of the *Habilitationsschrift* entitled *On the Concept of Number* that Husserl presented at Halle in 1887. In that work he does not cite Frege's 1884 *Foundations of Arithmetic,* which he apparently did not know before 1887.[6] A mere glance at the index of his 1891 book, however, shows that Husserl had by that time acquired a profound knowledge of Frege's book.

In September 1906 Husserl would write:

> I read a good deal in the *Philosophy of Arithmetic.* How immature, how naive and almost childish this work seemed to me. It was with good reason that my conscience bothered me when I published it. In actual fact I was already beyond it when I published it. It basically stemmed from the years 86/87. I was a beginner. . . .[7]

In May 1891 he had written to Meinong:

> The work [PA] is largely a work of earlier years and is in so many respects the result of adverse circumstances and restrictions that it will hardly give the impression of being a harmonious balanced whole.[8]

In order to complete his studies under the direction of Carl Stumpf (who had studied under both Brentano and Lotze),[9] Husserl left Brentano in 1886. In Halle, under Stumpf's influence, Husserl became increasingly interested in Platonic ideas; he drew progressively away from Brentano's ideas (ILI, pp. 34–35), finally finding that he had to refuse much of what he had learned from him (LI, pp. 856–69). Brentano had managed to draw Husserl to philosophy, but the mathematician in Husserl ultimately resisted many of Brentano's teachings.[10] Husserl would dedicate the *Logical Investigations* to Carl Stumpf.

Georg Cantor was also on the faculty at Halle during those years,[11] and he and Husserl became close friends (ILI, p. 37). In his 1885 review of Frege's *Foundations,* Cantor had, in the name of logical purity, praised Frege's eschewal of psychologism and decried his recourse to extensions. Frege, he complained, had "unfortunately completely failed to take into account the fact that the extension of a concept is generally completely indeterminate; only in certain specific cases is it determinate," Cantor maintained.[12] Cantor was also at that time promoting Bolzano's work on the paradoxes of the infinite.[13]

The earlier date should, then, be set back to 1887. In 1887 Husserl's position was definitely psychologistic. We know that he had misgivings about it in the years that immediately followed and that during that time he was impressed by his reading of Frege's *Foundations.*

The later date, the point at which Husserl's break with psychologism can be said to have been complete, is more problematic. The authority most often cited for establishing it at 1896 is Husserl's introduction to the second edition of the *Logical Investigations.* It is less well known, though, that this is a shortened, reworked version of another introduction he wrote in the same year, but which was not published until after his death (ILI). In the longer version Husserl provides a detailed account of his movement away from psychologism. Concerning his refutation of psychologism in the *Prolegomena* he begins as he does in the final version (cited in chapter 1). The arguments, he says, were drawn from a series of university lectures given in Halle, but he dates them 1895, rather than 1896. He concludes by writing, "The only section that was really freshly composed was the concluding chapter, whose thought-content, however, stems entirely from the older logical-mathematical studies, on which I had not worked any further since 1894." (ILI, pp. 35–36).

The examination of Husserl's published writings of the period shows that notions that are central to his phenomenology, and in conflict with the kind of psychologism he espoused in *Philosophy of Arithmetic,* were in place before 1894. J. N. Mohanty points this out in a 1974 article on Husserl and Frege:

> the basic change in Husserl's mode of thinking which by itself could have led to the *Prolegomena* conception of pure logic had already taken place by 1891. . . . If pure logic is defined in the *Prolegomena* in terms of the concept of ideal objective meanings, then already the 1891 review of Schröder's work contains this concept. If the major burden of Frege's 1894 review of *PA* is the lack of distinction, in that work, between the subjective and the objective, between *Vorstellung* and *Begriff,* then Husserl already had come to distinguish between *Vorstellung* meaning and object in his 1891 review.[14]

Mohanty's conclusions corroborate Husserl's own account and provide a likely explanation of why the "largely completed" (PA, p. ix) second volume of the *Philosophy of Arithmetic* did not come out within a year of the first volume, as the author promised it would. That in the early 1890s Husserl was already working on what would become the *Logical Investigations* and no longer continuing in the vein of the *Philosophy of Arithmetic* is reinforced by the fact that portions of Husserl's 1894 article "Psychologische Studien zur elementaren Logik" were directly incorporated into the *Logical Investigations.*[15] Husserl himself wrote that the *Logical Investigations,* and logical investigations 3 and 5, in particular, had been influenced by courses he gave in 1891–92.[16]

I believe, then, that the change took place between 1887, the date "On the Concept of Number: Psychological Analyses" was published, and 1891, the date *Philosophy of Arithmetic, Psychological and Logical Investigations* was written. In 1891 Husserl was already expressing his dissatisfaction with his work, and surely by 1894 he was well into the revision of the psychologism of his earliest philosophical endeavors, so that his conversion, if it is to be linked with Frege at all, is more likely linked with Husserl's encounter with the *Foundations* than with a reaction to Frege's critical review. By 1894 Husserl was no stranger to the kind of attack Frege launched upon him there.

§3. Husserl's account

In the posthumously published introduction cited above, Husserl himself provides a highly plausible account of his turn from psychologism in which he excludes all mention of Frege. He explains how during the ten years of hard solitary work he spent in preparing the *Logical Investigations* he broke both with tradition and with the philosophy of his time:

> I lost that intimate contact with the contemporary literature and, hence, with the very readership to which I was to address myself. . . . I still saw all around me only undeveloped, ambiguously iridescent problems and deep-delving but unclear theories. Weary of confusions and fearing lest I sink into the ocean of endless criticism, I felt myself compelled . . . to risk the attempt of starting someplace on my own. . . . [ILI, pp. 16–17]

Husserl does not single out Frege from among his contemporaries, and there is no indication that he did not class him with the rest. This could explain why his collection of Frege's works stops at 1894.

Husserl discusses the development of his thought in depth in this second introduction. He says that from 1886 to 1895 his studies were primarily confined to the

> very comprehensive but still limited areas of formal mathematics and formal logic. The dissociation from psychologism takes place first of all on the basis of studies in this area. . . . This transformation was prepared by the study of Leibniz and by the considerations occupying me ever anew of the sense both of the distinction between truths of reason and truths of fact and also at the same time of Hume's . . . "relations of ideas" and "matters of fact." I became keenly aware of the contrast between this latter distinction and Kant's distinction between analytic and synthetic judgments, and this became important for the later positions which I took. [ILI, p. 36]

It was Lotze, he claims here, and in the *Logical Investigations* (p. 224), that had the decisive influence on him. To the list of thinkers who influenced Husserl that Osborn compiled, Husserl himself added, writing in the margins of his personal copy, the name Lotze.[17] Brentano and Cantor had drawn his attention to Bolzano's writings (ILI, p. 37), and now he accidentally came across one of Bolzano's books in a bookstall.[18] Initially Bolzano's ideas had seemed strange, incomprehensible, and phenomenologically naive to him, but his assimilation of Lotze's philosophy gave him the key to understanding Bolzano. He writes:

> If previously for me, as indeed for all his earlier readers, Bolzano's *Sätze an sich* seemed to be mythical entities suspended between being and not-being, it all of a sudden became clear to me that this was fundamentally a completely understandable conception the value of which had been underestimated by traditional logic, i.e. *Sätze an sich* were none other than what was, in everyday, ideal objectifying language, called the *Sinn* of an assertion and were what was declared to be one and the same when one says of different people that they affirm the same thing.[19]

These propositions, ideas, and truths "in themselves" were not, however, meanings of "ideal" entities, and Husserl believed that Bolzano would have firmly rejected the idea of a pure logic as Husserl conceived it (ILI, p. 48).

Husserl had, by his own account, long seen serious problems with psychologism. The work of Lotze and Bolzano was decisive in showing him a path out of psychologism and into the realm of ideal meanings, which would become the proper domain of phenomenology. Those who have held that Frege had a decisive impact on Husserl's thought have not adequately explained away Husserl's own explicit and quite plausible description of his intellectual progress during those crucial years. Proper attention paid to his explanations would have made unnecessary much of the discussion of these matters that has taken place in the literature in recent years.

§4. PSYCHOLOGICAL VERSUS TRANSCENDENTAL ANALYSES

In his 1874 masterwork, *Psychology from an Empirical Standpoint*,[20] Brentano formulated his famous thesis of intentionality:

> Every mental phenomenon is characterized by . . . reference
> to a content, direction toward an object. . . . In presentation
> something is presented, in judgment something is affirmed
> or denied, in love loved, in hate hated, in desire desired, and
> so on.[21]

Brentano's psychological analyses were not finally adequate to Husserl's ambitious goals. But the intentionality of mental acts Brentano preached eventually opened Husserl the way to the deeper analyses of the consciousness and its objects that would be the stuff of phenomenology (CM, §17).

Throughout his life Husserl maintained that philosophy began in subjectivity. "Without a doubt," he affirmed in *Cartesian Meditation,* "at the beginning science can posit nothing but the ego and what is included in the ego" (CM, §13). But valid knowledge could only be possible if there was a link between the consciousness and what lay outside it. So after his foray into psychologism, Husserl's big question became, "How can this business going on wholly within the immanency of conscious life acquire Objective significance? How can evidence (clara et distincta) claim to be more than a characteristic of consciousness within me?" (CM, §40). How do the natural order and the realm of the objective a priori interrelate? Brentano's theory of intentionality supplied Husserl with this bridge between the mind and objective reality. Philosophers had to begin in subjectivity, but that was not where they wanted to go. Intentionality pointed the way out of the mind to things.[22]

As Husserl developed his phenomenology he began to prescribe a series of techniques by which, he believed, one could reach out beyond (CM, §20), transcend isolated subjective processes and the vicissitudes of ordinary experience of an everchanging world, and so gain access to the objective domain, the realm of transcendental knowledge. These rigorous mental exercises were designed to purge the philosopher of anything prejudicial to scientific objectivity.

Psychological analyses fall short in three ways that concern us here. First, Husserl decided, they were naive because they involve a relatively uncritical acceptance of the information the knower receives from experience. They do not force him to leave behind his presuppositions, beliefs, prejudices, or personal tendencies, needs, or desires to interpret phenomena in particular ways.

Second, they are superficial because they do not take sufficient note of the myriad mental acts in which judgments are formed, determinations are made and corrected, hypotheses are developed, logical connections are established, and so on. The psychologistic thinker takes his cognitive acts to be much more transparent than they possibly could in fact be.

Third, psychological analyses are shortsighted, according to Husserl, because they only provide information about an object as it is given in a certain way in the here and now. Most of what could be truthfully predicated of any object eludes the grasp of these analyses, which do not adequately account for variability, for potential or actual changes that may intervene, or may have intervened, to alter, even radically, the conclusions to be drawn.

So Husserl worked out a series of procedures designed to overcome these shortcomings and to produce deep, comprehensive analyses that could provide access to truly objective knowledge. The philosopher was to start with what Husserl called the *epoche* and the reductions.[23] Once intentionality has laid out the whole vast world of the consciousness and its objects, the *epoche* enters as a sort of purging process by which one can gain access to the real of "pure" consciousness.

Husserl considered the *epoche* and the attendant reductions to be a radicalization of the systematic doubt Descartes advocated (CM, §§ 1, 2, 3). To perform the *epoche* I must put the natural world and everything I have learned about it from the natural sciences "in parentheses." I neither affirm nor deny the world's existence. Nor do I doubt it. The world is just for me something that *claims* being. I refrain from believing any theory or thesis, from deciding anything, from forming my judgment whatsoever concerning the spatio-temporal order as viewed naturally and as known through experience, since all these activities presuppose belief in the world's existence, or beliefs about its meaning. As a radically meditating philosopher, there is no longer any science that I accept, no natural world, no people or animals. Once I have done this I have broken into the transcendental attitude. Now I apprehend myself as ego with my own pure conscious life. Everything that previously existed for me in straightforward consciousness is now taken exclusively as phenomenon, as a sense meant (CM, §44).

My regard is focused. I am now prepared to move on to the next task: the strict delineation and explication of the unmapped, and largely overlooked, workings of the human consciousness.

Phenomenological analyses are guided by the basic conviction that objects are not really known in the simple transparent way we imagine they are (CM, §20). In phenomenology, the intentional object acts as "transcendental clue" unlocking the way "to the infinite multiplicities of possible *cogitationes* that in a possible synthesis bear the intentional object within them . . . as the same object meant" (CM, §21).

The human mind can search through time and form hypotheses about what might be, but it is not just then. It can integrate what the different senses experience now with knowledge acquired in the past. It can sort through data, compensate for errors and discrepancies, entertain contradictory propositions. It can retrieve what it has tossed out, correct itself, study itself, and review its findings at will. It can skip illogically through facts and time. It ferrets through evidence, weighs possibilities, delves back into its memory, synthesizing its findings and providing unity as it gleans objective knowledge from a fluctuating world.

The various ways in which the mind positions itself in relation to objects to give them meaning Husserl called the noeses. He called the objects correlated to these noeses the noemata (noema in the singular). In intentional acts noeses are inseparably united with their corresponding noemata.

Further inquiry uncovers another fundamental trait of intentionality: each subjective process has a "horizon" of potential subjective processes that are "implicit" and "predelineated" within it. Every intentional act is "transcending." It posits more about its object than is actually given, or can be given at the time (CM, §55). Noeses and noemata are inextricably bound together, and so each actual intentional object also contains with it an infinite horizon of potential things that might be predicated of it:

> . . . there belongs to every external perception its reference from the "genuinely perceived" sides of the object of perception to the sides "also meant"—not yet perceived, but only anticipated. . . . Furthermore the perception has horizons made up of other possibilities of perception, as perceptions that we could have, if we *actively directed* the course of percep-

tion otherwise: if for example, we turn out eyes that way instead of this, or to one side . . . to every perception there
always belongs a horizon of the past. . . . [CM, §19]

For example, I usually say I can see the dome of the Pantheon
from my window. But in fact I only see part of a dome. From the
side, one only ever sees half of any dome. I do not strictly perceive
the structure underneath the dome part, but my memory supplies
me with a mental image of it. Even if I had never seen the whole
building, various experiences I have had inform me that dome parts
do not float freely in the sky above Paris. Much else that I do not
strictly perceive is "there" too. Earnestly pursuing my reflections
on the dome I realize that every bit of information I acquire about
it through successive intentional acts opens up new vistas and
possibilities of knowledge (CM, §55). "Evidently actual, intellec-
tually necessary, inconsistent, thinkable, probable, and the like—all
these are characteristics that occur within the realm of my consciousness as characteristics of the intentional object in question"
(CM, §40). Each fact I acquire points to other possible facts. I always
have before me an open undetermined horizon that I must go about
"explicating systematically by conversion into possible fulfilling
evidence, and then incessantly explicating in like manner the new
horizons that incessantly arise within the old" (CM, §29).

All this takes place "according to a definite style" (ibid.). My
experiences are governed by certain rules. For example, though
I face an "infinity of actualities and potentialities, not all possible
types are compossible, and not all compossible ones are compossible in just any order" (CM, §36).

> If one keeps no matter what object fixed in its form or
> category and maintains continuous evidence of its identity
> throughout the change in modes of consciousness of it, one
> sees that no matter how fluid these may be, and no matter
> how inapprehensible as having ultimate elements, still they
> are by no means variable without restriction. They are always
> restricted to a set of *structural types* . . . as long as the objec-
> tivity remains intended as *this* one and as of this kind, and
> as long as, throughout the change in modes of consciousness
> evidence of objective identity can persist. [CM, §21]

The systematic explication of these structural types is the task
of transcendental theory of the transcendental constitution of the

object. Progressively the phenomenologist comes to understand

> *how,* within the immanency of conscious life and in thus and
> so determined modes of consciousness belonging to this in-
> cessant flux, anything like *fixed and abiding objective* unities
> can become intended and, in particular, how this marvelous
> work of "constituting" identical objects is done. [CM, §20]

An example can help make clear how Husserl's noetic-noematic analyses operate in a way that will pertain to the discussions of the later chapters. Perhaps it can also make those practices seem less arcane.

§5. THE RADICALLY MEDITATING PHILOSOPHER MEETS NAPOLEON

Suppose, as Husserl's radically meditating philosopher, I can step back in time to go off in search of Napoleon in exile on St. Helena. I have only a reproduction of David's portrait of the emperor to guide me. Natives of the island lead me to an emaciated man known to them as Boney. He is the only person who could possibly fit the description I have given them.

I am apparently now in the presence of the man who, in the "natural attitude," had been the object of my myriad intentional acts. He had been the goal of my quest, the stuff of my expectations, the object of my awe. It was he I had thought about, dreamed of, studied, sought.

Reining in my emotions I shift into the transcendental attitude: the existence of a world, and accordingly of this dying man, is "parenthesized." I am left with my pure stream of consciousness replete with the objects of my intentional acts, *as* these objects exist for my consciousness.

Now I bracket out the infinite number of things that might otherwise capture my attention. I focus on the complex bundle of sensations associated with this strange figure sitting before me. I am bombarded with sensory impressions, recollections, expectations, valuations, and so forth. Facts stored in my memory mingle freely with present sensations and impressions. I recall that Napoleon was both defeated and victorious, married to both Josephine and Marie Louise, but not a bigamist. I mentally account for these disparate facts, and also for the difference between reality and my expectations, between the reality I perceive and my portrait.

Then come the inevitable questions. Is this defeated man the victor of Jena? Is this prisoner the emperor of France? Is this emaciated man the subject of David's portrait? I find I can truthfully predicate heterogeneous and even contradictory things of my *intentional* object, things that I could not simultaneously predicate of an object that was only given to me in a particular guise at a particular point in time.

Husserl's noetic-noematic techniques afford me this freedom and flexibility. Information culled by the noeses is regulated by the information provided from the noematic side, which acts as a continuous check on what the mind can do. Boney is "given continuously as an objective unity in a multiform and changeable multiplicity of manners of appearing" (CM, §17), which is more than an incoherent sequence of subjective processes. Though Husserl has advised me to exercise my imagination abundantly, the information I garner in my intentional acts is constantly monitored, refined, modified, held in check by entirely objective factors. These factors may be material and actualized, or true outside the confines of the present moment — that is, true of Napoleon in the past, but not true of him now.

As I use my intelligence to sift through all the possible, true, false, and apparently and genuinely contradictory things predicable of this man who could be Napoleon, I begin weaving the information I am culling into a noematic conception of Napoleon that is flexible enough to weather change, permanent enough to withstand the assaults of time. This conception of Napoleon is not exactly the object immediately present to my senses because little can now be said of it that was true of the famed emperor. The noema corrects for that discrepancy and accounts for the superficially misleading information of the present moment. It adjusts any of my subjective appraisals that do not accord with the facts. It is abstract enough to provide continuity and unity in spite of rupture and disparity. It is ideal in that it is not found some place in space and time. It is composed of material gleaned from appearances, but it is not the appearances themselves. Though it is the result of my mental activity, it is conditioned and determined by the demands of realities existing independently of me. I merely acted as an agent—a midwife, Socrates would have said. I conclude that the man sitting before me is not *identical* to the man in the portrait I have, and that these differences are not in my head. But my noetic-noematic analyses indicate that Boney and Napoleon are the same man. By making this identification I have increased mankind's store of knowledge about Napoleon's fate.[24]

3

SENSE, MEANING, AND NOEMA

HUSSERL AND FREGE BOTH studied language in its relationship to what it describes. Their inquiries led them to recognize the importance of distinguishing between the expressions used to describe objects and the objects themselves. They both distinguished the essentially subjective elements presumed to have a bearing on meaning from the abstract, objective, intensional component in meaning by whose agency they held truth was passed on from generation to generation. These distinctions were not original to either of them. They merely adopted and used to their own ends variations of distinctions that had been drawn earlier[1] and were in use at the time. They did so quite independently of each other, as a look at their earliest writings shows. Neither Husserl nor Frege reduced the intensional element in meaning to its linguistic expression, nor did either consider it to be analogous to any mental image.

Frege sought to apply these distinctions systematically. In his writings he continually deplored the mixing of concept and object, thought and subjective presentation, sense and denotation. These differences must be respected, he argued, if the errors of psychologism, empiricism, formalism, and subjective idealism are to be avoided. He harshly criticized his contemporaries for their failure to respect the objective order. The scientist is engaged in the pursuit of truth; he must respect what is objective and rigorously separate it from all intrusions from the outside. In the preface to the *Basic Laws of Arithmetic* Frege is particularly explicit about this, but he makes analogous points in *Foundations* and throughout his other writings as well. His reviews of his contemporaries' works (Husserl's among them) frequently turn on his perception that they had not respected these differences.

For Husserl, however, the logico-linguistic realm was but a stepping stone to an infinitely vaster realm of inquiry. So after devoting many years to the study of mathematics, logic, and language, he undertook to do something that was radically different from anything Frege and his successors ever tried, or ever considered worth doing: he "plunged into the task of laying open the infinite field of transcendental experience" (CM, p. 31). Not just interested in the meaning of linguistic expressions, Husserl made it his life's work to investigate as thoroughly and painstakingly as humanly possible the meaning conferred upon objects by the intentional acts of consciousness. To explain how the human mind confers meaning on its objects, Husserl posited the presence of structures analogous to the intensional "meanings" used by his contemporaries and predecessors in their discussions of the meanings of words. These structures were the noemata discussed in the previous chapter.

§1. IDENTIFYING SENSES AND NOEMATA

In his influential 1969 paper on Husserl's notion of the noema, Føllesdal points out that Husserl considered his noemata to be a generalization of the notion of meaning to the realm of all acts.[2] He cites several texts to substantiate his claim and compares and contrasts Husserl's theory with Frege's theory of intensional meaning.

Føllesdal's article itself is conservative and his claims are modest. And the article has played an invaluable role in making Husserl's thought accessible to those trained in analytic philosophy. Though other interpretations are possible, there is good textual evidence for most of Føllesdal's claims.[3] Big problems arise, however, when Husserl's noemata become too closely identified with Frege's senses, and this was one of the consequences of Føllesdal's article. Misconceptions about the role Frege played in Husserl's rejection of psychologism encouraged exaggerations about Frege's influence on Husserl.

Ronald McIntyre and David W. Smith have stated that

> Husserl's notion of noematic Sinn is basically the same as Frege's notion of meaning or sense (Sinn) and that noematic Sinne play essentially the same role in Husserl's theory of intentionality that senses play in Frege's theory of reference.[4]

Jaakko Hintikka has claimed that "Husserl's theory is both historically and systematically a further development of Frege's views."[5]

These philosophers further postulate analogies between Husserl's
horizon analysis and work done in possible worlds logic. They
argue that Husserl's work on noemata and horizons can provide
clues as to how to answer questions posed by intensional contexts
and by the logic of propositional attitudes in particular. I do not
agree at all with their conclusions, but I hope I can show in later
chapters why such analogies can be made and carried as far as
they have. In this chapter I need to show where the analogies
between Husserl's and Frege's notions of meaning obtain, and
where they break down. First, we need to review what Frege and
Husserl each had to say about linguistic meaning.

§2. Word, Object, and Meaning in Frege

Frege believed that it was "one of the tasks of philosophy to break
the domination of the word over the human spirit and to free
thought by laying bare misconceptions arising from the imprecise
use of words" (BS, p. 7). His work to perfect scientific language
and to supply secure foundations for arithmetic ultimately led him
to distinguish between what he called the sense and the Meaning
of linguistic expressions. Normally, he noted, words, signs, combinations of signs, expressions, and so on denote or refer to
something, to an object in the broadest sense of the word. In the
early 1890s Frege began to call the denotation or reference of an
expression its *Bedeutung,* Meaning (GB, pp. 29, 56–78).

There are many possible ways in which a word can relate to
an object, Frege observed. Many words or other signs may denote
a single object (BS, §8). The classic example Frege provides is
that of the expressions "the evening star" and "the morning star"
(GB, pp. 57, 62). Both these expressions denote the same planet,
otherwise called Venus. Because these expressions have the same
reference they can generally be substituted for each other without
changing the truth or falsehood of the statements in which they
figure (GB, pp. 64–65).

But, as Frege was quick to notice, the statement "the morning star is identical to the evening star" is not trivial. It is not a mere tautology of the form a=a. It is informative (of the form a=b) and as such may "contain very valuable extensions of our knowledge" (GB, p. 56). So as early as 1879 Frege was writing that the "existence of different names for the same content . . . is the very heart of the matter if each is associated with a different way of determining the content" (BS, §8). These different ways of determining the content became, in Frege's odd vocabulary, senses *(Sinne)*.

For Frege a single object may have many senses and may be denoted in many different ways, but not every word that has a sense has a denotation. One example Frege gives is that of "the celestial body most distant from the earth" (GB, p. 58). For him, these words have a sense, but it is "very doubtful if there is also a thing they Mean." Another example is the expression "the least rapidly convergent series," which, he writes, "has a sense but demonstrably there is nothing that it Means. . . ." (ibid.) That languages contain expressions that fail to designate an object is due to an imperfection in language that would not arise in a logically perfect language (GB, pp. 69–70). Studies of Frege's reflections on the sense and reference of expressions have played a preeminent role in analytic philosophy.

§3. WORD, OBJECT, AND MEANING IN HUSSERL

Husserl also accorded an important role to the study of language and logic. "Everyone knows," he wrote in the *Logical Investigations,* "how readily and how unnoticeably an analysis of meaning can be led astray by grammatical analysis" (LI, p. 257). "We all know that words mean something, and that, generally speaking, different words express different meanings" (ibid.). But the problems surrounding the correspondence between words and what they mean are apparent enough to make "us naturally tend to seek logical distinctions behind expressed grammatical distinctions" (LI, p. 258).

Many sections of Husserl's first Logical Investigation remind one of Frege's reflections on language. For example, Husserl writes, "Each expression not merely says something, but says it *of* something: it not only has a meaning, but refers to certain objects" (LI, p. 287). This relation can hold "in the plural for one and the same expression. But the object never coincides with the meaning" (ibid.). "Both," he maintained, however, "only per tain to an expression in virtue of the mental acts which give it sense" (ibid.). Frege categorically refused any analysis of meaning in terms of individual mental operations.

It is necessary, Husserl argued, to distinguish between meaning (Frege would say sense here), and object (Frege would say Meaning) because "a comparison of examples show us that several expressions may have the same meaning but different objects, and again that they may have different meanings but the same object. There is of course also the possibility of their differing in both respects and agreeing in both" (ibid.).

Husserl gives "the victor at Jena" and "the vanquished at Waterloo," and "the equilateral triangle and the equiangular triangle" as examples of names that differ in meaning but name the same object. Though each of these expressions has a distinctly different meaning, the first two expressions refer to the same person, and the second two to the same geometrical configuration (LI, p. 288). Conversely, two expressions may have the same meaning, but a different objective reference. "Whenever a word has *one* meaning," Husserl further observes, "it also names *one* object" (ibid.).

Such examples led Husserl

> to regard the distinction between an expression's meaning and its power to direct itself as a name to this or that objective correlate — and of course the distinction between meaning and object itself — as well established . . . an expression only refers to an objective correlate *because* it means something, it can be rightly said to signify or name the object *through* its meaning, an act of meaning is the determinate manner in which we refer to our object of the moment, though this mode of significant reference and the meaning itself can change while the objective reference remains fixed. [LI, p. 289]

Any deeper understanding of these relationships can only be had through undertaking phenomenological analyses, Husserl believed.

§4. HISTORICAL CONSIDERATIONS

Although there has been considerable debate about what Frege's *Sinn/Bedeutung* distinction actually is and what it can do for us now, philosophers as divided as to the answers to these questions as Quine, Carnap, Putnam, Church and Føllesdal all agree that, to the degree to which it resembles the old distinctions between comprehension or intension and extension, depth and breadth, or denotation and connotation, the *Sinn/Bedeutung* distinction has been around for a long time.[6] In particular, Bolzano had drawn and applied the distinction in a way that moved Husserl's and Frege's contemporaries to point out the similarities in the ideas of these three thinkers,[7] similarities that Føllesdal also acknowledges.[8] Husserl dedicates several pages of the *Logical Investigations* to discussing the importance Bolzano's *Wissenschaftslehre* had for him, and after *Logical Investigations* was published, Husserl felt the need to take up the pen to defend himself against charges that he had unjustly borrowed from Bolzano.[9] The examination of Husserl's personal copy of the *Wissenschaftslehre* (now in the Husserl library in Leuven) reveals that Husserl wrote in the margins and underlined those very passages in which Bolzano outlines and discusses the distinctions in question.[10] Husserl even wrote: "Presentation means for Bolzano 'presentations-in-themselves' *(Vorstellungen an-sich)*, which correspond to our concept of meaning *(Bedeutung)*" (LI, p. 499 n. 1). The fact that Husserl himself pointed out the kinship between his own ideas and those of Bolzano holds, I contend, more weight than speculation about some debt owed to Frege.

In his first letter to Husserl, Frege himself acknowledged the presence of the three-way view of meaning in Husserl's *Philosophy of Arithmetic*. He notes that Husserl conceives the relations among these notions differently than he does and he takes care to outline and discuss the differences (PMC, pp. 63–64). In so doing he presents the view of the matter that he would express in greater detail a year later in his famous article.

That Husserl's concerns already paralleled Frege's as early as 1891 is shown in this passage from the *Philosophy of Arithmetic:*

> Each abstract name has a twofold meaning. On one occasion it serves as a name for the abstract concept as such. On another occasion as the name of any object that falls under this concept. It designates the concrete thing via the abstract contained in this concrete thing or related to it. Language often operates with abstract names and uses them to designate concrete things and processes. [PA, p. 151]

The only time that Husserl discussed Frege's 1892 distinction in print, it was with disfavor (LI, p. 292). That Husserl ultimately turned a deaf ear on Frege's distinction between sense and Meaning while continuing to respect the differences between expression, meaning, and object in his own way is seen in this passage from the *Logical Investigations.* In reference to Frege's article, and by extension, to his letter, Husserl wrote:

> 'Meaning' is further used by us as synonymous with 'sense.' It is agreeable to have parallel, interchangeable terms in the case of this concept, particularly since the sense of the term 'meaning' is itself to be investigated. A further consideration is our ingrained tendency to use the two words as synonymous, a circumstance which makes it seem a rather dubious step if their meanings are differentiated, and if (as G. Frege has proposed) we use one for the meaning in our sense, and the other for the objects expressed. [LI, p. 292]

§5. TERMINOLOGICAL CONSIDERATIONS

Frege managed to change the history of logic, mathematics, and philosophy, but I think that the extent to which his senses and Meanings were terminological innovations has been underestimated. Frege adapted a view of meaning in use among his contemporaries. He tried to express it in his symbolic language and integrate it into his work on the foundations of arithmetic. In his quest for clarity he used the German language in innovative ways. He liked to distinguish between words normally taken to be synonymous, so, beginning in the 1890s, he chose to use two common German words for meaning to distinguish between the intensional and extensional meanings of terms but, conceptually speaking, the distinction is that used by his contemporaries and by him in his earlier works.

Since the basic distinction between intension and extension was in standard use among the logicians that Frege studied, Frege could not have considered it original to himself. He, Husserl, and others (see chap. 6, §§2, 3) weighed the merits of *Inhaltslogik* (intensional or content logic), as opposed to extensional logic. Although Frege only began using the words *"Sinn"* and *"Bedeutung"* in his special way in 1891 (GB, p. 29), he was talking about intensions and extensions in reference to Boole's work as early as 1880 (PW, pp. 9–47). Section 8 of the *Begriffsschrift* and Section 67 of *Foundations* are sometimes cited as evidence that the 1892 distinction was present implicitly in Frege's earlier works, but Frege himself seemed to take it for granted that the distinction was present in *Foundations*[11] when in a letter to Husserl (May 24, 1891) he schematizes his 1884 *Foundations* view of meaning and compares it with what he found in Husserl's *Philosophy of Arithmetic* (PMC, pp. 63-64). One of the chief indications that Frege introduced the words *"Sinn"* and *"Bedeutung"* as terminological innovations is in fact found in this letter. Here Frege deceptively begins the passage concerned: "In the *Foundations* I did not yet draw the distinction between sense and Meaning." But then he indicates that the change is primarily terminological and instructs as how to change into his new vocabulary: "I should now prefer to speak of 'having a Meaning' instead of 'having a sense.' Elsewhere too, e.g., in sects. 100, 101, 102 I would now often replace 'sense' by 'Meaning'" (PMC, p. 63). Note that in each case Frege is replacing the intensional word "sense" by the extensional "Meaning," not vice versa (PW, p. 123).

Further on, he writes that two of his early lectures on the concept-script

> do not quite accurately reflect my present position as you can see by comparing them with "Function and Concept." But since they can be easily translated into my present terminology, they may nevertheless serve to give an idea of my conceptual notation. [PMC, p. 64]

The idea that the distinction between *Sinn* and *Bedeutung* was not present conceptually in the earlier works was probably initiated by Russell when he wrote:

> Frege did not possess this distinction in the first of the two works under consideration [the *Begriffsschrift* and the *Grundlagen der Arithmetik*]; it first appears in 'Begriff und Gegenstand' (cf. p. 109) and is specially dealt with in 'Sinn und Bedeutung'. . . . His *Begriffsschrift,* owing to the absence of the distinction between meaning and indication, has a simpler theory than his later works. [PofM, p. 502]

But even Russell suggests that he himself had much the same distinction in his work independently of Frege: "The distinction between meaning *(Sinn)* and indication *(Bedeutung)* is roughly, though not exactly equivalent to my distinction between a concept and what the concept denotes" (PofM, p. 502).

Even as a terminological distinction Frege's distinction may not have been as odd at the turn of the century as it is to us now. After all, Frege wrote in "On Sense and Meaning":

> It is *natural,* now, to think of there being connected with a sign . . . besides that which the sign designates, which may be called the Meaning of the sign, also what I should *like to call* the sense off the sign, wherein the mode of presentation is contained. [GB, p. 57]

Husserl wrote in the *Logical Investigations:*

> Meanings are *often* spoken of as signifying the *objects* meant, a usage that can scarcely be maintained consistently, as it springs from a confusion with the genuine concept of meaning. [LI, p. 293]

* * * *

> The word 'meaning' is no doubt likewise equivocal so that men do not hesitate at times to call the object of a presentation a 'meaning' and at times to say the same of its intension (the sense of its name). [LI, p. 431]

In his 1891 "Review of Schröder" Husserl decries Schröder's confounding the usual sense with the object named by calling them both meaning (RS, p. 120).

Frege's successors have always been ill at ease with his choice of vocabulary. They have translated *"Sinn"* as both "meaning" and "sense" and have rendered *"Bedeutung"* as "denotation," "nominatum," "nomination," "indication," "reference," and most recently as "significance."[12] The 1922 translation of the *Tractatus* (that Wittgenstein himself oversaw) is almost alone in respecting Frege's choice of distinguishing between the synonyms (see 3.203, 3.3, 4.061, 4.241–43, 5.4733, 6.126, 6.232). It has only been recently that some philosophers have actually chosen to respect Frege's decision by translating *"Bedeutung"* as either "meaning" (GB, p. ix) or "Meaning."[13] This still is misleading since, when Russell initially translated *"Sinn"* as "meaning," he was respecting the logical tradition both he and Frege were working from by recognizing the *Sinn* intension as the meaning proper, or *the* meaning (see chap. 6).

§6. THE FUNDAMENTAL DIFFERENCES

It is, then, not a question of influence here. But is it a matter of significant kinship? The discussions of this chapter show kinship, but reveal significant divergences. First of all, the kinship observed concerns genuine similarities in theories of linguistic meaning. Even here, however, Husserl brings in epistemological considerations foreign to Frege's ideas. Husserl always believed it was the mind that conferred meaning on words (the first Logical Investigation, for example).

The question however, concerns comparisons between a theory of linguistic meaning and a theory of noematic meaning. And here the differences are more dramatic. Though Husserl drew analogies between the way the mind confers meaning on objects and the word-meaning-object relationship, he considered his theory of noematic meaning to be a radically new way of approaching logic, philosophy, *and* language. He used the more familiar notion of meaning as a conceptual tool to explain phenomena he believed no one had ever described before. He used it as a metaphor to describe the structures and features of the mind in both the natural attitude *and* the transcendental attitude. Husserl generalized the notion of meaning to include all mental acts, including those of the transcendental ego. So while it is possible to say that Husserl's theory of linguistic meaning as sketched in §3 is roughly equivalent to Frege's one cannot go so far as to identify the noemata with Frege's senses.

The most significant differences between noemata and Frege's senses, therefore, derive from the fact that Husserl had been the disciple of Brentano and that his phenomenology is the science of intentionality. It is the long and painstaking study of how the human consciousness can grasp the ideal unities of meaning in question. The philosopher, Husserl argues, must approach them in a special way. He must, while philosophizing, loose his consciousness from all connection with the world as known from the natural viewpoint. He suspends judgement on the objects in the world around him to concentrate on the noemata occasioned by (but dependent on) those objects.

Those who have sought to identify Husserl's noemata with Frege's senses have not fully appreciated the radical nature of this separation from the world and oneself in the natural viewpoint. And they have not adequately come to terms with the extent to which the grasping of the noemata depends on this radical shift in perspective.

In the author's preface to the English translation of *Ideas* Husserl insists that "those who set aside the phenomenological reduction as a philosophically irrelevant eccentricity . . . destroy the whole meaning of my work and of my phenomenology . . ." (ID, p. 16).

While Husserl's noemata share certain properties with Frege's senses, the role noemata play within Husserl's philosophy is very far removed from the role senses play for Frege. The noemata are necessarily fused with noeses. They are the object of Husserl's quest and will provide him with the secure ideal foundations for the sciences he seeks. Husserl's senses and his noemata can, by virtue of the intentional act, relate in a scientifically profitable way to imaginary, nonexistent, and even impossible objects. Husserl insists on this. The "meaning intention" need not be fulfilled by actually existing objects. Scientists, and mathematicians in particular, need to use expressions established by indirect, complicated demonstrations which, a priori, have no object. If one identifies the meaning with the object of the expression, Husserl complains at one point, then names that can have no object, like the golden mountain or the round square, become meaningless, lack of an object and lack of meaning become confused (LI, pp. 293–94).

Frege, on the other hand, warns against the difficulties mathematicians encounter when they appeal to combinations of signs that have no Meaning. In a piece from his *Nachlass* dated 1892–1895 (in which he makes special reference to Husserl), Frege writes that when it is a question

> of the truth of something — and truth is the goal of logic — we also have to inquire after Meanings; we have to throw aside proper names that do not designate or name an object, though they may have a sense; we have to throw aside concept-words that do not have a Meaning . . . for fiction the sense is enough . . . but not for science. . . .
> [PW, p. 122]

This echoes what he wrote in his 1891 letter to Husserl: "For poetic use it is enough that everything has a sense, for scientific purposes the Meaning also must not be missing" (PMC, p. 63). Considered in this context, Husserl's view of the role of poetry in the pursuit of truth is quite telling:

> Thus one can really say, if one loves paradoxical talk; and if one accounts for the ambiguity in meaning, one can say in strict truth, that "fiction" is the life of phenomenology, as of all eidetic science, that fiction is the source from which the knowledge of "eternal truths" draws its sustenance. [ID, §70]

For Frege, then, it is the quest for truth that drives him away from the senses to the Meaning or extension. In Husserl, on the other hand, the quest for truth leads us away from the object in search of senses.

With regard to the linguistic rendering of noemata, Husserl himself reminds:

> It is clear that all these descriptive assertions, in spite of
> the fact that they can read just the same as assertions
> about reality [*Wirklichkeitaussagen*] have undergone a
> radical modification in sense, just as that which is described
> has, although it behaves as if it is "precisely the same," none-
> theless it is something radically different, as it were by vir-
> tue of a complete change in signs. "Within" reduced percep-
> tion (in phenomenologically pure experience) we find, as
> belonging inseparably to its essence, the perceived as such
> to be expressed as "material thing," "plant," "tree," "bloom-
> ing," etc. The quotation marks are obviously important; they
> express that change in sign, the radical modification in the
> meaning of the word. [ID, §89]

That there is an essential quite unbridgeable difference between
the sciences of the ideal and the sciences of the real, the a priori
and the empirical, and that this is one of the decisive points that
divides psychologists and antipsychologists is one of the principal
planks of the antipsychologism of the *Prolegomena*. Noemata
rather decidedly belong to that other dimension.

Finally, Husserl himself addressed charges that his phenomenology amounted to the linguistic analysis of meaning in the introduction to the *Logical Investigation* that he wrote in 1913, at the
very time he was propounding theories of sense and noemata:

> And since the logical element in logical phenomena is
> given to the consciousness and since the logical phenom-
> ena are phenomena of predicating and thus of a certain
> signifying [*Bedeuten*], the investigation begins after all
> with an analysis of these phenomena. Whoever has read
> the introduction . . . and then some sizeable portions of
> the work must surely over and over again hit upon the
> fact that phenomenology is spoken of in an incomparably
> broader area, that analyses are carried out on perception,
> fantasy, pictorial-representation and thus on many sorts
> of experience-types that occasionally occur in connection
> with verbal phenomena and that occur especially where
> these phenomena are to become logical cognitions sup-
> plying evidence but for which this connection with the
> Logos is entirely extra-essential. [ILI, p. 50]

§7. CONCLUSION

The view that Husserl's theory of noema is historically and
systematically the further development of Frege's views on sense

Meaning must, then, be erroneous on the grounds that—

1. the three-way distinction in question was already in use at the time.

2. although for some it is the way Frege drew the distinction in 1892 that invites comparison with Husserl's notion of noema, Husserl was already distinguishing between the sense of an expression and its reference before Frege's article appeared. Frege himself acknowledged this in his first letter to Husserl (see also PW, p., 124).

3. Frege's terminological innovation, and its particular relationship to the concept-script and the extensional methods he was promoting, represent the specifically Fregean contribution.

4. like Russell and his successors, Husserl refused Frege's terminology. He offered his reasons for doing so in print.

5. Husserl refused Frege's concept-script and his extensional logic, and there is no indication that he ever seriously considered adopting them. This was clear as early as 1891, as I hope to make clear in the next chapter.

6. for Husserl phenomenology involved a radical shift in perspective. He believed he had broken with his contemporaries and with tradition. No exception was made for Frege.

7. by the time Husserl developed his theory of noemata he had radically departed from anything Frege or his successors ever took into consideration.

4

HUSSERL'S 1891 CRITIQUE OF FREGE

FREGE'S REVIEW OF Husserl's *Philosophy of Arithmetic* has played a prominent role in speculation as to the role Frege may have played in Husserl's philosophical development. But the fact that Husserl thoroughly criticized Frege's logical theories three years before Frege's famous review appeared has gone virtually unnoticed.[1] Few have studied Husserl's book, and no one, to my knowledge, has managed to overcome the substantial linguistic hurdles standing in the way of an evaluation of the significance of Husserl's criticism for contemporary philosophy. It has most often been assumed that Husserl and Frege were so fundamentally different in their philosophical orientation that Husserl did not really grasp what Frege was talking about.[2] One could, in fact, fairly easily conclude that Husserl's disavowal of psychologism in the *Logical Investigations* implied a rejection of all the arguments of the *Philosophy of Arithmetic*. As many believe it was Frege who actually turned Husserl around, Husserl's earlier appraisal of Frege's work may then have seemed of little interest. Husserl, however, only ever retracted three pages of the *Philosophy of Arithmetic* (LI, p. 179). He left almost all of his criticism of Frege intact.[3]

As interest in Husserl's work increases, and as more texts become accessible, the usual assessment comes to seem more and more problematic, and it becomes increasingly apparent that Frege's review was not a soliloquy, but rather took its place within the framework of a larger exchange between the two authors. In the next two chapters I continue to piece together the parts of that exchange. In this chapter I argue that Husserl did understand Frege's logic and rejected it on valid grounds. The chapter will probably have to be reread in light of the discussions of part two of this work. I must begin with some brief remarks concerning the role of identity in analytic philosophy.

§1. IDENTITY AND ANALYTIC PHILOSOPHY

Since the main arguments of this chapter concern Husserl's criticism of the role identity plays in Frege's logic, it is important to note some points about identity and analytic philosophy. First of all, Frege was already arguing in *Begriffsschrift* that questions of identity and denotation of signs were "the very heart of the matter" (BS, §8). "On Sense and Meaning" begins and ends with reflections of the problem of identity (GB, pp. 56, 78). So does *Foundations.* "With numbers," Frege argued, "it is a matter of fixing the sense of an identity" (FA, p. x, §§62, 107). The crucial Basic Law V of the *Basic Laws of Arithmetic* mandated some things about identity (BL, §§3, 20) that lead to Russell's paradoxes (GB, pp. 214–24; PW, pp. 181–82). Identity considerations play a prominent role throughout Russell's influential article "On Denoting" (LK, pp. 41–56). Without the vital (PM, pp. xliii, 56, 58, 76), but problematic (PM, pp. xiv, 59; LK, p. 325) Axiom of Reducibility of *Principia,* or another like it, Russell believed identity was indefinable (PM, p. 58). Wittgenstein called identity "the very devil" in a 1913 letter to Russell. He said it was "the occurrence of the same argument in different places of a function" that especially troubled him.[4] Identity, in fact, became an important issue in the *Tractatus.* Ever since Frege, Russell, and Wittgenstein worked on extensional logic, logical discussions have been rife with questions about identity, and the substitutivity of identicals in particular, as any cursory glance at the writings of Marcus, Carnap, Kripke, or Quine shows.

§2. EQUALITY AND IDENTITY

Husserl rejected Frege's use of Leibniz's law—"Things are the same as each other of which one can be substituted for the other without loss of truth"—on several grounds. First of all, he complains, it defines identity and not equality (PA, p. 104).[5]

Frege replied in his review of *Philosophy of Arithmetic* (FR, pp. 327, 331) and insisted throughout his writings (GB, pp. 22–23, 120–21, 141 n., 146 n., 159–61, 210; PMC, p. 141; PW, pp. 120–21, 182) that within his logic there was no difference between equality and identity. Of Leibniz's law he had written in *Foundations,* §65:

> This I propose to adopt as my own definition of equal-
> ity.[6] Whether we use "the same," as Leibniz does, or
> "equal," is not of any importance. "The same," may in-
> deed be thought to refer to complete agreement in all
> respects, "equal," only to agreement in this respect or that;
> but we can adopt a form of expression such that this dis-
> tinction vanishes. For example, instead of "the segments
> are equal in length," we can say "the length of the segments
> is equal," or "the same," and instead of "the surfaces are
> equal in color," "the color of the surfaces is equal" . . .
> in universal substitutability all the laws of identity are con-
> tained. [FA, §65; see also PMC, p. 141]

Frege repeats in "On Sense and Meaning," "Equality . . . I use this word in the sense of identity and understand 'a = b' to have the sense of 'a is the same as b' or 'a and b coincide'" (GB, p. 56).

The issue Husserl has brought up is not minor. Frege's logical project requires the removal of those logical considerations which mark the difference between equality and identity. But his thesis is rife with difficulties that become apparent when §65 of *Foundations* is submitted to closer scrutiny.

Frege's conviction that logic had followed language and grammar too closely "drove" him to rewrite the statements of ordinary language in a way that revealed their true logical form (BS, p. 7). So Frege began rewriting traditional subject and predicate constructions in ways that seemed better suited to his logic. In the text cited above Frege has used two statements to illustrate his point about equality:

1. The segments are equal in length.
2. The surfaces are equal in color.

Both are statements about objects that are "equal" from a specific point of view (i.e., length and color, respectively). He has rewritten them to read:

3. The length of the segments is equal.

4. The color of the surfaces is equal.

These new statements, he claims, express complete coincidence. By this Frege meant that the "objects" (now length and color, instead of segments and surfaces) are equal from all points of view, hence virtually identical. If two objects are equal as given in a certain way then, he has reasoned, for all intents and purposes they are equal in all ways. If two objects have one property in common that is all that is important.

But 1 and 2 were statements about objects (i.e., lines and surfaces). In 3 and 4, however, Frege has tried to convert the properties ascribed to those objects into the objects the extensionalist logician needs (chap. 6, §4). He has taken the ill-fated step of reifying properties, and in trying to avoid one linguistic trap he fell into some other very pernicious ones: we can make an adjective into a noun by putting a definite article in front of it, we can use an abstract concept as if it designated a concrete thing, and we can move the predicate of a sentence into subject position. Ultimately, though, descriptions of objects, adjectives, predicates, and concepts do not exhibit the same logical behavior as names, nouns, subjects, and objects. The particular way in which a term is given is not, logically speaking, a synonym or a substitute for the term. For though language lets us reify properties (concepts, attributes, etc.), is it unclear how length or color are objects in the same way lines or surfaces are. Not only does this offend any robust sense of reality, but, as became clear to Frege, logic rebels. He and Russell linked this problem directly to the paradoxes (discussed in chap. 8, §3). When language is juggled in a way that makes the difference between equality and identity disappear, other subtle, but vital differences are obscured as well.

§3. SO LONG AS THE LEAST DIFFERENCE REMAINS

So long as the least difference remains, Husserl continues his argument, there will be judgments in which we cannot make substitutions *salva veritate* (PA, p. 104). Frege tried to rewrite statements so that the difference between equality (there is a specific way in which x and y are the same), and identity (x and y are the same in all ways), vanishes. If the difference between identity and equality can be abolished or neutralized, then the innumerable possible predicates that could possibly intervene to alter the truth or falsity of the statement "$x=y$" will presumably vanish too. Frege (and others), in fact, tries to say that if two objects are equal under a given description, whatever else is, or might be predicated, of them is irrelevant.

Husserl protested that if it can be shown that there is a property F such that F is true of x, and F is not true of y, then it is not true that x and y have all their properties in common, so y cannot always be substituted for x. Intuitively this seems undeniable, and perhaps this is the reason Frege held that the law that was to guarantee this operation (Basic Law V) was undemonstrable (GB, pp. 26, 159, 161; PW, p. 182), for it is precisely the wealth of properties that all objects (though mathematical objects may be an exception) enjoy that finally brought about its failure.

One fundamental problem is that since there are no property-less objects (there are not even any single-propertied objects), a statement of identity or equality cannot be a statement about objects only. "The universe consists of objects having various qualities and standing in various relations," Russell wrote in *Principia* (p. 43). "Objects can only be mentioned in connection with some definite property," he wrote in his introduction to the *Tractatus*.[7] In "On Denoting" he had remarked, ". . . every object can be denoted by an infinite number of denoting phrases" (LK, p. 50). Innumerable properties (possible or impossible) can be predicated of any given object, and no one can manipulate, conceive of, control, or account for them all. These differences are neither psychological[8] nor merely linguistic. Even the case of the evening star and the morning star, Frege's classic example, is not as simple as Frege would have it be.[9] This is probably the state of affairs to which Kant was referring when he wrote: "Since one cannot become certain by any proof whether all characteristics of a given concept have been exhausted by complete analysis, all analytic definitions must be held to be uncertain."[10]

Reference is chronically undetermined. So analytic definitions remain uncertain. I believe this consideration played an important role in the development of Husserl's theory of noema and horizons. Attempts to remove, extinguish, neutralize, eclipse, or, alternatively, to accommodate the predicates that begin proliferating when two things are identified in an informative statement have managed to play a preeminent role in twentieth-century philosophy, both on the Continent and in English-speaking countries. This leads to Husserl's next point.

§4. INFORMATIVE IDENTITY STATEMENTS

Next, Husserl complains that Frege's method defines the extensions, not the intensions of concepts and that, though all his definitions become true propositions when taken extensionally, they are then completely self-evident and worthless (PA, p. 134).

The problem to which Husserl is alluding has in recent years come to be known as Frege's puzzle: "How can $\ulcorner a=b \urcorner$, if true, differ in "cognitive value"—that is, in cognitive information content—from $\ulcorner a=a \urcorner$?[11] The problem is built right into Frege's logic because his logic depends on ambiguities inherent in the notion of identity. In general, an identity statement can be said to be true or false (1) on the basis of its signs, (2) because of the objects those signs denote (i.e., extensionally), (3) because of the properties those objects may have (i.e., intensionally), or (4) some combination of these: The truth conditions for identity statements vary according to whether one appeals to signs, objects, or properties; philosophers today are still working to draw out the full implications this equivocation has for the questions that interest them.

In *Philosophy of Arithmetic* Husserl argued that there was no problem establishing the equality of two simple contents, but when it came to complex contents, language was misleading. If two complex objects are equal, he reasoned, then all their corresponding properties must be equal to each other (their physical components as well, since they too are properties). So much is obvious, he claims, but the inverse does not seem to be valid. Sometimes properties are equal on both sides and in spite of this we do not speak of the equality of the objects (PA, p. 108). As Russell put it in *Principia:*

It is plain that if x and y are identical, and ϕx is true, then ϕy is true. . . . The statement must hold for any function. But we cannot say conversely: "If, with all values of ϕ, ϕx implies ϕy, then x and y are identical" . . . we cannot without the help of an axiom be sure that x and y are identical if they have the same predicates. Leibniz' "identity of indiscernibles" supplied this axiom. [PM, p. 57]

It can even happen, Husserl continues, that we say that two objects are the same in one situation and not the same in another (PA, p. 108). Appealing to one of Frege's own examples, Husserl writes: "Two segments of a straight line are said to be equal if they have the same length, but we sometimes say they are unequal because we understand equal segments of a straight line to mean lines of equal length which are parallel and have the same direction. . . . There is a simple explanation for this apparent fluctuation in modes of expression," he declares. "We purely and simply say that two objects are equal if the properties that form the focus of interest are equal. . . . To say that two properties are equal is for the geometrician an abbreviated way of saying they are equal from a specific point of view, one in conformity with the purposes of the investigation" (PA, 108–9). In his review of *Philosophy of Arithmetic*, Frege condemned this analysis (FR, p. 327).

Frege had thought that he could, as against Kant, show how analytic statements could be both true and informative (FA, §§88, 89, 109; BS §§23-24). He attempted to do this by showing that both $a=b$ and $a \neq b$. To do this he split the identity statements of the *Begriffsschrift* §8 into senses and Meanings. "$a=b$" is to be true if the two signs "a" and "b" refer to (Mean) the same thing; it is informative, and therefore consequential if they differ in sense (PMC, pp. 127–28, 152, 157–58, 163). In other words, the statement "$a=b$" is true if we are talking about the extensions of "a" and "b", and "a" and "b" have the same extension. It is false if we are talking only about the intensions of "a" and "b" and there is the difference in sense the statement must have to have cognitive worth and to suit Frege's theories of analyticity and knowledge. It is a tautology and therefore empty if $a=b$ both extensionally and intensionally. On the level of signs it is absurd because the sign "a" can in no way be the same as the sign "b". Dummet writes:

> Given that a particular object is the bearer of two names,
> no information is acquired by learning that that object
> has to itself a relation which every object has to itself: but
> the truth conditions of an identity statement determine
> that it can be true only when the same object is the bearer
> of both names. The informativeness of an identity state-
> ment thus turns entirely on the sense of the two names.[12]

So to Quine's observation that "actually of course the statements
of identity that are true and not idle consist of unlike statements
of identity that refer to the same thing,"[13] one must add with
Dummett and Husserl that they are only not empty by virtue
of their intensions. A true identity statement like "the morning
star=the evening star" is important and not idle according to
Frege's theories precisely because it affirms that what is the same
(extensionally) is different (intensionally). A philosopher as seemingly removed from all of this as Friedrich Nietzsche spotted
the contradiction: "Strictly speaking, knowing takes the form
of a tautology and is empty. Any advance in knowledge is identification of the nonidentical and the similar (i.e., it is essentially illogical). This is the only way we acquire a concept."[14]
Frege enshrined this contradiction and made it the cornerstone
of his logic.

Translated into class talk (as inspired by Russell's discussion
of Cantor and the contradictions of set theory (PofM, chap. 10)
this means that if "β" designates the class of all b's and $a=b$,
then $a\varepsilon\beta$. But a has at least one property that distinguishes it
from b: it is in fact not b. It is a. Therefore $a\bar{\varepsilon}\beta$.

The elements of an informative identity statement both do
and do not belong to the same class. Even if a actually turns
out to be the same object as b, as is the case with the morning
star and the evening star, if "$a=b$" is true, then a would both
belong and not belong to the class of all things designated by "b."

Consider the class α of all objects having n predicates. a has
n predicates, so $a\varepsilon\alpha$. Now $a=b$, and the statement "$a=b$" is by
its form alone not a tautology—that is, b necessarily has at least
one quality that a does not have. So b has at least $n+1$ predicates.
Since a is to be a b, by Leibniz's law it follows that a has $n+1$
predicates. Thus both $a\varepsilon\alpha$ and $a\bar{\varepsilon}\alpha$.

Or, if $a=b$, $b\varepsilon\alpha$, but if b is an α it must possess the defining property of α. This property demands that b should have n predicates, but if "$a=b$" is not to be trivial, then at least one thing must be predicable of b that is not predicable of a. So b has $n+1$ predicates and both $b\bar{\varepsilon}\alpha$ and $b\varepsilon\alpha$.

So once played out, the contradiction Nietzsche pointed to begins to look like the contradiction that worried Russell so much: both $a\varepsilon\alpha$, and $a\bar{\varepsilon}\alpha$. Basic Law V would have alleviated the problems by making identity statements concerning properties, attributes, concepts, senses, intensions equivalent to statements about the identity of objects (extensions, references). But it could not work, and no effective way of juggling properties so that a is both the same as b and different from b has been, or I think can be, found. Reality, in the form of Russell's contradiction, enters in to utter a robust no. This is all discussed in depth in later chapters.

§5. NO BACKWARD ROAD FROM REFERENCE TO SENSE

Husserl further pointed out to Frege as early as 1891 (PA, p. 104), that although identical properties yield identical judgments (i.e., $F \equiv G. \supset. (x) Fx \equiv Gx$), coincidence of properties does not assure their identity (i.e., $(x) Fx \equiv Gx. \supset .F \equiv G$, does not hold). Borrowing from Quine's "Two Dogmas of Empiricism,"[15] one can illustrate the first point by noting that if being a bachelor is the same as being an unmarried man, then anyone who is a bachelor is an unmarried man. To illustrate the latter point Husserl himself gives examples of terms that, like the famous "creature with heart," "creature with kidneys," are equal in extension, but not in intension (PA, pp. 134–36). When Russell wrote to Frege of the paradoxes he had found this is precisely where Frege located the problem (GB, p. 214). When in his appendix to the second volume of *Basic Laws* Frege tries to track down the origin of the contradiction, he finally locates it in his Basic Law V, which Geach and Black render thus:

> VA amounts to the assertion: if two functions always have the same value for the same argument, then they have the

> same graph; in particular, if whatever falls under either one of two concepts falls under both, then they are equal in extension. VB makes the converse assertion. If functions have the same graph, then they always have the same value for the same arguments; in particular, if concepts are equal in extension then whatever falls under one falls under the other. [GB, p. 218]

In his search for the problem Frege concludes that the mistake can only lie in part b of the law which must be false.

> Along with [Vb], V itself has collapsed but not Va. There is nothing to stop our transforming an equality that holds generally into an equality of graphs (in accordance with Va). All that has been shown is that the converse transformation (in accordance with Vb) is not always allowable . . . we cannot in general take the words "the function of $\phi(\xi)$ has the same graph as the function $\psi(\xi)$" to Mean the same as the words "the functions $\phi(\xi)$ and $\psi(\xi)$ have the same value for the same argument." [GB, p. 219]

✳ ✳ ✳ ✳

> If in general for any first level concept we may speak of its extension, then the case arises of concepts having the same extension, although not all objects that fall under one fall under the other as well.
>   This, however, really abolishes the extension of the concept in the sense we have given the word. We may not say that in general the expression 'the extension of one concept coincides with that of another' means the same thing as the expression 'all objects that fall under the one concept fall under the other as well,' and conversely. We see from the result of our deduction that it is quite impossible to give the words 'the extension of the concept $\phi(\xi)$, such a sense that from concepts' being equal in extension we could always infer that every object falling under one falls under the other and likewise. [GB, p. 221]

Frege had begun this discussion writing: "Identity is a relation given to us in such a specific form that it is inconceivable that various kinds of it should occur" (GB, p. 215; also p. 141). But it is precisely the disparity between the truth conditions for statements concerning extensions and statements concerning intensions that would lead Carnap and others to develop logics that could cope with the differences. "Identity is different for extensions and intensions . . . and since identity is different for extensions and intensions a neutral formulation cannot speak about identity," Carnap would write in *Meaning and Necessity*.[16]

The statement "$x=y$" can be true extensionally, but that does not mean that x and y are intensionally equivalent. This statement of difference opens a Pandora's box of possibilities. Properties, concepts, attributes, senses, intensions, what we can know or predicate of things are too multiple, too fickle and diverse, and finally too elusive to be captured by Frege's extensional logic. Neither in reality nor in logic are they tame enough to meet his demands. This would seem to be a consequence of the fact that in Frege's theory of meaning it is the senses that pick out and determine the reference and not vice versa. Russell echoes Kant's statement that there is no way of being certain that we have exhaustively analyzed all the properties of a concept. . . . when he writes, "There is not backward road from denotations to meanings . . . because every object can be denoted by an infinite number of different denoting phrases" (LK, p. 50). This intensional indeterminacy finally means that (in Quine's words) the extension itself goes inscrutable.[17]

Perhaps this is one reason that in his 1885 review of the *Foundations* Cantor deplored the fact that in his efforts to ground arithmetic logically Frege turned to extensions.[18]

§6. SUBSTITUTIVITY PRESUMES IDENTITY

Lastly, Husserl asks what gives us the right to substitute one content for another? His answer: The equality or the identity of the contents (i.e., $x=y . \supset . Fx \supset Fy$). But, he reasons further, coincidence of properties does not insure their identity so the reply to the inverse question — two contents are equal to each other because they can be substituted for each other in true judgments (i.e., $Fx \supset Fy . \supset . x=y$) — is obviously off the mark and has absurd consequences. If we cannot be sure x and y are identical if they have the same predicates, then we cannot say that, because x and y can be substituted for each other, $x=y$.

If, Husserl continues, we must always establish substitutivity before we can establish equality, then each time we ascertain the equality of two things we must first have had to verify their substitutivity. But, he argues, doesn't this latter process itself consist in an even infinite number of acts, each implying that equality has been established. To establish all these equalities he complains, one would again have to know that the *same* true judgments are valid for each pair of judgments, and all this leads to a veritable labyrinth of infinite regression (PA, p. 104–5).

In Dummett's more contemporary prose:

> . . . the truth of an identity statement cannot be established by an appeal to Leibniz's law since, apart from the impossibility of running through the totality of first level concepts, there will often be no other way of ascertaining that a particular predicate which is true of the bearer of one name is also true of the bearer of the other except by establishing that the two names have the same bearer. There is, for instance, no way of showing that the predicate 'is visible shortly before sunrise,' which is plainly true of the Morning Star, is also true of the Evening Star, which does not depend upon showing that the Morning Star and the Evening Star are one and the same celestial body.[19]

§7. CONCLUDING REMARKS

So it is not true that, as Russell has suggested, his "paradoxes followed from premises which were not previously known to require limitations" (PM, p. 59). By 1891 Husserl had already detected the basic flaws in Frege's premises that would mean the dismantling of his logical edifice.

Though Russell owned a copy of *Philosophy of Arithmetic* as early as 1898, he never mentions having read or studied it. I am trying to show, however, the extent to which *Principia* is an effort to overcome difficulties first expressly formulated in the *Philosophy of Arithmetic*.

It has recently been discovered that Russell changed §128 of the *Principles of Mathematics*. He deleted portions from the printer's copy of the manuscript in which he had accepted that (in Michael Byrd's words) "logicalism, as regards the cardinal numbers, fails, because the equivalence classes which are to be identified with the numbers, cannot exist in a theory which adequately handles the contradictions."[20] Husserl had concentrated much of his attack on the theory of equivalence in Frege (PA, pp. 129–35).

Perhaps it was because Husserl's criticisms had been so apropos that Frege expressed reservations about his Basic Law V when he published his *Basic Laws of Arithmetic* three years later (GB, p. 118). This would explain the virulence of Frege's attack on Husserl and also why, when finally confronted with Russell's paradox, Frege located the difficulty just about exactly where Husserl had indicated it would be (GB, p. 219).

I do not believe, however, that Husserl ever carried his reasoning far enough to link his objections to Frege's logic directly to anything like Russell's paradox. The fact that in 1891 he discussed a contradiction like Russell's in his review of Schröder's *Vorlesungen über die Algebra der Logik,* which he did not link with Frege's ideas (RS, p. 137), indicates that he was blind to the connection.[21] He did, though, have the insight to locate the source of Frege's difficulties in the theory of identity, sense, and denotation that forms the basis of Frege's logic: he attacked Frege's use of Leibniz's "law," which is a theory of identity, sense, and denotation. In so doing he indicated a source of contradiction that is written right into the foundations of the logic deriving from Frege's work.

I hope these contentions will seem less contestable after the discussions of this chapter. But here I have only been able to lay the groundwork for the discussions of later chapters because many layers of language, history, and perhaps deceit still conceal the import and contemporary nature of Husserl's critique.[22]

5

FREGE'S REVIEW AND THE DEVELOPMENT OF HUSSERL'S THOUGHT

AFTER 1891 FREGE IS most conspicuous in Husserl's writings by his absence. Of Frege's writings Husserl appears to have consulted only the *Foundations* in the period between 1887 and 1891. He studied Frege's book thoroughly in the *Philosophy of Arithmetic,* three years before Frege's famous review appeared. Husserl then corresponded with Frege and read many of Frege's other writings. Frege's theories, though, proved no more helpful to Husserl than Brentano's empirical psychology had been in coping with the vast area of inquiry that opened up as Husserl confronted philosophical problems his mathematical studies raised, problems that Frege never worked through in print and that logicism never resolved.

Husserl read extensively in logic in the 1890s and he was keenly aware of his intellectual isolation. He considered the view of logic that he finally espoused as the response to problems first suggested to him in his study of arithmetic to be a radical departure from the work of his contemporaries and a breakthrough to an entirely different way of approaching problems of logic and knowledge (ILI, §6). By the time Husserl published the *Logical Investigations,* he had become wholly engrossed in a set of problems that was substantially removed from anything that might be termed Fregean. He does not study Frege's work, there or in any of his subsequent writings, either to approve it or to refuse it. To some extent the *Logical Investigations* may even be read as the implied refusal of all of Frege's logical innovations.

Still, in spite of these considerations, there is Boyce Gibson's report that Frege's criticism of *Philosophy of Arithmetic* was the

57

only one for which Husserl was really grateful: "It hit the nail on the head." And despite indications that this statement is not representative of Husserl's opinion as to the worth of Frege's ideas, there is still something in the statement that rings true. How, then, can this remark be integrated into the discussions of the present study? What might the nail have been?

In each of the four sections of this chapter I examine one of Frege's fundamental criticisms of Husserl's *Philosophy of Arithmetic* as expressed in the 1894 review. I use Frege's charges as springboards to the discussion of the broader issues concerning the evolution of Husserl's thought in the 1890s and to a thorough examination of the effect of Frege's review on Husserl's thought.

§1. PRESENTATION

Frege's review to a large extent consists of an attack on the role *Vorstellungen,* presentations, play in Husserl's philosophy of arithmetic, but confusions, past and present, regarding *Vorstellungen* have blocked attempts to understand and appraise Frege's criticism of Husserl's efforts. The term is so notoriously ambiguous that Husserl once proposed avoiding its use as much as possible.[1] In the *Logical Investigations,* he claims a "fourfold or fivefold ambiguity attaching to the word" and then proceeds to outline at least thirteen different understandings of it (LI 5, §44).

Frege further confused an already confused situation by insisting on his own personal use of the term. By refusing to come to terms with Husserl's use of the word, Frege, in his review of *Philosophy of Arithmetic,* sidestepped the real issues. The situation is even more complicated for readers of English because "*Vorstellung*" has no exact philosophical or linguistic equivalent in English. These factors have combined with others to displace the issues and have been responsible for many of the mistaken ideas about the nature of the exchange that took place between Husserl and Frege and, as a consequence, for misunderstanding regarding the development of Husserl's thought.

The same confusions have obscured many of the issues Bertrand Russell was tangling with as he engineered the linguistic turn, for although a good deal of effort has since been devoted to eliminating *Vorstellungen* from analytic philosophy, Russell toyed with his own version of them, and they figured prominently in some of his most influential writings. Though the validity of Frege's charge probably rests on whether he accurately pinpointed something that Husserl was, in some sense, doing wrong, a thorough study of the issues shows that what is more relevant now is that, ironically, since Bertrand Russell got his views on presentation from Franz Brentano, the man to whom *Philosophy of Arithmetic* is dedicated, Russell's thoughts on the matter rather resemble those Frege found so aggravating.

The situation has been obscured by layers of conceptual confusion, by substantial misunderstanding with regard to the philosophical climate that reigned in Austria, Germany, and England at the turn of the century, and by the fact that Russell's logic was designed to meet philosophical ends that Frege judged abhorrent. Through a misreading of the facts that I try to redress here and in chapter 7, followers of Russell have not seen how Frege's admonitions might apply to Russell at all.

DEFINING *"VORSTELLUNG"*

Husserl, Frege, and their contemporaries recognized the ambiguities inherent in talk of presentations. They also recognized the fundamental importance of the term for philosophy and saw its use as unavoidable. Aware of the problems, Frege wrote (note that he has not yet distinguished between sense and Meaning):

> A *Vorstellung* in the subjective sense is what is governed by the psychological laws of association; it is of a sensible pictorial character. A *Vorstellung* in the objective sense belongs to logic and is in principle non-sensible, although the word which means an objective *Vorstellung* is often accompanied by a subjective *Vorstellung* which nevertheless is not its meaning. Subjective *Vorstellungen* are often demonstrably different in different men; objective *Vorstellungen* are the same for all. Objective *Vorstellungen* can be divided into objects and concepts. I shall myself, to avoid confusion, use *Vorstellung* only in the subjective sense. [FA §27n.; see also p. x]

In "On Sense and Meaning" Frege gives more information about what *Vorstellungen* are for him:

> We may include with *Vorstellungen* direct experiences; here sense-impressions take the place of the traces which they have left in the mind. The distinction is unimportant . . . since memories of sense impressions and acts always go along with such impressions and acts themselves. . . . One may on the other hand understand direct experience as including any object in so far as it is sensibly perceptible or spatial. [GB, p. 59]

In his review of *Philosophy of Arithmetic,* Frege applies his view of *Vorstellung* when he writes in a passage that itself displays the difficulties this term and Frege's special use of it present:

> The components of a thought, and even more so the things themselves, must be distinguished from the *Vorstellungen* which in the soul accompany the grasping of a thought and which someone has about these things. In combining under the word *Vorstellung* both what is subjective and what is objective, one blurs the boundary between the two in such a way that now a *Vorstellung* in the proper sense of the word is treated like something objective, and now something subjective is treated like a *Vorstellung*. [FR, p. 325]

Husserl apparently dismissed Frege's interpretation entirely. The author of *Philosophy of Arithmetic* had studied Frege's *Foundations* thoroughly, but he refused Frege's approach in favor of a more empirical interpretation that could take into account a relationship of the knower to the known that was intolerable to Frege. Although Husserl uses the term throughout the *Philosophy of Arithmetic,* he only discusses it explicitly in chapter 11 where he contrasts authentic *Vorstellungen* and symbolic *Vorstellungen:*

> . . . a symbolic or improper presentation is, as the expression indicates, a presentation through signs. If a content is not given to us directly as it is, but only indirectly through signs which characterize it univocally, then, instead of a proper presentation, we have a symbolic presentation. . . . We have a proper presentation (of a house) if we are actually looking at a house; a symbolic presen-

tation if it is given to us indirectly: the house on the corner
of such and such a street and on such and such side of
the street. [PA, pp. 215-26]

It was Brentano, he tells us, who made him first profoundly
realize the "extreme importance" of symbolic presentation in the
life of the mind. No one before Brentano, Husserl believes, had
ever fully grasped this. Nonetheless, his definition of presentation differs from that of Brentano:

> The above definition is not identical to the one Brentano
> has given. I believed I especially had to stress the unicity
> of the characterization so as to maintain the difference
> between symbolic presentations and general presentations.
> Specifically, we will not call the general presentation "a
> man" a presentation, (even symbolic) of a specific man,
> Peter. The first expression contains only a part of the
> characteristics [*Merkmale*] appropriate to the characteriza-
> tion of the latter and must be completed by adding other
> characteristics so that we can designate [*bezeichnen*] it as a
> symbolic presentation of the individual, a presentation
> which can go proxy for [*surrogieren*] the proper presen-
> tation of this individual. [ibid.]

As for Russell, he borrowed his ideas on presentation from
Brentano, and from Brentano's student Meinong, as I hope to
show in what follows. In *Principles of Mathematics* Russell
wrote:

> An object can be present to the mind without our know-
> ing any concept of which the said object is *the* instance;
> and the discovery of such a concept is not a mere improve-
> ment in notation. The reason why this appears to be the
> case is that as soon as the definition is found, it becomes
> wholly unnecessary to reasoning to remember the actual
> object defined, since only concepts are relevant to our
> deductions. In the moment of discovery the definition is
> seen to be *true* because the *object* to be defined was already
> in our thoughts; but as part of our reasoning it is not true,
> but merely symbolic, since what reasoning requires is not
> that it should deal with *that* object but merely that it
> should deal with the object denoted by the definition.
> [PofM, p. 63]

But Russell's views on the matter also shifted significantly more than once during the crucial period in his philosophical career (1900–1919) (MPD, p. 134), and he never seems to have gotten Brentano's, Frege's, or Meinong's views exactly straight.[2] At one point Russell actually seems to have thought they were all alike, as the following 1904 passage from his series of articles on Meinong seems to indicate:

> That every presentation and every belief must have an object other than itself and, except in certain cases where mental existents happen to be concerned, extramental; that what is commonly called perception has as its object an existential proposition, into which enters as a constituent that whose existence is concerned, and not the idea of this existent; that truth and falsehood apply not to beliefs, but to their objects; and that the object of a thought, even when this object does not exist, has a being which is in no way dependent upon its being an object of thought. . . . Except Frege, I know of no writer on the theory of knowledge who comes as near to this position as Meinong. In what follows, I shall have the double purpose of expounding his opinions and of advocating my own; the points of agreement are so numerous and important. . . .[3]

Russell confused his own views with those of Frege and Meinong. Though Frege did not suffer the cultural and linguistic barriers that now separate us from Husserl's early thought, he misconstrued Husserl's views through the application of his own personal, subjective idea of the term *"Vorstellung,"* an interpretation he apparently shared with no one. Husserl's usage, on the other hand, was the common property of a whole tradition.

A COMPARISON WITH RUSSELL ON DENOTING

It is interesting to compare Husserl, Frege, and Russell further. Here I want to point out certain similarities between Husserl's early thought and Russell's ideas on acquaintance and denoting.

In the third of his series of articles on Meinong, Russell wrote, "Two distinct attitudes occur toward objects, one that of presentation, the other that of judgement. . . . We may say that the first gives acquaintance, while the second gives knowledge, or at least belief."[4] In his article "On the Nature of Acquaintance" (LK, pp. 125–75), Russell specifically identified his view of knowledge by acquaintance with *Vortstellungen* when he wrote, regarding Meinong, "I think the relation of the subject and object in presentation may be identified with the relation I call acquaintance" (LK, p. 169). The Meinong passage to which he refers is a discussion of *Vorstellungen*.[5]

In "Knowledge by Acquaintance and Knowledge by Description," he had been more expansive:

> I say that I am acquainted with an object when I have a direct cognitive relation to that object, i.e. when I am directly aware of the object itself. When I speak of a cognitive relation here, I do not mean the sort of relation which constitutes judgements, but the sort which constitutes presentation. In fact, I think the relation of subject to object which I call acquaintance is simply the converse of the relation of object and subject which constitutes presentation. That is, to say that S has acquaintance with O is essentially the same thing as to say that O is presented to S. [ML, pp. 209–10]

When we read the Husserl text in a way that accounts for the differences in word choice and terminology, Husserl's distinction between proper and symbolic presentations begins to resemble Russell's later distinction between knowledge by acquaintance and knowledge by description. In his famous article "On Denoting" Russell, aware that he has considerably departed from Frege's views, was to write:

> The distinction between acquaintance and knowledge about is the distinction between the things we have presentations of, and the things we only reach by means of denoting phrases. It often happens that we know that a certain phrase denotes unambiguously, although we have no acquaintance with what it denotes. In perception we have acquaintance with objects of a more abstract logical character. . . . All thinking has to start from acquaintance; but it succeeds in thinking about many things with which we have no acquaintance. [LK, p. 41]

And further in "Knowledge by Acquaintance and Knowledge by Description" Russell wrote, "I shall say that an object is 'known by description' when we know that it is 'the so and so' i.e. when we know that there is one object, and no more, having a certain property" (ML, pp. 214–15) and knowledge by acquaintance "brings the object itself before the mind" (ML, p. 213). In *Principia* he wrote:

> To Socrates himself the word "Socrates" no doubt stood for an object of which he was immediately aware. . . . But to us, who only know Socrates by description, the word "Socrates" cannot mean what it meant to him. It means rather "the person having such and such properties" (say, "the Athenian philosopher who drank the hemlock"). [PofM, p. 50]

RUSSELL AND BRENTANO

The relationship between Husserl's early thought and Russell's thought is less surprising when we remember that Russell and Moore had been favorably impressed by Brentano's route to realism, and that until 1919 Russell held a view of presentation that he specifically linked to Brentano's teachings on intentionality. He acknowledges this when he writes:

> During 1918 my view as to mental events underwent a very important change. I had originally accepted Brentano's view that in sensation there are three elements: act, content and object. I had come to think that the distinction of content and object is unnecessary, but I still thought that sensation is a fundamentally relational occurrence in which a subject is 'aware' of an object. I had used the concept 'awareness' or 'acquaintance' to express this relationship of subject and object, and had regarded it as fundamental in the theory of empirical knowledge. [MPD, p. 134]

Echoing Brentano on intentionality, he had written in 1912, "The faculty of being acquainted with things other than itself is the main characteristic of a mind. Acquaintance with objects essentially consists in a relation between the mind and the other than the mind."[6]

As this comparison with Russell helps to make clear, Husserl's early theory of presentation is a theory of how we know objects—and Husserl did distinguish objects from presentations of objects, and concepts from presentations. For Husserl and Russell, we get to know objects either by acquaintance (proper presentation), or via denoting phrases (symbolic presentations). Frege is not interested in the epistemological questions Russell and Husserl pose and as an anti-empiricist (FA, pp. x–xi) places sensory apprehension of objects under the category of subjective *Vorstellungen* rigorously to be avoided. Indeed, Russell might just as well have said of Frege what Russell wrote of James: "Immediate experience, which I should regard as the only real knowledge of things, he refuses to regard as knowledge at all" (LK, p. 159).

Frege was clearly interested in denoting phrases as a logician, but his perspective is again colored by the fact that what Husserl and Russell deemed properly epistemological questions, Frege considered psychologism. Husserl's and Russell's distinctions were clearly drawn to serve empiricist ends, so that knowledge by description as distinguished from knowledge by acquaintance, as Husserl or Russell would define those terms, can no longer resemble Frege's view of presentation. In the Fregean sense of the word Husserl remained psychologistic all his life—that is, he remained a person whose interests were dominated by the relationship of the subjectivity of the knower to what is known. But on these same grounds, we have seen, Russell's thought was psychologistic. Husserl, in 1891, resisted much in Frege that Russell would later find he had to modify, and in 1894 Frege resisted much in Husserl that Frege presumably would have resisted in Russell had he been asked. Many of Russell's most influential theories would have been the object of Frege's attacks.

Compare, for example, this account by Russell of what we can know by acquaintance with Frege's definition of subjective presentation.

> Sense data, as we have already seen, are among the things with which we are acquainted. . . . The first extension beyond sense data to be considered is acquaintance by memory. . . . The next extension to be considered is acquaintance by introspection.[7]

Or Frege on Husserl:

> If I want to have a symbolic presentation where I do not
> have a proper one, I idealize (p. 251) my powers of presen-
> tation; i.e. I imagine or present to myself that I have a
> presentation which I, in fact, neither have had nor can
> have; and thus what I imagine would be my symbolic pre-
> sentation. [FR, p. 335]

Russell:

> What happens, in cases where I have true judgement with-
> out acquaintance, is that the thing is known to me by
> description, and that, in virtue of some general princi-
> ple, the existence of a thing answering to this description
> can be inferred from the existence of something from
> which I am acquainted.[8]

Frege:

> According to the author (p. 215) a symbolic presentation
> is a presentation by means of signs which uniquely
> characterize what is to be presented. [FR, p. 334]

Russell:

> We know a description, and we know that there is just
> one object to which this description applies, though the
> object itself is not directly known to us.[9]
>
>   ✻ ✻ ✻ ✻
>
> We must attach *some* meaning to the words we use, if we
> are to speak significantly and not utter mere noise; and
> the meaning we attach to our words must be something
> with which we are acquainted.[10]

EARLY HUSSERL AND LOCKEAN IDEAS

Russell's successors have not generally been very sympathetic
or discriminating when they have suspected that some variant
of the "idea" idea might be present. In "Knowledge by Acquaintance and Knowledge by Description," Russell defines this "idea"
theory:

> The view seems to be that there is some mental existent which may be called the "idea" of something outside the mind of the person who has the idea, and that, since judgement is a mental event, its constituents must be constituents of the mind of the person judging. But in this view ideas become a veil between us and outside things — we never really, in knowledge, attain to the things we are supposed to be knowing about, but only to the ideas of those things. The relation of mind, idea and object, on this view, is utterly obscure, and, so far as I can see, nothing discoverable by inspection warrants the intrusion of the idea between the mind and object. [ML, p. 222]

Unfortunately, several factors have combined to make it seem that in his review of Husserl Frege was attacking the presence of the kind of ideas Russell came to find so offensive. Among these factors are: (1) the fact that *"Vorstellung"* is frequently translated as "idea" (GB, p. x; PW, p. vii; LI, p. 38). (2) When *"Vorstellung"* is understood in the Fregean way only, as referring to a subjective mental state, then it may seem that Husserl was talking about "ideas." (3) There is a fair amount of debate as to whether or not Brentano trafficked in ideas.[11] (4) Husserl did get involved in ideas, in another sense of the word, in his later career.[12]

Husserl's earliest use of the term *"Vorstellung,"* I am arguing, rather resembled Russell's theories on presentation. That presentation or acquaintance in Russell's sense can be separated from the view that we know things via ideas is indicated by Russell's statement in "On the Nature of Acquaintance": "I do not think that, when an object is known to me, there is in my mind something which may be called an 'idea' of the object, the possession of which constitutes my knowledge of the object" (LK, p. 147).

That Russell could argue for knowledge by acquaintance and still consider himself free of Frege's charges that in direct experience things *become* subjective presentations is apparent when he writes that it is wholly false "that if anything is present to me that thing is part of my mind. The upholders of 'ideas,' since they believe in the duality of the mental and the physical, infer from this assumption that only ideas, not physical things can be immediately present to me" (LK, p. 147). Though there is a fair amount of debate as to whether Brentano thought that the consciousness is immediately directed, not to the real objects of our acts, but toward some kind of mental contents, this was certainly not Husserl's view in the *Philosophy of Arithmetic:*

First of all, Husserl never in this work defends the abstractionist theory of concept formation that had its roots in British empiricism. He plainly says:

> From our point of view the presentation of the number of a specific quantity does not arise from the comparison of the objects concerned there and their subsumption under the generic concept *(Gattungsbegriff)* (horse, apple, sound, pencil) that becomes evident through this comparison. [PA, p. 159]

Husserl never speaks favorably of John Locke in *Philosophy of Arithmetic;* he even denounces his theories as absurd (p. 92) and obviously mistaken (p. 139). Though at times Husserl allies himself with John Stuart Mill (pp. 181, 189), he often criticizes him (pp. 11–12, 33, 67), and he condemns Mill's theory of abstraction in no uncertain terms (pp. 92, 167).

Second, Husserl devotes almost an entire chapter (chap. 9) to refuting Frege's views on mediation by concepts. The relationship between the concept and what is numbered is in certain respects the opposite of what Frege maintains Husserl contends (PA, p. 186). His own position turns on his observation that in the numbering process, the numberer can count the same objects in different ways according as he focuses his attention on different aspects of the objects to be counted. The conflict between them turns on the fact that for Frege a number asserts something about a concept that exists prior to any individual act of counting or any individual apprehension of the quantity, amount, group, or aggregate to be counted. And this for Frege is very basic. It constitutes one of the major planks of his antipsychologism.

The crux of the matter is that Husserl and Frege are not really talking about the same thing. They are each focusing on different sides of the same issue. Both authors subsume the things counted under a concept, but for Frege this concept is a preexisting relation. "Two" asserts something about the concept shoes: two individual shoes fall under this concept. "One" asserts something about the concept pair; two matching shoes fall under this concept. "Zero" asserts something about the concept moon of Venus. Nothing falls under this concept (FA, §46). The concept can be empty and still have meaning. Frege does not see how Husserl's theory can accommodate empty concepts (PMC, pp. 63–64).

Husserl is inquiring into the counting process, and all his observations pertain to the way things are actually counted by us. For Husserl, the concept is the concept of "anything to be counted" (PA, p. 159), anything whatsoever, as he repeatedly reminds us. This concept is generated within the counting process itself and varies from situation to situation. The way the counter himself collects and arranges what he is counting is primary. Two shoes are two shoes if we choose or need to look at them that way; they make one pair if that is the relationship under which we group them as we count. Their "shoeness," or their "pairness," or any other of their intrinsic or merely accidental qualities may or may not be relevant to us in the numbering process. Neither the shoes themselves nor any of their properties evaporate or disappear (PA, pp. 84–85), as Frege ridiculously charges (FR, pp. 323–24, 330); they just do not constitute the focus of our interest as we count.

Once it is understood what Frege and Husserl each meant by *"Vorstellung,"* it becomes clear that Frege was objecting that Husserl counted objects directly; his counting was not mediated by concepts that would intervene between the subject and objects to guarantee objectivity. A number asserts something, not about a concept, but rather about the extension of a concept, Husserl insisted (PA, p. 189). "This much is certain," Frege countered in his review, "that neither the extension of a concept, nor a totality are designated directly, but only a concept." (FR, p. 328) ". . . in a statement of a number there is invariably mention of a concept . . . if a group or aggregate is mentioned it is invariably determined by a concept, that is by the characteristics an object must have in order to belong to the group" (BL, pp. vii–ix). Since Husserl still insisted on unmediated knowledge in the *Logical Investigations* (6, §§47, 49),[13] it can be assumed that he did not find Frege's arguments compelling. As for Russell, who labored to free philosophy from the "odium of the a priori"

(LK, p. 128), it is only reasonable that he would find Frege's concepts odious and seek to remove them.

§2. CONFUSING CONCEPTS AND OBJECTS

In the late 1880s Husserl and Frege both engaged in the analysis of the concepts of arithmetic. The nature of their insights differed, however, as Frege was interested in purely logical analyses as they could be accommodated by his *Begriffsschrift* and Husserl was interested in *both* the mind's relationship to objects in the intentional act and properly logical studies of the concepts themselves. In *Philosophy of Arithmetic* Husserl provided both psychological and logical analyses of the major concepts of arithmetic. The book is subtitled "Psychological and Logical Investigations."

As a disciple of Brentano, Husserl held that each mental act was directed toward an object. In love, something is loved; in presentation something is presented. So in the mental act of counting, something is counted. It is within this context that Husserl takes up his investigations of the intentional relationship binding the counter to the counted. This is the study he labels psychological, and, though it overlaps in many fundamental ways (PMC, pp. 61–65) with Frege's investigations, it naturally contrasts with his more rationalist, Leibnizian perspective.[14]

For Husserl there were two things involved in the study of concepts: the study of the concepts themselves, and the study of the objects that fall under these concepts, as those objects are known to us via our proper and symbolic presentations. For answers to questions of a purely conceptual nature, prior to any counting process, Husserl appealed to logical analyses. The numbering process that was the object of his psychological analyses was bounded and determined a priori by logical, conceptual considerations. Logical and psychological considerations overlap, but they are not the same, and neither kind of analysis reduces to the other. Temporal succession, for example, may very possibly be necessary to the psychological analysis of addition, but logically it is contingent. Husserl cites other examples of the gap between logical and psychological analyses in chapter 11 of

Philosophy of Arithmetic (pp. 217, 244, 245, 247, 249), a chapter Frege found particularly offensive (FR, p. 337).

LOGICAL AND PSYCHOLOGICAL ANALYSES IN EARLY HUSSERL

In *Ideas* §124 Husserl points to the following passage, identical in *On the Concept of Number* and *Philosophy of Arithmetic,* to show that even in his earliest works he drew the line between the psychological and the logical. These texts, in fact, contain the implied refutation of many of Frege's charges. In the passage cited, he had written:

> . . . a distinction generally has to be made between the phenomenon as such and its use for us or what it means to us; and then also between the psychological description of a phenomenon and the indication of its meaning. The phenomenon is the basis of meaning, but it is not the meaning itself. Suppose we have a presentation of a group of objects A, B, C, D. According to the order of succession in which the whole is formed, finally only D is given as a sensory presentation. The remaining contents are, however, merely given as imaginary presentations altered in time and content. If we go in the opposite direction, from D to A, the phenomenon is different. The logical meaning nullifies all these differences. The modified contents serve as signs, as stand-ins for the unmodified. While we make the presentation of grouping, we pay no attention to the fact that, in the grouping process, changes have occurred in the content. It is our intention to hold them together and unify them and so the logical content of that presentation is not, for example, some D, then C just before, B even earlier, until we get to the most radically changed, A, but rather: (A, B, C, D). [OCN, p. 309; PA, pp. 28–29]

The following passage provides a good illustration of how Husserl viewed the two types of analysis and their relationship to each other in his *Philosophy of Arithmetic* period. In a section of *Philosophy of Arithmetic,* entitled "Numbers in arithmetic are not abstracta" he tries to resolve the following difficulty:

2 and 3 make 5; but the concept 2 and the concept 3 always remain the concept 2 and the concept 3, and they never yield the concept 5. . . . Gold and gold always remain gold; Why do not 5 and 5 always remain 5? How can one, practically speaking, join number concepts, since each one remains identically what it is, and since each concept is unique in and of itself, how should one join equal concepts?

The answer is right at hand. The arithmetician does not work with number concepts as such at all, but rather with the objects generally presented by these concepts. . . . Thus 5 does not mean the concept (the abstractum) five, but 5 is a general name (and a calculational sign) for any group of things which ranges under the concept five. 5 plus 5 equals 10 means the same thing as: a group of any things whatsoever which fall under the concept five and any other group of things which range under the same concept yield, when they are brought together, a group of things which ranges under the concept ten. [PA, pp. 201–2]

The nature and the validity of Frege's charge that Husserl mixes subjective presentations, concepts, and objects becomes clearer when we compare Husserl's view on this subject with Frege's and examine it in the light of the material examined thus far. First we need to account for a difference in terminology.

THE TERMINOLOGICAL STUMBLING BLOCKS

To understand the exchange that took place between Husserl and Frege on this issue and to evaluate Frege's appraisal of Husserl's views, we must, once again, overcome certain terminological obstacles.

Both Husserl and Frege endeavored to come to terms with the confusions brought on by the fact that in everyday discourse the same word frequently is used to designate both a concept and the objects that fall under that concept.[15]

All abstract names (in Husserl's terminology), in as much as they are also used as general names are liable to be mistakenly considered to refer to the objects that fall under the concept. The word "book" used as an abstract name designates the concept book; used as a general name it names the individual books that fall under the concept book.

To avoid mixing concepts with the objects that fall under them, Frege coined the term "concept-word" to replace the commonly used "general" or "common name." According to his usage concept-words designate concepts; proper names designate the specific objects that range under a concept.

CONCEPT AND OBJECT IN FREGE

In the *Foundations* Frege outlines his view of the phenomena Husserl also tried to elucidate:

> The business of a general term is precisely to signify a concept. Only when conjoined with the definite article or a demonstrative pronoun can it be counted as the proper name of a thing, but in that case it ceases to count as a general term. The name of a thing is a proper name. . . . That a concept need not be acquired by abstraction from the things which fall under it has already been pointed out in criticizing Spinoza. . `. . We should not be deceived by the fact that language makes use of proper names, for instance moon, as general terms, and vice versa; this does not affect the distinction between the two. As soon as a word is used with the indefinite article or in the plural without any article, it is a general term [FA, §51]

Later, in "Concept and Object," he would write on the same subject:

> The word 'concept' is used in various ways; its sense is sometimes psychological, sometimes logical, and sometimes a confused mixture of both. . . . What I decided was to keep strictly to a purely logical use. . . . A concept (as I understand the word) is predicative. It is, in fact, the meaning of a grammatical predicate. On the other hand, a name of an object, a proper name, is quite incapable of being used as a grammatical predicate. [GB, pp. 42–43]

If one joins the objective and the subjective in the term *"Vorstellung,"* Frege reasoned, then one loses sight of the differences between the one and the other. Then concepts seem sometimes objective and sometimes subjective. Objective *Vorstellungen* properly divide into concepts and objects.

Concepts, for Frege, exist entirely independently of the individual knower, and though he never developed any theories as to how the knower gains access to the objective order, he recognized the significance of the question. Frege dismisses Husserl's attempts to elucidate this dynamic as psychological, but he does not dismiss the question itself as psychological:

> The word "white" ordinarily makes us think of a certain sensation, which is, of course, entirely subjective; but even in ordinary everyday speech, it often bears, I think, an objective sense. When we call snow white, we mean to refer to an objective quality which we recognize in ordinary daylight, by a certain sensation. . . . Often, therefore, a color word does not signify our subjective sensation, which we cannot know to agree with anyone else's . . . but rather an objective quality. It is in this way that I understand objective to mean what is independent of our sensations, intuitions, and imagination, and of all construction of mental pictures out of memories of earlier sensations, but not independent of our reason. [FA, §26]

In a passage from his posthumous writings dated 1897, Frege wrote on this subject:

> But still the grasping of this law [of gravitation] is a mental process! Yes, indeed, but it is a process which takes place on the very confines of the mental and which for that reason cannot be completely understood from a purely psychological standpoint. For in grasping the law something comes into view whose nature is no longer mental in the proper sense, namely the thought; and this process is perhaps the most mysterious of all. [PW, p. 145]

Frege's complaint that Husserl has confused concept-words with the objects that fall under them, then, does not apply. In his review of Husserl's book he had written:

> This unfortunate expression "common name" is undoubtedly the cause of the confusion. This so-called common name—better called concept-word—has nothing directly to do with objects, but refers to a concept. And perhaps

objects do fall under this concept; although it may also be empty without the concept-word referring any less because of this. [FR, p. 332]

The example he gave there was:

> If we designate Tom by "human being" and Dick likewise, we should indeed be committing the mistake. Fortunately, we do not do that. When we call Tom a human being we are thereby saying that Tom falls under the concept human being; but we neither write nor say "human being" instead of Tom. [ibid.]

HUSSERL'S VIEW

Husserl's work, Frege charged in his review, is "a confused mixture of both subjective and objective." Let us now take a closer look at Husserl's views on concepts and objects.

Husserl, we have noted, distinguishes between abstract names and general names. He defines abstract names as names for abstract concepts; general names name the objects falling under these concepts. By defining these terms in this way we overcome the ambiguity in question (PA, pp. 150–53). He gives the word "color" as an example:

> Thus, for example, color can mean [bedeuten] the logical part for itself which is common to reds, blues, etc. If we speak of colors, though, of "this color" or "that color" etc. then color is a general name for each individual color species as such. To mark off more distinctly this way of using the name, instead of "color," we say "a color," "a certain color," etc. when we refer to the abstractum, we stress the abstract concept color (or simply the concept color). In the plural there is naturally no need for such additions since then, eo ipso, only the objects of the concept can be referred to. [PA, p. 151]

Husserl, we have seen, would not have confused the abstract name "human being" with any object falling under it. He would, however, apply the general name "human being" to objects falling under that designation. In the previous chapter we noted that Husserl did "distinctly maintain the difference between symbolic presentations and general presentations. A general presentation 'a man' is not the presentation (even symbolic) of a specific man Pierre" (PA, p. 215–16).

CONCLUSION

So the word "concept," for Husserl, as for Frege, is ambiguous. By it we designate either an abstract entity, or the actual objects that range under the concept. In the first case, logical analyses are called for. In the second case, for Husserl, psychological analyses are appropriate. But Husserl clearly distinguishes between the two kinds of analyses and undertakes both kinds of analyses for the major concepts concerned. From *Philosophy of Arithmetic* he would progress to the logical studies that led to the *Logical Investigations* and from there to the studies of ideal structures and their relationship to the consciousness. The principal insights of his later work, I hope I am demonstrating, were already anticipated in the early work we are studying here. In these early works, Husserl was interested in the objects, or more broadly, the phenomena themselves as they are grasped in the intentional act.

Here, once again, Frege chose to apply an innovative terminology to conceptions he shared with many of his contemporaries, Husserl included. Once again Husserl drew the distinctions in question, but applied them within the context of his own philosophical preoccupations and to meet his own ends. The Frege criticism studied in this section is, then, mainly a terminological one since Husserl basically shared Frege's insights. Frege's intellectual heirs in English-speaking countries themselves deviated from Frege's views,[16] both terminologically and philosophically. These facts were obscured when Frege's thought went abroad, with the result that Frege's thought has seemed more original than it was.

§3. SUBJECTIVITY AND THE OBJECTIVITY OF KNOWLEDGE

Husserl espoused a version of empirical psychology, he subsequently denounced several versions of psychologism, and it will probably always be argued that he lapsed back into psychologism after his extensive refutation of it in the *Logical Investigations*. These are facts on which nearly everyone acquainted with Husserl's work will agree, and each reflects a stage in Husserl's lifelong struggle to grasp, elucidate, and detail the relationship of the subjectivity of the knower to the objectivity of the known.

The conflict in Husserl

In about 1890 Husserl's interests began to move away from empirical studies of the mind's grasp of objects in the natural viewpoint toward studies of the mind's grasp of ideal objects in the phenomenological stance. In 1906 he wrote of the conflicts he experienced as he completed the first volume of the *Philosophy of Arithmetic:*

> I was a beginner with no proper knowledge of philosophical problems, with no proper training of my philosophical abilities. And while I struggled to outline the logic of mathematical thought, and especially mathematical calculation, incredibly strange worlds tormented me, the world of pure logic and the world of act-consciousness, which I would now call the phenomenological and the psychological. I did not know how to bring them together and yet they had to stand in some relation to each other and form an inner unity. . . . Extension to the entire region of pure logic mainly brought about a concern with logical calculus in Winter 1890, then came the 1891–92 Psychology course, which caused me to take a look into the writings on descriptive psychology, drawing me longingly to them.[17]

In his posthumously published introduction to the *Logical Investigations,* Husserl discusses the battle that ensued:

> The reader of the "Prolegomena" is made a participant in a conflict between two motifs within the logical sphere which are contrasted in radical sharpness: the one is the psychological, the other the purely logical. The two do not come together by accident. . . . Somehow they necessarily belong together. But they are to be distinguished namely in this matter: everything "purely" logical is an "in itself," is an "ideal" which includes in this "in itself"—in its proper essential content—nothing mental, nothing of acts, of subjects, or even of empirically factual persons. . . . [ILI, p. 20]

His fight culminates in analyses like the following:

> There is an essential, quite unbridgeable difference
> between sciences of the ideal and sciences of the real. The
> former are *a priori,* the latter empirical. . . . Ultimate ob-
> jects are, in the former case, empirical facts. . . . A correct
> assessment of these differences presupposes the complete
> abandonment of the empiricistic theory of abstraction,
> whose present dominance renders all logical matters
> unintelligible. [LI, p. 185]

PHILOSOPHY OF ARITHMETIC IN A NEW LIGHT

Husserl transformed his early work, but he never completely
repudiated it. The things-in-themselves that had previously only
been of interest to him in as much as they made themselves
known in objects in the natural standpoint now became the over-
riding focus of his concern. This radical shift in the nature of
the objects to be grasped and studied required radically new
analyses of the grasping process. This opened up whole new
vistas of inquiry, but it largely allowed Husserl to leave in place
many of the analyses he had made from the natural viewpoint.
Thus we find this evaluation of *Philosophy of Arithmetic* in the
foreword to the *Logical Investigations:*

> Where one was concerned with questions as to the origin
> of mathematical presentations, or with the elaboration of
> those practical methods which are indeed psychologically
> determined, psychological analyses seemed to me to pro-
> mote clearness and instruction. But once one had passed
> from the psychological connections of thinking, to the
> logical unity of the thought-content (the unity of theory),
> no true continuity and unity could be established. I
> became more and more disquieted by doubts of principle
> as to how to reconcile the objectivity of mathematics, and
> of science in general, with a psychological foundation for
> logic. . . . I felt myself more and more pushed towards
> general critical reflections on the essence of logic, and on
> the relationship, in particular, between the subjectivity of
> knowing and the objectivity of the content known. [LI,
> p. 42]

The extent to which Husserl—for questions concerning the natural order—retained the basic elements of his early analyses becomes apparent when one compares passages like the following (in which he cites Frege favorably) with his earlier analyses of the counting process:

> Counting and arithmetical operations as *facts*, as mental acts proceeding in time, are of course the concern of psychology, since it is the empirical science of mental facts in general. Arithmetic is in a totally different position. . . . The number Five is not my own or anyone else's counting of five, it is also not my presentation of anyone else's presentation of five. . . . If we make clear to ourselves what the number Five truly is, if we conceive of it adequately, we shall first achieve an articulate collective presentation of this or that set of five objects. In this act a collection is intuitively given. . . . Looking at this intuited individual, we perform an 'abstraction', i.e., we not only isolate the non-independent moment of a collective form in what is before us, but we apprehend the Idea in it: the number Five as the species of the form that swims into our conscious sphere of reference. [LI, pp. 179–80]

THE PARADOXES

Understood on his own terms, Husserl did not confuse psychological analyses with logical or phenomenological analyses. He held them distinct while trying to understand the necessary interplay among them. It was just as much the intention of the *Logical Investigations* to separate the knower from the known as it was to join them again in a new way, to show how, though utterly distinct, they still must interact.

Nonetheless, certain confusions and misunderstandings necessarily result from the paradoxes that arise from this state of affairs. Three such paradoxes concern us here:

1. Husserl both did and did not repudiate the *Philosophy of Arithmetic*.

2. Husserl manages to transform the specific analyses of *Philosophy of Arithmetic* while leaving them intact.

3. It was Husserl's lifelong ambition to join what he held to be radically separate.

Husserl did not mix the subjective and the objective in the manner in which Frege argued he did in his review, and, as I have said, understood on his own terms, Husserl did not exactly mix them at all. Still, Husserl's particular attempts to define the relationship of the subjective to the objective is framed in paradoxes that lend some legitimacy to Frege's charge.[18]

§4. THINGS-IN-THEMSELVES

In his review of *Philosophy of Arithmetic* Frege approvingly acknowledges the presence in Husserl's work of "numbers-in-themselves which are independent of our thinking, which exist even when they are not accessible to us" (FR, p. 336). Frege expresses his pleasure that these elements of a nonempiricist view of number appear more frequently in the last chapters of Husserl's work, thus, it would seem, indicating progress toward a view more compatible with his own. In this section I want to document the steps in Husserl's passage from the views he entertained in *Philosophy of Arithmetic* to the view he takes up in the *Logical Investigations*. I will argue that even as *Philosophy of Arithmetic* was published Husserl had come to hold that arithmetic was an analytic discipline and that it and other formal analytic disciplines had been "left in the lurch" by logics that were inadequate to the broader epistemological issues involved in the relationship between the knower and the known that were the abiding focus of his concern throughout his lifetime.

NUMBERS-IN-THEMSELVES IN THE EARLY WRITINGS

First, we need to point out that things-in-themselves, and numbers-in-themselves specifically, appear in Husserl's writings as early as *On the Concept of Number*. In material almost identical in *On the Concept of Number* and *Philosophy of Arithmetic,* Husserl had written:

> . . . it is clear that to call numbers pure mental creations of internal intuition is an exaggeration and a distortion of the real situation. Numbers are mental creations to the

> degree to which they result from activities we perform on
> concrete contents. . . . But these activities do not produce
> new absolute contents which we can then find again some-
> where in space or in the external world. . . . What is in-
> tuitively present, what we can find and notice in space
> are not numbers-in and for-themselves, but only spatial
> objects and their spatial relations. No number is, however,
> given in that way. . . . [OCN, p. 317; see also PA, pp. 45–46]

References to numbers-in-themselves, and things-in-themselves
appear in *On the Concept of Number* and are found frequently
throughout the *Philosophy of Arithmetic,*[19] but ideal entities are
far from constituting the focus of these works. Husserl primarily
intended them to be studies in empirical psychology, and as we
have seen, that meant the study of the mind's relationship to the
objects falling under the concepts in question. Concepts-in-
themselves did exist, in his theory, but they were only interesting
to the degree in which they were manifest in particular objects.

Again on the subject of general names and abstract names,
Husserl writes:

> In conformity with practical needs, most names usually
> function as general names. By preference our interest is
> directed toward concrete things and relations. Nonethe-
> less, in life and in science, there are many occasions to
> consider the abstract as such. . . . Naturally, the abstract
> concept in question was already formed when the general
> name emerged; but it was only of interest to the degree
> to which there were objects that contained it as a charac-
> teristic *[Merkmal].* Interest in the abstractum for itself can
> then very well only have come about later and given rise
> to a special designation. [PA, p. 152]

THE ROLE OF THE CARDINAL NUMBER

The role ideal entities played in Husserl's thought shifted in
the early 1890s. This shift went hand in hand with Husserl's
refusal of empirical analyses of number concepts and with his
new conviction that arithmetic and mathematics in general could
not be derived from an analysis of the cardinal number. He came
to reject his earlier empiricist orientation because of the dif-

ficulties he encountered as he tried to apply Brentano's techniques to the mathematical phenomena he had hoped to explain in the second volume of *Philosophy of Arithmetic*. The mathematician in him balked before empirical analyses of mental experiences of fractions and imaginary, negative, and irrational numbers.

Frege attempted to derive arithmetic from logical analyses of cardinal numbers and failed. Although he assigned other numbers (i.e., negative, fractional, irrational, and complex numbers) a place in his theories, he never provided analyses for them. Frege concluded his *Foundations* with the following passage:

> Our earlier treatment of the positive whole numbers showed us the possibility of avoiding all importation of external things and geometrical intuitions into arithmetic, without, for all that, falling into the error of the formalists. Here once again the task is the same, to fix the content of a recognition-judgement. Once supposed this everywhere accomplished, and numbers of every kind, whether negative, fractional, irrational or complex, are revealed as no more mysterious than the positive whole numbers, which in turn have no better claim to reality, or to existence or to intelligibility, than they. [FA, §109]

Nine years later, in 1893, he would begin his *Basic Laws* with the following words:

> In this book there are to be found theorems upon which arithmetic is based, proved by the use of symbols, which collectively I call *Begriffsschrift*. . . . It will be seen that negative, fractional, irrational and complex numbers have still been left out of account, as have addition, multiplication and so on. [BL, p. v]

Husserl also began his philosophical, logical, and mathematical inquiries with conceptual analyses of cardinal numbers, and in *On the Concept of Number* he was convinced that arithmetic and mathematics in general could be derived from them.

By the time *Philosophy of Arithmetic* was published he no longer held this to be true, and it was precisely his inability to provide adequate analyses of negative, fractional, irrational, complex, and imaginary numbers that forced him to change his orientation. He gave up both his empirical analyses and his view of the primacy of the cardinal number. The first would meet with Frege's approval; the second could not. No logic of his time was adequate to the problems Husserl faced. Frege's logic, oriented as it still was toward the analysis of the cardinal number as the basis for arithmetic, could not help Husserl.

In the next section I will document the progression described above.

THE MOVEMENT AWAY FROM EMPIRICISM DOCUMENTED

In *On the Concept of Number,* Husserl expressed his confidence in his methods and the very fundamental role of the cardinal number in mathematics in the broadest sense of the word:

> It is nowadays generally held that the whole of the *arithmetica universalis* in Newton's sense of the word . . . would have exclusively to come from the elementary arithmetic in which it is grounded. . . . The sole foundation of elementary arithmetic, however, is the concept of number, or to be more exact, that infinite series of concepts which mathematicians call "positive whole numbers." All the more complicated and more artificial constructions which we as well call numbers i.e., fractions and irrational numbers, negative and complex numbers have their origin and support in elementary number concepts and in the relations which bind them. If these latter concepts fall; the former fall with them and even mathematics must, then, begin with the analysis of the concept of number. This analysis is the goal of the present study. The means that it uses to this end must belong to psychology if this kind of inquiry is ever to provide any sure results. [OCN, p. 294–95]

By comparing his *On the Concept of Number* position with his views on the same question in *Philosophy of Arithmetic* we are witness to the evolution in his thinking. His introduction to the *Philosophy of Arithmetic* shows Husserl had reservations at the time he was writing the book:

> Other than the kinds of numbers belonging to practical life, there is still another important series of other numbers which are particular to the science of arithmetic. These

are positive and negative numbers, rational and irrational numbers, quaternions, alternative numbers, ideal numbers, etc. As dissimilar, however, as the arithmetical expression of these numbers may be, they still include the numerical signs 1, 2, 3 . . . and so cardinal numbers seem in a certain way to be the basis for arithmetic. [PA, p. 5]

This position is going to serve as his point of departure for the time being and he will provisionally begin with the conceptual analysis of cardinal numbers but he warns, "Do not expect from that, in any way, a final verdict. Perhaps even a further development in volume II will show that the position we have assumed is untenable" (PA, p. 6).

The preface to *Philosophy of Arithmetic,* written in 1891, at the time of its publication, documents the next decisive step in Husserl's movement away from his early position. In it Husserl promises that the second volume, "already largely worked out, will appear in a year's time" (PA, p. ix). The first part of this second volume was to deal with, among other things, fractions and negative, imaginary, and irrational numbers (PA, p. vii). This study was to provide ample opportunity to

consider the question whether it is the domain of cardinal numbers, or which conceptual domain if it be another, regulates general arithmetic in its ultimate, primary sense. The second part of volume II will be dedicated to this fundamental question. The conclusion is that exactly the same algorithm, the same *arithmetica universalis* regulates a series of conceptual domains which must be well separated, and that in no way does one single kind of concept *[Begriffsart],* whether it be the cardinal number, the ordinal number, or any other find universal application throughout. [PA, p. viii]

A letter Husserl wrote to Carl Stumpf (to whom he would dedicate the *Logical Investigations*) in late 1890 or early 1891 provides more information:

The results which I have attained are sufficiently noteworthy. The opinion by which I was still guided in the elaboration of my *Habilitationsschrift* to the effect that the concept of cardinal number forms the foundation of arithmetic, soon proved to be false. (I was already led to this by the analysis of the ordinal number.) By no clever devices, by no 'symbolic presentation' can one derive negative, irrational and the various sorts of complex numbers from the concept of the cardinal number. The same is true of the concept of the ordinal, of the concept of magnitude and so on. . . .[20] Since these various applications of arithmetic rely on no ordinary concept from which this science could be deductively derived, what is, then, its content, what are the conceptual objects to which these principles apply?[21]

Alongside these considerations Husserl writes in the same letter:

> The *arithmetica universalis* is not a science, but is rather a part of formal logic which I would define as a technique of signs . . . and which I would characterize as making up a special, and one of the most important, chapters in logic as theory of knowledge. . . .[22] My view requires important reforms in logic. I know of no logic that would even give an account of the very possibility of a genuine calculational technique.[23]

That in mid-1891 Husserl had set out in pursuit of the answers to these questions is indicated in a letter to Frege (July 18, 1891):

> . . . I still have only a rough idea of how you want to justify the imaginary in arithmetic. After many vain efforts I found a path leading to that goal, but in your discussion of it ('On Formal Theories of Arithmetic,' p. 8), you hold that path to be impassable. During the summer vacations I am thinking of turning my relevant drafts into a clear copy. [PMC, p. 65]

The continuation of *Philosophy of Arithmetic* was never published, and only notes for it were found in Husserl's *Nachlass*.[24] Instead, as his published writings of the period reveal, Husserl turned to properly logical studies.[25] Husserl himself mapped his passage from empirical psychology and the study of the concept of number, through the logic of his time to the new logic he would begin to unfurl in the *Logical Investigations*.

Husserl recalls how his training had prepared him to view the philosophy of mathematics as the radical analysis of the "psychological origins" of the basic concepts of mathematics, and how in *On the Concept of Number* and *Philosophy of Arithmetic* he had studied the "origins" of mathematical notions (ILI, pp. 33–34). It was in writing those works that he first encountered some of the structures he would outline more fittingly in *Logical Investigations,* and it was while working on them from 1887 to 1891 that he began to have doubts as to his method. He was tormented by doubts as to the true nature of number from the very beginning, and these doubts

> then extended to all categorical concepts as I later called them and finally in another form to all concepts of objectivities of any sort whatsoever. The customary appeal in the Brentano school to symbolic presentation . . . could not help. . . . The immense importance that "purely symbolic thinking" has for consciousness could, after all sorts of difficulties, theoretically be comprehended by external logic, as it were, in the case of mathematics. But how symbolic thinking is "possible," how the objective, mathematical, and logical relations constitute themselves in subjectivity, how the insight into this is to be understood, and how the mathematical in itself, as given in the medium of the psychical, could be valid, this all remained a mystery. [ILI, p. 35]

PURE LOGIC AND THE MATHESIS UNIVERSALIS

The nature of these difficulties soon led Husserl to reappraise the work of Bolzano and Lotze, which he now viewed as initial attempts to develop the pure logic he now sought. He would later write in the posthumous introduction to the *Logical Investigations* that

> pure logic develops through a step by step extension of that particular concept of formal logic which remains as a residue of pure ideal doctrines dealing with "propositions" and validity after the removal from traditional logic of all the psychological misinterpretations and the normative-practical goal positings. In its thoroughly proper extension it includes all of the pure "analytical" doctrines of mathematics (arithmetic, number theory, algebra, etc.) and the entire area of formal theories. . . . Thus no

psychologistic empiricism à la Mill can change the fact
that pure mathematics is a strictly self-contained system
of doctrines which is to be cultivated using methods that
are essentially different from those of natural science. [ILI,
pp. 28–29]

Of his new understanding of the relationship between mathematics, logic, theory of knowledge, and phenomenology, he
would write in the same introduction:

> The *mathesis universalis* in its so-to-say naive as well as
> its technical forms, as it has been grounded in the natural-
> objective orientation and can then be further cultivated,
> has at first no common cause with epistemology and
> phenomenology—just as little as ordinary arithmetic (a
> subdivision of *mathesis universalis*) has. However, if it also
> assumes the problem of phenomenological "elucidation"
> in the sense of the "Prolegomena" and of the second
> volume if as a consequence of this it learns from the
> sources of phenomenology what the solution is to the
> great riddles which here as everywhere arise from the cor-
> relation between being and consciousness, if in the process
> it learns as well the ultimate formulation of the meaning
> of concepts and propositions (a formulation which only
> phenomenology is capable of providing): then it will have
> transformed itself from the naive into the truly philosoph-
> ical pure logic. . . . it is not a mere coupling of phenome-
> nology of knowledge with natural-objective *mathesis* but
> is rather an application of the former to the latter. [ILI,
> pp. 29–30]

Of the extension of these same preoccupations beyond the
Logical Investigations, Husserl declared in 1925:

> The pressing need to universalize the perspective of the
> *Logical Investigations*—a need already awakened by the
> formal universality of the *mathesis universalis*—necessarily
> meant the extension of logic and of *a priori* and formal
> logic and mathematics to the idea of an all encompass-
> ing system for *a priori* sciences for all conceivable cate-
> gories of objective realities, consequently, *à la limite,* the
> need for a universal *a priori* of possible worlds in general
> next to that of formal mathematics, but also, and cor-
> relatively, the extension of the pure *a priori* consideration
> of the knowing consciousness concerning only formal

generalities up to the level of a knowing consciousness more determinant in its content, related to all categories of objectivities in general. And from that to a theory of the pure *a priori* consciousness in its total universality would finally develop. . . .[26]

If there are important arithmetical concepts of which we can have no direct access via our experiences of concrete phenomena, and which cannot be derived from any experiences we can have, then, Husserl apparently reasoned, these concepts must exist somehow independently outside the knowing process. So Husserl set out to find new answers to the fundamental questions this old philosophical problem was raising again.

Husserl's reflections led him to separate the ideal from the psychological. Understanding how the "being-in-itself" of the ideal sphere relates to the consciousness involves enigmas that, he concluded, could only be resolved by using the new phenomenological methods that he began to develop as he furthered and corrected work he had done on the philosophy of arithmetic.

As mathematicians, logicians, and philosophers, then, both Husserl and Frege suffered, already in the 1880s, the inadequacy of the logic of their time to the tasks that it was to facilitate. Both endeavored to develop a logic that could overcome the inadequacies they perceived. The efforts of both were inextricably bound up with their pursuit of objective scientific truth, and the results and implications of their work determined how subsequent generations of philosophers would define the philosophical enterprise.

Frege's attempts to derive arithmetic from logical analyses of the concept of cardinal number ultimately failed. Before Husserl had read any of Frege's writings, he had himself hoped to derive arithmetic from studies of the concept of cardinal number using the philosophical methods he had learned from Brentano. At the time he published *Philosophy of Arithmetic* he was already expressing reservations as to the feasibility of his project. He had thoroughly studied Frege's work on the philosophy of arithmetic and by 1891 was convinced that Frege's method was doomed to failure. It was the nature of the problems he encountered in his attempts to analyse various sorts of numbers that convinced him that there was as yet no logic adequate to the task he and Frege had set for themselves; Frege's 1894 attack on Husserl's early work was not the decisive factor in his movement toward phenomenology. Frege's review of the *Philosophy of Arithmetic* is probably the worst thing Frege ever wrote.

CONCLUSION:
ANALYTICITY

THROUGHOUT PART ONE I have argued that under the influence of men like Stumpf and Cantor in Halle in the late 1880s the young mathematician Husserl both gradually dissociated himself from empirical psychology and repudiated Frege's logicism. In 1885 Cantor had lauded Frege's eschewal of psychologism and decried his espousal of extensions; Cantor was recommending Bolzano's *Paradoxes of the Infinite*. Husserl studied Frege's *Foundations* thoroughly during those years and managed to pinpoint its chief failings in his *Philosophy of Arithmetic,* three years before Frege's famous review of that book appeared.

I have also argued that Husserl's notion of noema was not in any special way influenced by Frege's inquiries into meaning. So the question that remains to be answered here is, How can these conclusions be reconciled with Husserl's statement that Frege's critique had "hit the nail on the head?"

The most interesting answer, I believe, is that the crucial factor in Husserl's abandonment of psychologism concerned analyticity. Husserl said directly that his study of Leibniz's truths of reason and truths of fact, and a new "keen awareness" of the contrast between Hume's matters of fact and relations of ideas, on the one hand, and Kant's analytic and synthetic judgments, on the other, undermined his confidence in empirical psychology and set the stage for his conversion (ILI, p. 36). The whole approach whereby the overcoming of psychologism is phenomenologically accomplished, he said, showed that his earlier analyses of immanent consciousness must be considered as a pure *a priori* analysis of essence. . . . The starting point lay in intensive studies of Hume's relations among ideas as compared to Leibniz's truths of reason and to Kant's analytic truths, and, at the same time, to Lotze studies. . . . So for many years he strove to work out the proper concept of the analytical as opposed to the obscure Kantian one and to discover the boundary, fundamental for philosophy, which separates genuine analytic ontology from material ontology which must be essentially distinct from it (ILI, p. 42–43).

He called Kant's logic "utterly defective" (LI, Prolegomena §58). Kant neither saw how little the laws of logic are all analytic propositions in the sense laid down by his own definition, nor how little his dragging in of an evident principle for analytic propositions really helped to clear up the achievements of analytic thinking (LI 6, §66).

Among those who in the nineteenth century had attacked Kant's definition of analyticity were Husserl's mentors Brentano[1] and Bolzano.[2] Frege did, too (FA, §§88, 109). Husserl attacked it in one way when in the *Philosophy of Arithmetic* he, then suspicious of definitions, criticized Frege's attempts to ground arithmetic in the analysis and definition of concepts (PA, p. 129). All one can do in those cases, he contended then, is to show the concrete phenomena from which our concepts have been abstracted (PA, p. 130). These criticisms appear on the only three pages he ever retracted from *Philosophy of Arithmetic.*

As he worked on the foundations of arithmetic, Husserl came to believe that arithmetic and knowledge in general had to have the kind of objective underpinnings that psychologism could never provide. As he recalls in the foreword to the *Logical Investigations,* there were connections in which a psychological foundation for mathematics and for science in general never came to satisfy him. He came to doubt whether psychological analyses could establish any true unity or continuity, and his doubts shook his confidence in the psychologism favored by his contemporaries (LI, p. 42).

He did come to agree with Frege that there had to be some a priori structure to gird knowledge and guarantee the unity and continuity that empirical psychology could not provide, but the part of his critique of Frege that he never retracted shows plainly that he did not think Frege had the answer either.

Husserl's new reflections on analyticity led him to abandon an epistemological view that could provide only a fragmented view of reality. It may be presumed that he would also have balked before the kind of fragmentation that talks of rabbit parts, river stages and kinship, and according to which the ontologies of physical objects and mathematical objects are myths relative to an epistemological view that Quine so eloquently describes,[3] and so many of his contemporaries have seemed primed to embrace as a consequence of their logical endeavors. Quine's reflections on analyticity, reductionism, and the phenomenalism to which he has pledged his allegiance can in fact be compared in instructive ways to the considerations that conditioned Husserl's turn from psychologism. One cannot help but speculate that Quine's behaviorism would have incurred Frege's wrath, but all this extends beyond the bounds of this study.

An important point remains to be made about meaning in Husserl and Frege. Both their theories represented their efforts to overcome inadequacies they perceived in Kant's notion of analyticity. The new problem for Frege and his successors became that a potentially infinite number of predicates may coincide in extension and still differ (in ways significant for philosophy, though perhaps not for mathematics) in intension. Innumerably many things may be known, said or predicated of *any* object of discourse. Intelligent discourse involves reference, both implicit and explicit, to the multiple facts about objects that do actually intervene to alter the truth or falsehood of what we want to say about those objects.

In his work on Husserl and Frege, J. N. Mohanty cites a passage from Husserl's *Formal and Transcendental Logic* to show that Husserl held the object to be as unsaturated, ever incomplete, as what can be predicated of it. As Quine would later put it, ". . . what is indeterminate . . . is not just meaning, but extension, reference."[4] This is the deep reason why Husserl's theories on noema and horizons seem related to certain discussions in contemporary semantics. The passage Mohanty cites is reminiscent of points made by Frege in his later writings, after he became convinced that his logicism had failed. The case of the mountain variously called Aphla and Ateb (PMC, p. 80) is one of them; that of the loser of Waterloo and the victor of Austerlitz (PMC, p. 97) is another. In the passage Mohanty cites, Husserl had written:

> If we say *A is b*, and continue, *A is c*, the two propositions do not have an identical member. The same object A is meant twice, but in a different How; and this How itself appertains to the noematic meaning. . . . Occupy-

ing the corresponding places in the two propositions, we have differents, each with a content A, that is quite like that of the others; and these contents are formed differently.[5]

In 1914 Frege wrote to Philip Jourdain of the hypothetical case of two explorers who sighting the same mountain from two distinct vantage points accordingly gave it two different names. Later it is discovered that Aphla is the same as Ateb. The new proposition "Ateb is Aphla" is not of the form $a=a$, but rather $a=b$, and so contains a valuable piece of geographical knowledge. Studying this situation more closely, Frege concludes:

> An object can be determined in different ways and every one of these ways of determining it can give rise to a special name and these names then have different senses; for it is not self-evident that it is the same object which is being determined in different ways. [PMC, p. 80]

Five years later he wrote to Linke:

> . . . the property of being victor of Austerlitz cannot be gathered either without further ado from the designation 'the loser of Waterloo.' We can indeed know this or that property of the designated object from the individual name; but there is no reason why all the properties of the designatum should be capable of being known in this way. Why could the loser of Waterloo not have properties which are not characteristic of the concept loser of Waterloo? [PMC, p. 97]

As Husserl extended the notion of meaning to the realm of all acts, he worked to develop a theory that could account for the indeterminacy inherent in any particular perception of any given object. The intentional acts by which we apprehend objects are inherently perspectival, he concluded. No perceptual determination is ever complete in itself. It leaves open a horizon for further determination. That horizon includes both the various ways in which the object might be apprehended by the subject and the potentially infinite number of things that could be, but are not in this instance, predicated of that object. While the first point *might* be dismissed as being psychologistic, the second, that each object is given with its horizon of possibilities, that it can be apprehended under infinitely many descriptions no single one of which can exhaustively determine it, is a logical and ontological thesis that pertains to the truth and falsehood of any statements made about things.

Within very different contexts both Husserl's theory of the transcendence of the object and Quine's reflections on the inscrutability of reference recognize and attempt to account for this seemingly unavoidable fact common to both objects and objects of discourse in general — that is, their elusiveness.

Possible Worlds Logic also attempts to account for the difficulties this plethora of possible predicates poses for logicians, but it misses the point. The problem is that referents are radically undetermined in this world. Referents automatically come armed with a formidable number of senses. As Frege himself noted, one never attains to comprehensive knowledge of a thing (GB, p. 58). We do not need functions to multiple possible worlds. We need multiple functions for each object we need to treat in this world. Hintikka has conceded that, though the logical and semantical analysis we have makes it much more appropriate to speak of several worlds, it does sound somewhat weird, and it would be more natural to speak of different possibilities concerning the "actual" world.[6]

This comment seems to imply that these procedures are somehow equivalent, but they are not. The latter, Husserl's choice, leaves us with hard philosophical problems to solve about familiar objects. The former suggests a weird ontology that should offend any healthy sense of reality. The problems involved are necessarily more thorny for the extensionalist logician who needs to have a firm grasp on extensions, who needs to quantify over something, and who relies on the principle of substitutivity of identicals as a principle of inference. The answer cannot be to multiply worlds because that suits a logical notation that cannot cope with multiple possibilities concerning a given object in this world.

Part Two

CONCEPTUAL
CLARITY

INTRODUCTION

". . . the task of logic can hardly be performed without trying
to recognize the thought in its manifold guises."
Gottlob Frege [GB, p. 46]

Clear conceptual analyses have been a hallmark of analytic
philosophy. And, as this concern for conceptual clarity was one
of the fruits of the conceptually troubled atmosphere of the turn
of the century, it is perhaps an inevitable irony that when analytic
philosophy looks back to its origins,[1] its perception of what exactly
went on is muddled by conceptual equivocation that has been
exacerbated by uncertain translations.[2] Analysis succeeds analysis,
but no satisfying account seems to have surfaced to still the discussion, and the flurry of activity itself seems more and more a symptom of deeper problems. It is these root problems that I try to uncover in this study of concepts central to Frege's thought.

Numerous factors have in fact combined to disguise the issues,
so that as turn-of-the-century philosophical concerns continue,
as they must, to make their way into present-day discussions, philosophers increasingly run the risk of generating pseudoproblems
from the confusion. A philosophical housecleaning is in order, for
Frege and his successors have repeatedly warned against the mis-
takes that arise from the ambiguity of expressions.

One problem is that, for many reasons, the distinctions vital
to Frege's perspective have not come down to us in a very distinct
way. There was notoriously little clarity in philosophy at the time
Frege struggled with the questions that still concern us today. Frege
complained vociferously about this and his complaints are well
known. But he only voiced the frustrations others like him felt,
Husserl included. One gauge of the confusion we are considering
here is that *every* term studied in this section (i.e., *"Inhalt," "Um-
fang," "Begriff," "Gegenstand," "Vorstellung," "Gedanke," "Idee," "Sinn,"*
and *"Bedeutung"*[3] has been used as a synonym for "meaning" in

one or other of the contexts in question. This legacy of confusion has been passed down to us and we confront it today in a different guise to the extent that we can still fairly say that Frege's problems are our problems. Moreover, the equivalences we have overlap in deceptive ways with English concepts that have different associations or a very different history.

Russell signaled this problem early on when, in 1903, he introduced Frege to the English-speaking world:

> Frege is compelled, as I have been, to employ common words in technical senses which depart more or less from usage. As his departures are frequently different from mine, a difficulty arises as regards the translation of his terms. Some of these, to avoid confusion, I shall leave untranslated, since every English equivalent that I can think of has already been employed by me in a slightly different sense. [PofM, p. 501]

This terminological predicament would not in and of itself pose a problem if it did not yield confusion on a deeper conceptual, and even ontological level—if (to use Frege's words) philosophers were "grasping the thought in its various guises." To the extent, however, that they fail in this, they begin to undermine the whole task of philosophy as it has been conceived in English-speaking countries in the twentieth century. For if we are going to confront conceptual issues, we must know how to identify our concepts.

The recourse open to us, then is to undertake the philosophical activity of clarification, and thus to endeavor to fill a gap in the current literature by studying more closely the fate met by Frege's main semantical notions. Much recent scholarship has used Frege's ideas as springboards to the consideration of more pressing contemporary concerns. These studies suit well the intentions of what Frege's philosophy has become, but they require a complement. We need now, instead of working exclusively from our own vantage point, to work further to reestablish the context in which Frege thought his thoughts and to recapture some of the how and why of their immigration to English-speaking countries. In fact, once this is done and the superficial terminological barriers are removed, certain similarities and disparities disappear while others come to light as a clearer picture of the issues emerges to alter the philosophical landscape.

We have the privilege of undertaking this study with the distance and sophistication the passage of time affords. I propose to take advantage of this to obtain a more certain grasp on the present situation and so provide clearer foundations for the questions philosophers are asking now. I hope that, in addition to the goals just outlined, this account of the permutations wrought in Frege's thought over the years can—

1. begin to uncover and limn the structure of the preconceptions that have buttressed analytic philosophy, and so to provide additional insight into just how the conceptual routes were forged that brought philosophy into the twentieth century.

2. continue to illustrate the fact that, however little the Anglo-American and Continental schools of thought may now have in common, they started in about exactly the same place, since Husserl tangled with the same set of considerations that brought about the linguistic turn.

3. continue to point out why certain aspects of Husserl's thought seem to resemble certain issues in twentieth-century semantical theory.

4. continue to show how confusions in the concepts in question have displaced certain issues in contemporary semantics and have also been responsible for some of the mistaken ideas about the nature of the exchange that took place between Husserl and Frege—and, as a consequence, for misunderstandings regarding the development of Husserl's thought.

5. begin to show how the same confusions have obscured many of the issues Russell and Wittgenstein tangled with as they engineered the linguistic turn.

6. mark the passage from Husserl and Frege to the thought of their immediate successors, those who translated their insights into English (i.e., Russell, Wittgenstein, and Carnap.)

6

INTENSIONS AND
EXTENSIONS

The facts seem to be that while mathematical logic requires
extensions, philosophical logic refuses to supply anything but
intensions. —Bertrand Russell [PM, p. 72]

Intensions are creatures of darkness. . . . —W.V.O. Quine[1]

BY THE BEGINNING of the twentieth century it had long been
customary to distinguish between two kinds of meaning, a meaning in intension, and a meaning in extension.[2] The first term
referred to the properties something was said to have to be so named
and it was considered the meaning proper. The second designated
the objects, if any, to which the expression referred. It was considered natural to distinguish between the expression, its meaning,
and what it denoted, but it was also considered quite significant,
so that the principal logicians of the nineteenth century labored
to develop logics that could come to terms with issues such a distinction raises. The two kinds of meaning were considered complementary and inseparable.[3] Mathematicians were said to lean toward
extensional analyses, while philosophers were said to prefer intensional logic (PM, pp. 8, 22; PofM, §66). The foremost extensionalist logicians were English.[4]

These logical terms do not, however, have for us now the same
meaning they had for Husserl, Frege, Russell, and their contemporaries, and there is now no straight road that leads from their
understanding of these terms to the way we use them today.

Frege's views on extensions and intensions matured and changed,
and he finally altered them in a way that became decisive for

twentieth-century philosophy. Russell transplanted Frege's ideas onto English logical soil (where the terms in question already had their own history and meaning), and he adapted them to his own purposes without himself sorting through the quite significant philosophical issues that come up when the German word *"Inhalt"* appears in one context or another. In addition, Carnap, one of the rare people who had actually studied under Frege, added a new chapter to logical history when, in mid-century, he sought to reintroduce intensions to a logical world that had worked hard to eliminate them. The debate continues today, but the issues have been confused through long-term lack of attention paid to the philosophical issues such shifts must involve.

The school of philosophy that has in recent years begun to take a serious look at intensional logic, that has produced an abundant literature on sense and reference, and that has inquired into the nineteenth-century roots of its logic, still seems unconscious of the heritage of this concept and the difficulties in logic and in the interpretation of logical writings that an inadequate grasp of this notion carries with it.

What seemed clear has become abstruse. What once seemed to be the more significant of two elements in a quite ordinary theory of meaning has suffered an ignominious fate at the hands of the extensionally inclined. Intensions have been compared to the inhabitants of the nether world; they have been branded psychological or reduced to linguistic or logical constructs or fictions. In many contexts now the word "intensional" merely means refractory to the principles of extensional logic, or more succinctly put, abnormal. As logicians have struggled to slay what they say can hardly be, these logical considerations have begun to take on mythical proportions.

Perhaps in the final analysis these despised "creatures" are indeed worthy of contempt and so deserve the fate they have met. But earlier warriors in the fight against them had a clearer idea of the enemy they fought than we have had in recent years, and this is the situation I seek to remedy here.

§1. The terminological darkness

I think that inconstant renderings of the German word *"Inhalt"* have been the source of a good deal of confusion in logical matters in the twentieth century. In the nineteenth century, the word *"Inhalt"* was used to designate the content of a judgement, of a presentation, or of any act in general. It was also employed in philosophical discussions of form and content where in some contexts what we would call intensions would have been bound up in discussions of form, not content. To complicate matters further, the German word *"Gehalt"* often appears in these same contexts. Since there is no English equivalent for *"Gehalt,"* it too is often rendered "content."

In his *Prolegomena* to the *Logical Investigations,* Husserl pointed to some of the difficulties I want to discuss here when he wrote of the logician Herbart:

> It was certainly unfortunate that Herbart did not notice the basic equivocation in expressions like *Inhalt,* what is presented, what is thought. These expressions designate both the identical ideal content *[Bedeutungsgehalt]* of the corresponding expressions, and the objects presented at the time. As far as I can see, Herbart never said the one thing that clears up the definition of concept, namely that a concept or presentation in the logical sense is nothing other than the identical meaning *[identische Bedeutung]* of the corresponding expressions. [LI, p. 217; also LI5, §45]

The term *"Inhalt"* can also, as Husserl points out, designate the content or intension of an expression. And this is the sense of the word I want to discuss here. The logic that has accommodated the role intensions play in meaning, *Inhaltslogik,* has been variously translated "intensional logic" or "content logic." Husserlians seem to have preferred the latter translation (LI, p. 39), while English language successors of Frege have used both, indiscriminately it seems, without taking into account the complications that that has caused. For when we translate *"Inhalt"* as "content," or change back and forth between "content" and "intension," we block a natural route obtaining between Frege and his predecessors, between Husserl and Frege, and between Frege and Russell, Wittgenstein and Carnap. We block our own way back to their thought and handicap ourselves with respect to any exchange we might have with them on issues that concern us today.

§2. THE MEANINGS OF "INTENSION" AND PRIOR INTENSIONS

Like any other term, the word "intension" would have, in the nineteenth century, had a meaning in intension. This intensional meaning would have been those properties found to be common to all intensions that marked them out and distinguished them from other possible contenders for the title. For Frege, his contemporaries, and his predecessors, the intensional meaning of the word "intension" would have normally been given in one or more of the following ways—that is, any one of the following would have "picked out" the word "intension" for an interested party: (Note that no one of these linguistic descriptions of the meanings of "intension" fully captures all aspects of the meaning of that word, but each would have given a nineteenth-century logician enough information to identify an intension as such.)

1. The more important of two factors in meaning, the meaning proper.

> There is no part of the doctrines of Logic to which I would more urgently request the attention of the reader. . . . I speak of the double meaning which is possessed by most logical terms— the meaning in extension, and the meaning in intension. [Stanley Jevons, *Elementary Lessons in Logic*, 5th ed. 1875][5]

> . . . there are reasons for believing that the intensive or qualitative form of reasoning is . . . fundamental. It is sufficient to point out that the extensive meaning of a name is a changeable and fleeting thing, while the intensive meaning may nevertheless remain fixed. [Jevons, *Principles of Science*, 1873][6]

> . . . how does it come to pass that ideas or nouns are said to have two kinds of meaning, known as Intension and Extension? The meaning proper, the fixed content, is

obviously the Intension of the name or idea. . . . But it is clear, as Mill has well insisted, that the intension is the primary meaning, or, as we have said, *the* meaning. [Bernard Bosanquet, *Logic,* 1888][7]

Since concepts can be considered in two ways, according to *Inhalt* and according to extension, there are also "two possible ways of determining a concept" the indication of extension or division, the indication of *Inhalt,* or definition. [Husserl, RS, p. 123]

. . . the expression has primarily an intension and secondarily an extension. [Carnap, *Meaning and Necessity*][8]

Our two concepts (i.e., extension and intension) may be regarded, like Frege's, as representing two components of meaning (in a wide sense). The concepts of sense and intension refer to meaning in a strict sense. [Carnap, *Meaning and Necessity*][9]

2. The factor in meaning that gives the properties something must have to be called what it is called.

. . . the attributes which are thought of as embodied in particular cases are what constitute the Intension. [Bosanquet, *Logic,* 1888][10]

The first one to introduce the concepts and intension and extension into logic, the author of *Ars Cogitandi* . . . presented the concept of intension in such a way that he counted every property that necessarily belongs to the object of an idea (every attributum) with the idea's *Inhalt.* [Bolzano, *Theory of Science,* 1837][11]

These properties are common to all metals, or nearly all metals, and are what mark out and distinguish a metal from other substances. Hence they form in a certain way the meaning of the name metal, the meaning in intension, as it is called to distinguish it from the former kind of meaning. [Jevons, *Elementary Logic*][12]

Each concept, as partial concept, is contained in the presentation of things as a basis of knowledge, i.e., as characteristics are these things contained under it. In the first case, each concept has an *Inhalt;* in the other an extension. [Kant, *Logic,* 1800][13]

Sense is an ingredient in meaning: to give an account of
the sense of an expression is, therefore, to give a partial
account of what a speaker knows when he understands
an expression. [Dummett, *Truth and Other Enigmas*][14]

. . . in every symbol we separate what it means from what
it stands for. A sign indicates or points to something other
than itself; and it does this by conveying, artificially or
naturally, those attributes of the thing by which we
recognize it. [F. H. Bradley, *Principles of Logic*][15]

3. The factor in meaning that picks out or determines the
extension; the way the extension is given.

The presentations equilateral triangle and equiangular
triangle differ in *Inhalt* though both are directed
. . . toward the same object; they present the same
object, although in a different fashion. [Husserl, LI5,
§20]

It is natural, now, to think of their being connected with
a sign . . . besides that which the sign designates, which
may be called the Meaning of the sign, wherein the way
of being given is contained (*enhalten*). [Frege, "On Sense
and Meaning," GB, p. 57]

The intension of a predicate for a speaker X is, roughly
speaking, the general condition which an object must fulfil
for X to be willing to apply the predicate to it. [Carnap,
Meaning and Necessity][16]

The technical term 'intension,' which I use here instead
of the ambiguous word 'meaning,' is meant to apply only
to the cognitive or designative meaning component.
[ibid.][17]

4. The factor in meaning complementary to and inseparable
from the extension.

It is an old dispute whether formal logic should concern itself mainly with intensions or with extensions. . . .
Our theory of classes recognizes and reconciles two
apparently opposed facts, by showing that an extension (which is the same as a class) is an incomplete symbol whose use always acquires its meaning
through reference to an intension. [Russell, PM, p. 72]

. . . it is not possible for a predicator in an interpreted language to possess only an extension and not an intension, in customary terms, to refer only to a class and not to a property. [Carnap, *Meaning and Necessity*][18]

. . . a name or conception without Intension would be a name without meaning, and therefore, also without Extension; for it is only the meaning that prescribes the Extension. And a name or conception that should have no Extension would be one that would not apply to any particular thing or case, and therefore could have no Intension. [Bosanquet, *Logic*][19]

. . . a purely extensional specification is, in general, no way to define a concept; that all definitions of concepts are definitions of *Inhalten;* and that wherever we hear of the definition of a concept by means of its extension, what is meant, and alone can be meant, is an indirect definition of the *Inhalt* of the concept to be defined, by means of another conceptual *Inhalt* corresponding equivalently to the first in virtue of having the same extension. And this, by itself, suffices to make it known that the ideal of an "extensional logic," i.e., a logic which in principles considers *only* extensions of concepts, is futile. . . . [Husserl, RS, p. 123]

Definition by extension. Logically there is no such thing. The class whose members are a and b is defined by the intension "identical with a or identical with b"; and what one commonly calls definition by extension is really definition by intensions of this type. [Russell][20]

5. The factor in meaning that remains identical and unchanged, grasped by the subject but not perceived.

We distinguish . . . in every statement between *Inhalt* and object; by the *Inhalt* we understand the self-identical meaning that the hearer can grasp even if he is not a percipient. [Husserl, LI 1, §14, pp. 290–91]

By a thought I understand not the subjective performance of thinking but its objective content, which is capable of being the common property of several thinkers. [Frege, GB, p. 62]

... the meaning is other than the fact of which the meaning is true. The fact is an individual or individuals, and the idea itself is an universal. The extension cannot be reduced to intension. [Bradley, *The Principles of Logic*][21]

I shall follow Mr. Bradley in using 'idea' for a fixed content or logical meaning, not for the psychical images which pass through the mind and never recur. [Bosanquet, *Logic*][22]

6. The factor in meaning that stands in inverse relation to the extension.

We increase the intent of meaning of a term by joining to it adjectives or phrases equivalent to adjectives, and the removal of such adjectives of course decreases the intensive meaning. Now, concerning such changes of meaning, the following all-important law holds universally true: When the intent of meaning of a term is increased the extent is decreased; and vice versa, when the extent is increased the intent is decreased.

This law refers only to logical changes. The number of steam-engines in the world may be undergoing a rapid increase without the intensive meaning of the name being altered. [Jevons, *The Principles of Science*, 1873][23]

For example, it should be noted that the extension of a presentation does not diminish when its *Inhalt* is increased by a mere redundancy, that rule was not viewed as mistaken because of this, because the difference between redundant and non-redundant presentations was not looked for in the presentations-in-themselves, but in our mere thoughts or expressions of them. If I am so fortunate as to have avoided a mistake here which remained unnoticed by others, I will openly acknowledge what I have to thank for it, namely it is only the distinction Kant made between analytic and synthetic judgements, which could not be made if all of the properties of an object had to be components of its presentation. [Bolzano, *Theory of Science*, 1837][24]

The *Inhalt* and extension of a concept stand in inverse relationship one to the other: the more that is included under it, the less is included in it and vice versa. [Kant, *Logic*, 1800][25]

The *Inhalt* of a concept decreases when its extension increases; when the latter is all-encompassing, then the intension completely disappears. [Frege, FA, §29]

Extension and intension, we are told, are related and must be related in a certain way. The less you have of one, the more you therefore must have of the other. This statement has often passed itself off as both true and important. I confess that to me it has always seemed either false or frivolous. [Bradley, *The Principles of Logic*]²⁶

§3. FREGE'S INTENSIONS

Frege's *Begriffsschrift* was, as the title page indicates, a concept-script, "a formal language of pure thought modelled on the language of arithmetic." It was not an object-script. The word "extension" does not appear in the *Begriffsschrift* at all.

In opposition to Kant, Frege believed that arithmetic was analytic and that analytic statements could have cognitive worth. He hoped his concept-script could disclose the true nature of and limn the structure of arithmetical concepts, and that it would ultimately prove to be an effective tool for manipulating those and other concepts (FA, §§87–91). His initial orientation was rationalist and intensional. Throughout his life he denounced what was empirical and individual as subjective, psychological, and fleeting (FA, introduction).

But the mathematician, as Frege insisted, manipulates signs that stand for objects. And as it seems to be one condition of the universal applicability of arithmetical concepts that these objects, like notches on a bedpost, be relatively void of properties, Frege's work on the foundations of arithmetic forced him to take a hard look at his views on meaning, and he became increasingly receptive to the ideas promulgated by the extensionalist logicians of his time. Nonetheless, it was with reluctance that he began to talk of extensions; it seems he was finally only able to do this by considering, as did his contemporaries, the objects in question as one of two complementary components in logical meaning—that is, as an intrinsic part of a concept, its Meaning in extension. He went one step further than many of his contemporaries and actually labeled extensions, Meanings. This step ultimately had the effect of disguising his thought once it went abroad.

The shift toward extensions began in the *Foundations* and was completed with the *Basic Laws*. For a time in the 1890s Frege actually seemed convinced of their value. But when the transition from concepts to their extensions, which Frege had come to advocate, proved impossible, Frege did not hesitate to say that he had always had reservations about extensions.

This brief summary of Frege's views on extensions and intensions counters the commonly held view that (to paraphrase Gareth Evans): Frege originally concentrated exclusively upon extensional fragments of language and he later grafted on *Sinne*, laying aside non-extensional contexts as special or abnormal.[27] The summary, however, agrees with Frege's own accounts, and there is rather considerable evidence that, in spite of all the literature on the subject, Frege's views on these matters have been widely misunderstood.

Frege himself recounted (1912):

> . . . when classes are introduced, a difficulty (Russell's contradiction) arises. In my fashion of regarding concepts as functions, we can treat the principal parts of Logic without speaking of classes, as I have done in my *Begriffsschrift,* and that difficulty does not come into consideration. Only with difficulty did I resolve to introduce classes (or extents of concepts) because the matter did not appear to me quite secure— and rightly so as it turned out. The laws of numbers are to be developed in a purely logical manner. But numbers are objects. . . Our first aim then was to obtain objects out of concepts, namely extents of concepts or classes. By this I was constrained to overcome my resistance and to admit the passage from concepts to their extents. . . . I confess . . . I fell into the error of letting go too easily my initial doubts, in reliance on the fact that extents of concepts have for a long time been spoken of in logic.[28]

Early reviewers of the *Begriffsschrift,* citing the names of prominent extensionalist logicians, noted that Frege had failed to take into account the work of others on his subject (Boole was among those named).[29] Frege immediately took up the pen to defend himself against these charges. In two posthumously published replies to critics of his *Begriffsschrift,* Frege speaks of extensions for the first time.[30] His comments are critical:

> My concept-script commands a somewhat wider domain that Boole's formula language. This is a result of my having departed further from Aristotelian logic. For in Aristotle, as in Boole, the logically primitive activity is the formation of concepts by abstraction, and judgement and inference enter in through immediate or indirect comparison of concepts via their extension. [PW, p. 15]

> . . . we do justice to the distinction between concept and individual which is completely obliterated in Boole. Taken strictly, his letters never mean individuals but always extensions of concepts. [ibid., p. 18]

Boole's symbolic logic, Frege complained, "only represents the formal part of language" (PW, p. 13) . . . "there is no concern about *Inhalt* whatsoever" (ibid., p. 12). "In contrast we may now set out the aim of my concept-script. Right from the start I had in mind the expression of an *Inhalt*" (ibid., pp. 46–47).

Inhalten in fact abound in the *Begriffsschrift,* but Frege had not yet introduced his special vocabulary that distinguishes between the objective *Inhalten* (thoughts, concepts, objects, senses . . .) and the subjective *Inhalten* (sense impressions, memories. . .) of presentations (see chap. 7). He had begun his work to separate the *Inhalten* of possible judgments into functions and arguments, but the *Inhalten* of expressions (as opposed to their linguistic form) remained undifferentiated. In his discussion of equality of *Inhalt* in §8 of the *Begriffsschrift* (GB, pp. 10–12), he implicitly recognizes a division of *Inhalten* into the meaning and the thing meant,[31] but the dual meaning he speaks of there is rather that of sign and signified. He did not explicitly divide the latter until after his encounter with Boole. When he did, I argue, he divided them into *Inhalten* (intensions) and extensions of concepts. The *Inhalten* of concepts he came to call senses and the extensions, *Bedeutungen.* When philosophers[32] translate the "*Inhalt*" in this passage (BS, §8) as "referent," they reflect a certain disposition to read more extensionalism into the *Begriffsschrift* than is actually there.[33]

In spite of his protests, Frege must have immediately seen the need to come to terms with extensions because they begin to play an integral role in his plans to logicize arithmetic in the *Foundations*, published shortly after the reviews in question. Nonetheless, in one of the last pages of the *Foundations* he declares:

> In this we take for granted the sense of the expression "extension of the concept." This way of overcoming the difficulty will not win universal applause, and many will prefer to remove the doubt in question in another way. I attach no decisive importance to bringing in the extension of a concept. [FA, §107; also §68n.]

His discomfort is further reflected in his preface to the *Basic Laws:*

> If anyone should find anything defective, he must be able to state precisely where, according to him, the error lies. . . . A dispute can arise, so far as I can see, only with regard to my Basic Law concerning courses-of-values (V), which logicians perhaps have not yet expressly enunciated, and yet is what people have in mind, for example, when they speak of extensions of concepts. I hold that it is a law of pure logic. In any event the place is pointed out where the decision must be made. [BL, p. vii]

In the years immediately preceding and following the publication of the *Basic Laws* Frege made his most positive statements concerning extensions (see BL, §9). So we read in his posthumously published "Comments on Sense and Meaning" dating from 1892–1895:

> . . . we have, I believe, made an important concession to the extensionalist logicians. They are right when they show their preference for the extension as against the *Inhalt* of a concept, that they regard the Meaning and not the sense of words as the essential thing for logic. The *Inhaltslogiker* are only too happy not to go beyond the sense; for what they call the *Inhalt*, if it is not a *Vorstellung* is nothing other than the sense. [PW, p. 122]

Still he concludes:

> Logic must demand not only of proper names but of con-
> cept words as well that the step from the word to the sense
> and from the sense to the Meaning be determined beyond
> a doubt. [ibid., p. 125]

and his published reflections on the same subject from the same
period are more conservative with respect to extensions:

> Someone may get the impression from my procedure that
> in the battle between extensionalist and intensionalist
> logicians I take the side of the latter. I do in fact maintain
> that the concept is logically prior to its extension. [GB,
> p. 106]

And so he maintained all his life — for example, in 1893:

> In §46 [of the *Foundations*] I expressed my most basic
> finding that the assignment of a number includes a state-
> ment of a concept . . . the properties an object must have
> to belong to the group. [BL, p. ix; GB, p. 120]

in 1906:

> What may I regard as the result of my work? It is almost
> all tied up with the concept-script. A concept construed
> as a function. A relation as a function of two arguments.
> The extension of a concept or class is not the primary
> thing for me. Unsaturatedness in case of concepts and
> functions. The true nature of concept and function real-
> ized. [PW, p. 184]

in 1910:

> . . . to belong to a certain set of values properly means
> to fall under a certain concept; for this can only be deter-
> mined by giving the properties that an object must have
> in order to belong to this set, that is, the set of values will
> be the extension of a concept.[34]

* * * *

But concepts are something primitive which cannot be
dispensed with in logic. We can only determine a class
by giving the properties which an object must have in

order to belong to the class. But these properties are the characteristics *[Merkmale]* of a concept. We define a concept, and pass over from it to the class.[35]

in a letter to Peano (no date):

> Of course, one must not then regard a class as constituted by the objects (individuals, entities) that belong to it; for in removing the objects one would then also be removing the class constituted by them. Instead one must regard the class as constituted by the characteristics i.e., the properties an object must have if it is to belong to it. It can then happen that these properties contradict one another or that there occurs no object that combines them in itself. The class is then empty, without being logically objectionable for that reason. [PMC, p. 109]

Concepts are primitive, but arithmetic requires that we pass from concepts to their extensions. This is the dilemma Frege faced. "I define number itself as the extension of a concept," he wrote in the *Basic Laws*, "and extensions of concepts are by my definition courses of values. Thus we just cannot get on without them" (BL, p. x). Frege's logic was fundamentally intensional, and he never successfully managed the transition from intensions to extensions of concepts that Basic Law V was to guarantee. Frege's attempt to introduce extensions set Meaning against meaning. In his 1885 review of the *Foundations* Cantor had warned Frege that extensions could not provide the secure foundations Frege wanted.[36]

Frege replied to Russell in the appendix to the second volume of the *Basic Laws:*

> I have never disguised from myself its lack of the self-evidence that belongs to the other axioms. . . . I should gladly have dispensed with this foundation if I had known of any substitute for it. And even now I do not see how Arithmetic can be scientifically established; how numbers can be apprehended and brought under review; unless we are permitted — at least conditionally — to pass from a concept to its extension. [GB, p. 214]

And to Russell himself Frege wrote in 1902:

I myself long resisted admitting truth values and with them classes; but I saw no other possible way to ground arithmetic logically. It comes down to the question: how do we apprehend logical objects? And I have found no other answer to it than this, we apprehend them as extensions of concepts, or more generally as ranges of values of functions. I have always been aware that there are difficulties connected with this and your discovery of the contradiction has added to them. But what other way is there? [PMC, pp. 140–41]

And so Frege believed for the rest of his life. In 1925 he wrote to Hönigswald:

The expression 'the extension of F' seems naturalized by reason of its manifold employment and certified by science, so that one does not think it necessary to examine it more closely; but experience has shown how easily this can get one into a morass. I am among those who have suffered this fate. When I tried to place number theory on scientific foundations, I found such an expression very convenient. While I sometimes had slight doubts during the execution of the work, I paid no attention to them. And so it happened that after the completion of the *Basic Laws of Arithmetic* the whole edifice collapsed around me. [PMC, p. 55]

§4. OBTAINING OBJECTS FROM CONCEPTS

Frege had to obtain objects out of concepts.[37] He thought he could do this by taking the subject-predicate constructions of ordinary language and translating them into extensional language. To understand what Frege did we need to look at some concrete examples. The following are taken from Frege's writings and from *Word and Object* by Quine, the premier defender of this practice today. Example 7 is from Russell's *Principia:*

1. In regard to the equals sign we shall do well to keep our convention that equality is complete coincidence, identity. Of course, bodies equal in volume are not identical, but they have the same volume. The signs on either side of the equals sign must thus in this case be taken as signs

not for bodies but for their volumes. . . . We shall not speak of equal vectors, but rather of a certain attribute of the vectors (let's call it the length which can be the same in different vectors). [BL II, §48; GB, p. 141n.]

2. . . . take 'Mabel loves none but George.' This amounts to an identity having the definite singular term 'George' as one side and the indefinite singular term 'everyone whom Mabel loves' as its other side. [Quine, p. 117]

3. 'Every square root of 1 is a binomial coefficient of the exponent -1 and every binomial coefficient of the exponent -1 is a square root of 1' ⇔ 'the extension of the concept square root of 1 is equal (coincides with) the extension of the concept binomial coefficient of the exponent -1. . . . and so 'the extension of the concept square root of 1' is here to be regarded as a proper name. . . . [PW, p. 182]

4. 'Agnes is a lamb' then ceases to be seen as 'Fa' and comes to be seen as 'a=b' where 'b' represents an indefinite singular term of the form 'an F,' 'Agnes bleats' and 'Agnes is docile' retain the form 'Fa,' and the 'is' of 'is docile' retains the status of a copula, or a particle for converting adjectives to verbs; but the 'is' of 'is a lamb' becomes '=.' [Quine, p. 118]

5. "If a thought is an equation," Frege reasoned, "This does not exclude its also being a subsumption. The proposition 'Napoleon is the loser of Waterloo' can be changed into 'Napoleon is identical with the loser of Waterloo,' and here Napoleon is subsumed, not indeed under the loser of Waterloo, but under the concept 'identical with the loser of Waterloo.' [PMC, p. 98]

6. The equation 'x=a' is reparsed in effect as a predication 'x=a' where '=a' is the verb, the 'F' of 'Fx.' [Quine, p. 179]

7. The most perfect being exists. [PM, p. 31]

Translated into extensional terms the subject-predicate construction becomes Fx equivalent to $x=a$:

1a. "The bodies are equal in volume" is equivalent to "the volume of the body A=the volume of body B."

b. "The vectors are equal" is equivalent to "The length of vector A=the length of vector B."

2. "Mabel loves none but George" is equivalent to "Everyone Mabel loves=George."

3. "Every square root of 1 is a binomial coefficient of the exponent -1 and every binomial coefficient of the exponent -1 is a square root of '1'" is equivalent to "The extension of the concept square root of 1=the extension of the concept binomial coefficient of the exponent -1."

4. "Agnes is a lamb" is equivalent to "Agnes=lamb."

5. "Napoleon is the loser of Waterloo" is equivalent to "Napoleon=the loser of Waterloo."

6. Fx is equivalent to x=a.

7. $(\exists c)$: x is most perfect . $\equiv_x . x=c$.

It was Basic Law V that was to guarantee this transition from concepts to their extensions. Frege never believed any proof could be found to justify his axiom (BL, p. vii; GB, p. 214; PW, p. 182), but he thought it could provide him with the results he needed. It was bound to fail, though, because (as Husserl had pointed out to him in 1891 — PA pp. 104–5 — and as he himself acknowledged in his 1903 appendix to the *Basic Laws* — GB, pp. 214-24) Frege had things backward: if x and y are identical then if Fx is true, Fy is true, but we cannot say that x and y are identical if they have the same predicates.

Frege wanted to banish the words "subject" and "predicate" from logic entirely (PW, p. 120). He held that the basic logical relation was that of an object's falling under a concept and that subject-predicate analysis leads us to confuse this relation with that of a concept's being subordinated to another. In his effort to avoid this linguistic trap, though, he fell into at least two others: (1) language is replete with ambiguities concerning the notion of identity and (2) language lets us convert predicates into subjects — that is, we can talk about adjectives, qualities, attributes, properties, or concepts as if they were things. Frege thus managed to reify intensions and to confuse the "is" of equality or identity with the "is" of predication.

Frege, Russell, and Quine all explicitly recognize the differences between the "is" of identity and the "is" that expresses posses- sion of a property or class membership.[38] Properties (attributes, concepts, intensions), though, have the inconvenient property that they do not respond to extensional treatment in the same way that the objects that flank an identity statement do. No proper criterion for the identity of properties has been found at all and in particular, the fact that two properties have the same extension does not mean that the properties themselves are the same. Nonetheless, statements involving properties are just too numerous and significant to be dismissed.

Properties stand in a many-one relationship to the object that they describe. By overlooking the differences between identity and equality, or by mandating that there is no difference,[39] the many-one relationship is artificially reduced to a one-to-one rela- tionship. The objects no longer need to have all their proper- ties in common. They need only be alike as given in a certain way. Frege's analyses left off here, but led to gross problems with substitution (notably that from statements of the form "Socrates is wise" and "Tully is wise" we can conclude that Socrates is Tully). Russell introduced procedures by which an entity could be so precisely defined that any other entity so defined would be identical to it. With his axiom of reducibility he banished any extra properties. Quine noted the circularity in Russell's argu- ment and tried to neutralize the differences between entities and properties by presupposing classes — that is, by saying that expres- sions that follow the "is" of predication indicate the class the predicate picks out. "Classes," he writes, "may be thought of as properties if the latter notion is so qualified that properties become identical when their instances" are identical.[40] Quine's reasoning is circular too. The "is" of predication is reduced to the "is" of identity. The price paid: the introduction of abstract entities that correspond to properties but exhibit desirable behavior as regards identity. More is said on this subject in chapter 9.

Frege's formula for making intensions into objects and the intensions Frege's analyses create have generated problems for logicians ever since.[41] Extensionalist logicians manipulate objects (extensions) and must ban intensions. Intensions are for them aberrant and abhorrent things.

§5. A NOTE REGARDING OPAQUE CONTEXTS

I have argued that the senses that make their entry in "On Sense and Meaning" were not last-minute imports devised to patch holes in an otherwise parsimonious logical project. Quite the contrary, the logic Frege wanted to symbolize had a basic intensional orientation that rejected Basic Law V and also rebelled in other, more subtle ways when extensions were brought in. Arguing thus I counter the more usual claim, here represented by Quine:

> Failures of substitutivity of identity . . . were in Frege's view unallowable; so he nominally rectified them by decreeing that when a sentence or term occurs within a construction of propositional attitude or the like, it ceases to name a truth value, class or individual concept. [Word and Object, §32]

In his 1943 review of Quine's "Notes on Existence and Necessity," Church points out that Frege had contended with the cases of opaque reference that Quine discussed in his article.[42] In a letter to Russell about the paradoxes (PMC, pp. 152-54), Frege asks Russell if he has not read "On Sense and Meaning," where Frege's most thorough discussion of nonpurely designative contexts appears. "Wherever the coincidence of *Bedeutung* is not self-evident, we have a difference of *Sinn*," he tries to tell Russell (PMC, p. 152).

Senses were not "ad hoc devices imposed to avoid paradoxical consequences."[43] Frege began with intensions. When he tried to change his intensions into extensions he encountered fragments of language that would not comply. In those cases intensions resisted the change in a way that could not be ignored because their recalcitrance affected the truth value of those contexts. He ended up with a mostly extensional logic, and this is what he bequeathed to posterity. The logical problems found in opaque contexts are an intensional logic's reaction to the introduction of extensions.

Contemporary semantics has largely been conditioned by the view that it was the opposite that occurred. When Frege's successors—whether Russell, Marcus, Quine, or Carnap—sought to further what Frege had begun, they ran into his intensions again. Now they appeared as the exceptions rather than the rule, and, for some, appealing to them seemed a strategy for saving extensionality.

Senses stand out when substitutivity is not logically guaranteed, and when one does not heed the differences between intensions and extensions, substitutivity cannot be guaranteed. Simple identity statements are one place in which the difference stands out. In his correspondence with Russell, Frege repeatedly appeals to statements identical in extension, but differing in senses to show the necessity of the latter. *Oratio obliqua*, Frege claims, can only be rightly understood if there are senses as well as *Bedeutungen* (BL 1, p. x; GB, p. 122). To Russell he wrote:

> Let e.g. 'M' and 'N' (indirect speech) be names of the same class so that M=N is the true. But I assume that these names have a different sense in that they determine the class in different ways. Then M cannot be interchanged with N in indirect speech because their Meanings [*Bedeutungen*] are different. . . . The thought that all thoughts belonging to class M is true is different from the thought that all thoughts belonging to class N are true; for someone who did not know that M coincided with N could hold one of these thoughts to be true and the other to be false. [PMC, p. 153]

In these and other cases substitutivity fails because extensionalist philosophers have tried to substitute things that could not be substituted one for another. Names, extensions, and intensions all operate according to different rules. Although they may appear in the same linguistic clothing and sometimes behave in analogous ways, for very basic reasons one cannot predicate the same things of what belongs to one type as of what belongs to another. As Frege noted in "On Concept and Object," ". . . the words 'the concept square root of 4' have an essentially different behavior as regards possible substitutions, from the words 'square root of 4.' . . .The *Bedeutungen* of the two phrases are essentially different" (GB, p. 50).

Extensional logic was conceived in sin, in the sin of confusing concepts and objects. Frege needed to confuse properties and things. His attempts to develop an extensional logic forced the hypostatization of the intensions of traditional logic. Post-Fregean attempts to exorcize intensions cannot succeed because the logic that would remove them itself generates them. It has to have them. They are creatures of analysis. Frege's logic is an intension creating logic, and the history of analytic philosophy is to a large extent the chronicle of efforts to make the intensions it makes amenable to extensional treatment. That intensions now haunt logical discussions is an indication that something remains amiss about which more is said in later chapters.

7

Presentations
and Ideas

. . . we shall have to raise fundamental questions as to
the acts, or alternatively, the ideal meanings, which in
logic pass under the name of 'presentations.' It is important to clarify and separate the many concepts in which
the psychological, the epistemological and the logical are
utterly confused.   Edmund Husserl [LI, p. 259]

Everyone but a philosopher can see the difference between
a post and my idea of a post.   Bertrand Russell[1]

HUSSERL AND FREGE both philosophized in the wake of Kant's
blend of rationalism and empiricism. Each cast a cold eye on
the troubles the Kantian synthesis brought to the vulnerable concept-object relationship, and each carved a logic from the confusions they found.

The elusive German term *"Vorstellung"* stood at the heart of
these confusions, and the difficulties that abounded then per-
sist today, but in a different guise, so that the present-day version
of the difficulties Husserl and Frege fought continues to spawn
misunderstandings about the nature of Husserl's early psychologism, the nature and worth of Frege's attack on the same, and
the nature of the English realist rebellion at the turn of the century with its links with the thought of continental philosophers
Brentano, Meinong, Frege, Bolzano, Lotze, and again, of course,
Husserl in his psychologist phase.

As presentations and ideas interact intimately with intentions
and intensions, two subjects that analytic philosophers have

historically avoided, it is perhaps not surprising that the confusion has persisted. But these notions are as significant as they are muddled. With them we stand at the crossroads not only of empiricism and rationalism, but also of realism and idealism, of the twentieth century and the nineteenth century, of analytic philosophy and phenomenology, of English and German philosophy, of different interpretations of Kant, and so on.

§1. THE SOURCE OF THE CONFUSION IN KANT

In the nineteenth century the word *"Vorstellung"* was used quite broadly to describe the knowing subject's relationship to the external world. Its use varied widely according to the particular philosophical orientation (LI 5, chap. 6), and the word was quite indiscriminately employed (LI 2, §10) to designate either the *act* of presenting, the object that was presented, or various third entities (some would say intensional) that might be somehow interposed between the presenter and the presented. This third factor, often called the content (LK, pp. 127, 139, 147, 151, 156–57, 171–72), could be of empirical extraction, a Lockean idea for example, or, it might, like a Platonic idea, exist a priori outside space, time, and subjectivity. This latter element was called an *Idee* by Kant, and passages like the following from his logic set the stage for nineteenth-century idealism and the various revolts against it. This is probably one of the texts Frege had in mind when he wrote that Kant's doctrine had assumed "a very subjective idealist hue," because he associated subjective and objective presentations in a way that made his true views hard to discover (FA, §27n.):

> §1 All knowledge, i.e., all presentations that are consciously related to an object, are either intuitions or concepts. . . . Knowledge via concepts is called thought.
>
>   ❖ ❖ ❖ ❖
>
> §3 A concept is either empirical or *pure*. A pure concept is a concept which is not abstracted from experience, but which comes from the understanding, even in its *Inhalt*.

An Idea *[Idee]* is a concept of pure reason whose object is not to be found in experience.

Empirical concepts originate in the senses, through comparing the objects of experience. . . . The reality of these concepts is grounded in actual experience from which, with respect to *Inhalt,* they are produced.[2]

§2. Reactions to Kant

Although Kant held that it was absurd to try to derive logical principles from psychology because that could only lead to subjective, contingent laws, he claimed the necessary laws of pure logic had their source in the understanding,[3] and this thesis led to the widespread and pernicious psychologism that characterized much of nineteenth-century thought and conditioned twentieth-century thought by provoking a virulent reaction.

Husserl writes of the psychologism Kant unintentionally produced:

It is well-known that Kant's theory of knowledge has sides in which it strives and successfully gets beyond the psychologism of mental faculties as sources of knowledge. Here it is enough to stress that it also has prominent sides which fall within this psychologism. . . . Most Kantianizing philosophers fall in the field of psychologizing epistemologists, however little they may fancy the name. [LI, p. 122n.]

Two responses to Kant's view of knowledge, presentation, and concepts especially concern us here. One is the reaction of the empirical psychologists, headed by Brentano, who directly influenced Husserl (in his *Philosophy of Arithmetic* period), plus Meinong, Russell, and Moore (MPD, p. 134). The other is that of a group of philosophers who, refusing the subjectivity of the more empirical approach, responded to Leibniz and set out in search of the concepts of pure reason. Among these were Bolzano, Lotze, Frege,[4] and Husserl (after the publication of *Philosophy of Arithmetic*) (ILI, pp. 35–38).

A quite inaccurate view of the nature of the realist rebellion has come down to us. The mistaken view is probably due to Russell.[5]

In his rush to leave idealism and the a priori behind (LK, p. 128), Russell embraced and confused the thought of two quite different men. One was Brentano (the man whose psychologism Husserl embraced, then renounced).[6] The other was Frege.

In the preface to his 1874 masterwork *Psychology from the Empirical Standpoint* Brentano wrote:

> The title I have given this work indicates its subject matter and the method. As a psychologist I am an empiricist. My sole teacher is experience. Nonetheless, with other philosophers I share the conviction that a concern for the ideal is not incompatible with this perspective.[7]

In spite of Brentano's open espousal of a variety of nineteenth-century psychologism, Bertrand Russell and others (Sartre included) saw in Brentano's doctrine of intentionality the promise of a road out of psychologism, a way out of the mind to things. In an article in which Russell fights Lotze (the philosopher whom, ironically, Husserl claimed was the determinant factor in his own turn from psychologism [ILI, p. 36],) Russell writes:

> Lotze presumably holds that the mind is in some sense creative—that what it intuits acquires, in some sense, an existence which it would not have if it were not intuited. Some such theory is essential to every form of Kantianism—to the belief that is that propositions which are believed solely because the mind is so made that we cannot but believe them may yet be true in virtue of our belief. But the whole theory rests, if I am not mistaken, upon neglect of the fundamental distinction between an idea and its object. . . . Seeing that numbers, relations and many other objects of thought do not exist outside the mind, they have supposed that the thoughts in which we think of these entities actually create their own objects.[8]

Compare this text with Husserl's statement in *Philosophy of Arithmetic* on the same subject:

> Our mental activity does not *make* relations; they are simply there, and when interest is directed toward them they are noticed just like any other content. Creative acts, acts that would produce any new content . . . are absurd from the psychological point of view . . . the act can in no way generate its content. . . . [PA, p. 42]

Even in the darkest days of his psychologism, Husserl held to Brentano's view that all consciousness was consciousness *of* something, a conviction that offered others the hope of a way out of psychologism. Husserl never merited Frege's charges that for Husserl the external order alters or disappears according as we attend to it or not (GB, pp. 84–85).

The hope Brentano's doctrine seemed to hold for souls thirsting for a way out of subjectivity becomes clearer when we compare Sartre's discovery of intentionality with Russell's break into realism:
Sartre:

> Against the digestive philosophy of empirico-criticism, of neo-Kantianism, against all "psychologism," Husserl persistently affirmed that one cannot dissolve things into consciousness. . . .
>
> Imagine for a moment a connected series of bursts that tear us out of ourselves, throw us beyond them into the dry dust of the world, onto the plain earth, amidst things . . . you will then grasp the profound meaning of the discovery which Husserl expresses in his famous phrase, "All consciousness is consciousness *of* something."[9]

Russell:

> I felt . . as if I had escaped from a hot-house on to a wind-swept headland. I hated the stuffiness involved in supposing that space and time were only in my mind. I liked the starry heavens even better than moral law, and could not bear Kant's view that the one I liked best was only a subjective figment. I . . . rejoiced in the thought that grass is green, in spite of the adverse opinion of all philosophers from Locke onwards . . . I have never again shut myself up in a subjective prison. [MPD, p. 61]

§3. The terminological confusion

One immediate way of responding to the problem was to try to bring order to the confusion by prying apart and clarifying the several things and processes the nineteenth century had lumped together under the single word "*Vorstellung.*" Large portions of Husserl's *Logical Investigations* (e.g., LI 5, §§44–45) are devoted to just that, and Husserl's work probably provides the most lucid (once the terminological difficulties are removed for readers of English) and thorough discussion of this intricate affair. Although Husserl himself seemed on the point of abandoning all efforts to resolve the problem when he wrote in his 1894 "Psychological Studies,": "I think that it is a good principle to avoid everywhere that it is possible a noun as equivocal as presentation,"[10] he came to reconsider, and in the *Logical Investigations* we find: "However the notion of presentation is defined, it is universally seen as a pivotal concept, not only for psychology, but also for epistemology, and particularly for pure logic" (LI, 5, §45; also LI 2, §23). In any case the particular nature of Husserl's response to the confusion does not seem to have had much appeal in English-speaking countries. Indeed it is usually argued that Husserl lapsed quite rapidly back into the subjective idealism and psychologism that embracing this term seemed to involve.

The confusion becomes more confusing in English because the term *"Vorstellung"* has been frequently translated as "idea" (not to mention "imagination" or "representation,") and "ideas" can either refer to a priori concepts (in Frege, the mature Husserl, Bolzano, Kant, Leibniz, Lotze) or the products of empirical abstraction most frequently associated with Locke. Russell, we will see, wanted to eliminate both, and he along with certain of the philosophers just cited wished ardently to separate *Vorstellungen* as *acts* of presentation from *Vorstellungen* as the things themselves presented, the so-called content of the presentation. Where Russell sought to banish ideas or contents as an annoying third element, others, most notably Frege, sought to consolidate their role as the guarantors of objectivity in knowledge (GB, p. 85; pp. 111–12; ILI, pp. 34–40).

The new confusion we now confront is that most of the authors cited managed this dissection of *Vorstellungen* by tagging the newly separated parts in different and overlapping ways, a problem exacerbated by the disparity in translations this work is trying to circumvent. The precise nature of the terminological tangle we have inherited becomes clearer when we focus our discussion on the issues surrounding a specific term. In this case I have chosen Frege's term *"Gedanke."*

§4. Frege's thoughts

Frege, we have seen, made the decision to use the word "*Vorstellung*" only for what he considered to be subjective presentations. Into this category fell the testimony of the senses, memory, emotions, and so on (GB, pp. 59–60). Objective *Vorstellungen,* he claimed, properly divided into concepts and objects, and presumably that is what he went on to call them (FA §27). His senses and *Gedanke* would later fall into this category (GB, pp. 57–63; PMC p. 163).

"By thought [*Gedanke*]," he wrote in "On Sense and Meaning," "I understand not the subjective act of thinking, but its objective content, which can be the common property of many." (GB, p. 62). *Vorstellungen* are subjective: one person's *Vorstellung* is not that of another. A *Vorstellung* is essentially different from the *Sinn* of a sign, which can be the common property of many and so is not a part or mode of any individual mind. For no one can deny that mankind has a common store of thoughts that it transmits from generation to generation (GB, p. 59).

Frege departed from ordinary usage in order to distinguish the mental act from its content, but his choice of the word "thought" for the latter concept was potentially confusing too.

Frege was aware of the problem:

> What if it is objected that I am attaching to the word "thought" a sense that it does not ordinarily have, and that other people understand by it an act of thinking which is obviously private and mental. Well the important thing is that I remain true to my way of using it. [PW, pp. 135–36]

One could say that Frege himself used words in a private, individual way, but the terminology that described the concepts that had been passed on to his generation was in sore need of alteration.

> Psychological treatments of logic arise from the mistaken belief that a thought . . . is something subjective like a *Vorstellung*. This view leads necessarily to an idealist theory of knowledge . . . this means the breakdown of every bridge leading to what is objective. [PW, pp. 143–44]

The problem for us, of course, is that the subjective *Vorstellungen* Frege sought to banish were frequently called ideas in English, while the senses and the *Gedanken* Frege sought to promote were considered either linguistic or subjective entities. Frege himself would later complain that what he called a *Gedanke* is what Russell considered a *Satz* (PMC, pp. 149–53). Russell considered what Frege called thoughts to be ideas, by which Russell meant subjective entities. Frege's senses and *Gedanken,* though, I hope I am showing, were related to the *Ideen,* the concepts of pure reason of Kant, and were to be distinguished from Locke's ideas. "The *Idee* of unity" Frege wrote in the *Foundations,* before he had established his special vocabulary, "is not as Locke thought, brought to the mind by that object outside and each idea inside, but is known by us by virtue of the superior mental capacity that distinguishes us from animals" (FA, §31).

In the same vein, Husserl wrote in the *Logical Investigations:*

> Locke should, above all, have reminded himself that a triangle is something that has triangularity, but that triangularity is not itself something that has triangularity. The universal idea of triangle, as an idea of triangularity, is therefore the idea of what every triangle as such possesses, but it is not therefore itself the idea of a triangle. [LI 2, §11]

§5. RUSSELL'S IDEAS

At the time he did his most significant work in philosophy, Russell refused ideas, both Lockean and Kantian, and he did not discriminate between them. He lumped meanings, intensions, images, ideas, senses, and *Gedanken* all together. They were all contents to him, and as such acted as a veil between the philosopher and things. He never grasped Frege's distinctions (PMC, pp. 149–66), and the notation he borrowed from Peano (PMC, pp. 149–50, 125–29) could not accommodate them.[12]

That Frege's foray into the a priori made no sense to Russell is clear from this passage taken from their correspondence (Russell writes):

Concerning sense and Meaning, I see nothing but difficulties which I cannot overcome. . . . I believe that in spite of all its snowfields Mont Blanc itself is a component part of what is actually asserted in the proposition 'Mont Blanc is more than 4,000 meters high.' We do not assert the thought for this is a private psychological matter: we assert the object of the thought. . . . In the case of a simple proper name like 'Socrates,' I cannot distinguish between sense and Meaning; I see only the idea *[Idee]* which is psychological and the object. Or better: I do not admit sense at all, but only the idea and the Meaning. [PMC, p. 169]

Frege's 1906 letter to Husserl shows how completely Russell and Frege misunderstood each other on the terminological and conceptual level:

Logic, in no way, is a part of psychology. The pythagorean theorem expresses the same thought for all men, while each person has his own presentations, feelings, resolutions which are different from those of every other person. Thoughts are not mental creatures and thinking is not a manufacturing and shaping, but it is a grasping of thoughts which are already given. [PMC, p. 70]

When Jourdain later asked Frege "whether in view of what seems to be a fact, namely that Russell has shown that propositions can be analysed into a form which only assumes that a name has a *Bedeutung* and not a *Sinn*," he "would hold that the *Sinn* was merely a psychological property of a name," Frege replied without equivocation:

. . . I do not believe that we can dispense with the sense of a name in logic; for a proposition must have a sense if it was to be useful. . . . Now if the sense of a name was something subjective, then the sense of the proposition in which the name occurs, and hence the thought, would also be something subjective, and the thought that one man connects with it, a common store of thoughts, a common science would be impossible. It would be impossible for something one man said to contradict what another man said, because the two would not express the same thought at all, but each his own. [PMC, p. 70]

§6. RUSSELL, MEINONG, AND FREGE

Given his philosophical inclinations Russell could not but interpret Frege's senses and *Gedanken* as other than remnants of the psychologism Frege used them to guard against. Russell apparently overlooked, or chose to overlook, Frege's division of *Vorstellungen* into objective and subjective with all its anti-empiricist overtones.

Nonetheless, Russell wanted to free objects from mental acts and to maintain that "there is a duality that is essential in any form of knowledge. . . . We are aware *of* something, we have a recollection of something, and generally knowing is distinct from that which is known" (MPD, p. 139). And in the first years of the century Russell believed that Brentano's, Meinong's, and Frege's work pointed in that direction. For instance, Russell wrote of Brentano's student (in the same volume of *Mind* in which he published his famous article on denoting, where he criticizes Meinong's theories) that the value of Meinong's philosophy appeared to be very great, that its originality consists

> mainly in the banishment of the psychologism which has been universal in English philosophy from the beginning and in German philosophy since Kant. . . . Presentations, judgements and assumptions, Meinong points out always have objects, and these objects are independent of the states of mind in which they are apprehended.[13]

Russell had read this same message into Frege's theory of judgement. He wrote in his series of articles on Meinong that according to the theory of knowledge advocated by Moore and Frege we may hold that even in cases of erroneous judgement the object is always transcendent.[14] "Things which exist . . . really do exist, and are not merely judged to exist."[15] "Truth and falsehood apply not to beliefs but to their objects."[16] "A cowardly soldier may actually be retreating and the same time judge that he advanced."[17]

In another article in which he uses Frege's thought to combat Lotze and Kant, Russell again combines Frege's thought with that of the school of Brentano. Referring to Frege's *Basic Laws* Russell wrote:

Arithmetic must be discovered in just the same sense in
which Columbus discovered the West Indies, and we no
more create numbers than we created Indians. The
number 2 is not purely mental, but is an entity which must
be thought *of*.[18]

These observations corroborate conclusions drawn in previous
chapters about misconceptions surrounding the realist revolt
against nineteenth-century idealism and about the role that, for
better or for worse, confusions in very fundamental areas of
philosophy played in shaping twentieth-century philosophical
thought. The precise nature of Husserl's psychologism, and of
Frege's antipsychologism, has been misunderstood, I argue.
Russell misread Frege's works; Frege misread Husserl's works.
Many of Russell's ideas were closer to Husserl's ideas in the *Philosophy of Arithmetic* than to Frege's. The way back to Frege's
thought (and even to Russell's!) is strewn with linguistic obstacles, and the fact that there is now such confusion on the superficial terminological level is a symptom of deeper, conceptual
misunderstandings.

8

FUNCTION
AND CONCEPT

The metaphor which is really important, as it seems to me, is that whereby Frege speaks of concepts (properties) and relations in analogy with mathematical functions: it is by the appropriateness or inappropriateness of this analogy that Frege's account stands or falls.   Michael Dummett[1]

FREGE'S WORK ON meaning and arithmetic finally brought him to establish a vocabulary and a symbolism that respected what he considered to be the dual nature of meaning and could trace its course throughout expressions where the two parts of meaning figured like the two faces of one coin. And Frege held that perspicuous argumentation required the perspicuous separation of words, concepts, and things. The fruit of his attempts to accommodate these convictions and apply them to his work on mathematics and philosophy found its most mature expression in the well-known series of articles he published in the early 1890s. It found its most systematic application in his *Basic Laws*.

§1. THE CONFUSION

As Frege studied functions, concepts, and objects he came up against what finally proved to be insuperable difficulties. The problems first surfaced in the form of a linguistic dilemma that Frege described in his 1892 "On Concept and Object" (GB, pp. 42–55). Language, he complained there, forced him to mention an object when what he intended was a concept (GB, p. 54). In another piece from the same period he again complained about the "great obstacle" he faced when he wanted to speak about a concept. With "an almost irresistible force" language compelled him to use expressions that obscured and almost falsified his thought (PW, p. 119).

The verbal problem Frege refers to in these texts proved to be the symptom of deeper problems deriving from the particular nature of Frege's efforts to combine mathematics and philosophical logic. The philosophical riddles that riddle the concept-object relationship have always resisted unraveling and seemingly always will. They come from confusions about concepts and objects that are embedded right into language. We must use concepts to talk about objects, but when we in turn talk about concepts, they then become objects. The same word "horse" refers to both the set of conditions something must fulfill to be called a horse, and to each horse itself. It also names itself (PW, p. 270). Finally, and most determinantly for Frege, it was this tendency of language to form objects out of concepts that led to Russell's paradox. Both Frege and Russell located the problem there (PMC, pp. 55, 130; PW, p. 269). The paradox concerning concepts and objects that defied translation into language turned out to be *the* paradox.

Frege translators Peter Geach and Max Black have faced the linguistic obstacle. Black writes:

> Over the question what it is that is called a function in Analysis, we come up against the same obstacle, and on thorough investigation it will be found that the obstacle is essential, and founded on the nature of our language.[2]

> . . . on Frege's view it is logically impossible to express his thought literally and explicitly. If this is so, we seem to be committed to the quixotic task of trying to understand the ineffable.[3]

and Geach:

> . . . Quine . . . thinks the distinction between concept and object is unnecessary in logic. I hold with Frege that this distinction is founded in the nature of things, and that a logical system will express it somehow or turn out inconsistent.[4]

The as yet unmastered problems to which Geach and Black allude continue to spawn explanations,[5] and, as we could expect, the deep philosophical and linguistic difficulties are reflected in terminological confusion.

§2. THE TERMINOLOGICAL CONFUSION

Inadequate attention has been paid to the confusion introduced into analytic philosophy by diverse renderings and understandings of the key German word *"Begriff,"* the normal translation of which is "concept."

In a passage that uses almost every term discussed in these chapters on conceptual clarity, Husserl paints the confusion that he and Frege, and for that matter, Russell, Carnap, and Wittgenstein, faced and tried to clear. Leaving the key terms in German:

> The word *'Bedeutung'* is no doubt likewise equivocal so that men do not hesitate at times to call the object of a *Vorstellung* a *'Bedeutung,'* and at times to say the same of its *'Inhalt'* (the *Sinn* of its name). To the extent that a *Bedeutung* is also called a *'Begriff,'* the relative talk of *Begriff* and object of *Begriff* likewise becomes ambiguous. At one time one is dealing with the relation, just now taken as basic, between the attribute (Redness) and the object to which this attribute belongs (the red house), at another time with the totally different relation between the logical *Vorstellung* (the *Bedeutung*), e.g. (of the word 'redness,' or of the proper name 'Thetis'), and presented object (the attribute Redness and the goddess Thetis). [LI 2, §42, p. 431]

Unfortunately, the situation Husserl describes has never been cleared up, and the conceptual opacity that was the subject of his complaint has generated and continues to generate a good amount of philosophical activity that turns the issues over and over, never getting to their source:

> The distinction between meaning [*Sinn*] and indication [*Bedeutung*] is roughly, though not exactly, equivalent to my distinction between a concept as such and what the concept denotes. [Russell, PofM, p. 502]

The intension of a concept is made up of the properties common to the things designated by the common name. [Husserl, RS, p. 123]

. . . since 'concept' hints of mind and 'property' hints of a distinction between essence and accident, let us say attributes. . . . The attributes were called propositional functions in *Principia*. [Quine][6]

. . . the true idea is that the *Sinn* is itself the function. . . . It includes, Frege said, . . . besides the reference also the way in which this reference is given. And of course all such talk of 'ways of being given' must in the last analysis be understood functionally. Meanings of expressions and meanings of acts are simply the functions which determine their references or objects respectively. . . . Concepts, as meanings, are according to possible world semantics, functions from possible worlds to references. [Hintikka][7]

I use 'intension' as a technical term for the meaning of an expression. . . . For example, the intension of *'blau'* in German is the property of being blue. [Carnap][8]

According to Frege's original system, every attribute ϕ had a class $\hat{x}\,(\phi x)$ as its extension. [Quine][9]

If one calls the general meaning a concept, the attribute itself the concept's intension, and every subject having this attribute the concept's object, one can put the point in the form: It is absurd to treat a concept's intension as the same concept's object, or to include a concept's intension in its own conceptual extension. [Husserl, LI 2, §11, pp. 359–60)

. . . it seems reasonable to assume that what he [Frege] means by the sense of an individual expression is about the same as what we mean by an individual concept. [Carnap][10]

The word *Begriff* is used by Frege to mean nearly the same thing as propositional function. . . . [Russell, PofM, p. 507]

For a predicator (of degree one) its ordinary sense is the property in question and its intension is the same. [Carnap re: Frege][11]

I come now to a point in which Frege's work is very important and requires careful examination. His use of the word *Begriff* does not correspond exactly to any notion in my vocabulary, though it comes very near to the notion of an assertion. . . . [Russell, PofM, p. 505]

. . . for Frege functions are extensional entities. . . . [Evans][12]

§3. FREGE ON FUNCTIONS

If mathematics was to be logicized and if logic was to be symbolized in the way mathematics is, then some workable correlation between logical notions and mathematical symbolism had to be found (GB, p. 30).

There was, Frege observed, a far-reaching agreement between the cases in which mathematicians speak of a function and the cases in which we speak of a concept (PW, p. 235), so he came to believe it appropriate to understand a concept as a function (GB, p. 31). Just as functions appeared unsaturated, there was something in the realm of meanings that corresponded to them, and these unsaturated "somethings," according to Frege's theories, were concepts (PW, p. 177).

Looking at language, Frege also noted certain rather imperfect analogies between traditional grammatical analysis in terms of subject and predicate and mathematical analysis in terms of function and argument. He pursued these analogies. Statements, like equations or inequalities, can be divided into two parts, a part in need of completion and a part that is complete (GB, p. 31). Predicates need subjects, as functions need arguments, as properties need something that they are properties of.

The factual content of an expression, Frege further noted, could be cut up and studied in multiple ways; a sentence can be dissected and rearranged in various ways so that what in one case figured as the incomplete element, could in another be the saturated or complete part (GB, pp. 47, 49, 55; PW, p. 119). Function-argument analysis respected this fact in a way subject-predicate analysis could not, so the former might offer the clear, flexible, and effective way of manipulating expressions that his project to join logic and mathematics required. Once Frege had made his connection between functions and concepts he concluded that one should do away in logic with the subject and the predicate.

Or one should restrict these words to the relation of an object's falling under a concept (PMC, p. 68).

Although Frege maintained throughout his life that it was one of his abiding achievements to have recognized the true nature of the concept as a function to an argument (PW, p. 184), his theories had severe limitations the full implications of which have yet to be seen or drawn. Thoughts, statements, propositions, and so forth, can not be carved up indiscriminately, and they strenuously resist certain analyses. The obstacles Frege and Russell encountered when logic refused their efforts to make functions into objects provided an initial strong hint that something was basically, and perhaps irremediably, awry.

As he worked on the first and second volumes of the *Basic Laws,* Frege held that, though functions were fundamentally different from objects, functions did (and sometimes had to) take other functions as their arguments: "In logical discussions one quite often needs to say something about a concept and to express this in the form usual for such predication . . . " (GB, p. 46). So in some sense concepts had to become objects (GB, p. 38). "But the concept as such cannot play this part, in view of its predicative nature; it must be converted into an object" (GB, p. 46, 136n.; PMC, pp. 134, 141). When a function had to take another function as its argument, it then became a second-level function and was "fundamentally different from functions whose arguments are objects and cannot be anything else" (GB, p. 38). This distinction is not made arbitrarily, he insisted, but is "founded in the deep nature of things" (GB, p. 41). He repeatedly acknowledged this (PW, pp. 119, 177, 195, 235, 239, 250, 272) and it was this logico-linguistic trap that he finally blamed for the defeat of his logical project.

Russell flagged the problem and the well-known contradiction that it entailed in his first letter to Frege:

> On functions in particular I have been led independently to the same view even in detail. I have encountered a difficulty only on one point. You assert that a function could also constitute the indefinite element. This is what I used to believe, but this view now seems to me to be dubious because of the following contradiction: let w be the predicate of being a predicate which cannot be predicated of itself, can w be predicated of itself? From either answer follows its contradictory. [PMC, p. 130]

Frege replied, "Your discovery of the contradiction . . . has rocked the ground on which I meant to build arithmetic" (PMC, p. 132). Frege and Russell corresponded on the subject, but could come to no mutual agreement. Frege never comprehended Russell's way of solving the problem. When in 1914 Jourdain asked Frege whether Russell's theory of orders was not the same as Frege's theory of first- and second-level function (PMC, p. 78), Frege replied:

> Unfortunately, I do not understand Russell's *Principia* well enough to be able to say with certainty that Russell's theory (*Principia* 1, 54ff.) agrees with my theory of first and second level functions I find it very difficult to read Russell's *Principia*. I stumble over almost every sentence. [PMC, p. 81]

And Frege remained convinced until the end of his life that the confusion over concepts and objects had cost him his logical project. Shortly before his death he wrote:

> One feature of language that threatens to undermine the reliability of thinking is its tendency to form proper names to which no objects correspond. . . . A particularly noteworthy example of this is the formation of a proper name after the pattern of 'the extension of the concept a' e.g. 'the extension of the concept *star*.' Because of the definite article, this expression appears to designate an object; but there is no object for which this phrase could be a linguistically appropriate designation. From this has arisen the paradoxes of set theory. . . . [PW, p. 269]

And to Hönigswald the same year: "We must set up a warning sign visible from afar: let no one imagine that he can transform a concept into an object" (PMC, p. 55).

§4. CHARTING THE COURSE OF MEANING

In light of the discussions of the previous chapters and lucid about the controversy surrounding the issues raised, I propose the chart on page 144. The correlations I make there have all been partially drawn before and considerably disputed, but I do not believe that they have ever been systematically drawn or defended across the board.

CHARTING THE COURSE OF MEANING

Kind of meaning	Frege's terminology	In concept-script	Role in meaning	Objective level
"concept-word" has two kinds of meaning (predicate)				
A. intension	*Sinn*	function	gives the attributes a concept must have to be so named	sense of the concept-word
B. extension	*Bedeutung*	(a function requires an argument)	gives the actual embodiment of these attributes	the concept itself composed of characteristics → the object falling under the concept

Concepts and objects are on the same level, but we can in turn predicate things of specific concepts . . . words for objects falling under concepts have a dual meaning.

Kind of meaning	Frege's terminology	In concept-script	Role in meaning	Objective level
"proper name" has two kinds of meaning (singular term)				
A. intension	*Sinn*	— —	gives the attributes a concept must have to be so named	sense of the proper name
B. extension	*Bedeutung*	argument	gives the actual embodiment of these attributes	the object itself composed of properties

The chart is basically an extension of the schema Frege traced for Husserl in the letter dated May 24, 1891. According to the chart Frege's two kinds of meaning correspond to the *traditional* (i.e., pre-Russellian) division of meaning into intension and extension. This is the key to understanding the parallels outlined.

It is important to keep in mind in examining the chart that Frege held that perspicuous argumentation requires the perspicuous separation of symbols, words, concepts, and things. The correlations proposed on the facing page respect the categories that Frege traced—that his innovative vocabulary was meant to protect. So I am saying that intensions are to extensions, as functions are to arguments, as senses are to references, and so on. I do not claim that this chart solves the problem. Because the problem is precisely that there is a problem. This is less a matter of the ineffable, I contend, than a matter of logical impossibility clothed in confusion. The chart merely helps locate the problem.

§5. Some consequences

Substitution within the chart yields the following conclusions concerning Frege's logic:

1. *A*'s have been interchanged with *A*'s, and *B*'s with *B*'s throughout the literature.

2. *A*'s are predicative. Only in the case of *B*'s can one speak of identity.

3. *A*'s and *B*'s are complementary and interdependent.

4. *A*'s go with a *B* to make up a complete whole.

5. A *B* is incomplete; *A*'s need *B*'s.

6. *A*'s and *B*'s have no existence independent from each other.

7. *B*'s are only given via *A*'s; reference to *B*'s is only given via *A*'s.

8. *A*'s contain the ways in which *B*'s are given.

9. *A*'s pick out or determine *B*'s

10. Different *B*'s can have the same *A* without coinciding.

11. Many *A*'s correspond to one *B*.

12. *A*'s are in no sense entities; they can take on an entity-like status when something is asserted or predicated of them, but then they are *B*'s.

13. The linguistic expression of any *B* involves both *A*'s and *B*'s.

14. In cases of unique reference the difference between an *A* and its *B*'s disappears.

15. Even when just one *B* falls under an *A,* this *B* is not identical, equivalent to, or equal to the *B.*

16. In ordinary language an *A* can figure as the object of an assertion (i.e., as a *B*).

17. *A*'s can figure as *B*'s, but *B*'s can never play the role of *A*'s.

18. Because *A*'s can be *B*'s in certain situations, there is a confusing, but inevitable crossover and interchange.

19. There is no backward road from *B*'s to *A*'s.

20. A *B*'s falling under an *A* is an irreversible relation.

Frege was adamant about points 15, 17, 19, and 20. This was his way of avoiding psychologism, empiricism, subjectivity, formalism, and linguistic idealism. He never hid his contempt for those who mixed what he labored to separate.[13] But that is precisely what linguistic philosophy has managed to do as it has violated what Frege worked to preserve. Ironically, this disregard for Frege's efforts seemed to herald what Quine has called a "new era of clarity."[14] And the blend of words, concepts, and things that apparently arose from Russell's "robust sense of reality" ushered in a period of linguistic idealism that, though surely a distinct step up from subjective idealism (due no doubt to the inherently intersubjective nature of language), was probably all the reality that the twentieth century could bear.

9

ON DENOTING

> . . . my success in the article "On Denoting" was the source of all my subsequent progress. . . . as a consequence of the new theory of denoting, I found at last that substitution would work, and all went swimmingly. . . .
>
> Bertrand Russell, 1906[1]

> . . . inattention to referential semantics works two ways, obscuring some ontological assumptions and creating an illusion of others. . . .   W. V. O. Quine[2]

FREGE'S LOGIC LEFT Russell with a host of problems to solve, and the most significant contributions Russell would make to logic and philosophy resulted from his efforts to overcome the paradoxes Frege's logic produces. So the really interesting question that we confront as we complete this work is: Why was it that the new theories of denotation and identity expounded in *Principia* seemed to promise relief from the problems besetting Russell? To begin to answer this question we need first to take a look at what Russell thought denoting was, and why it was a problem. Peter Strawson notwithstanding,[3] Russell was not trying to give a correct account of the use of denoting expressions in ordinary language. His theory of definite descriptions does not even begin to account for the variety of ways in which expressions refer, and in recent years it has been neo-Russellians that have been the first to point this out.[4] What Russell was trying to do was to answer the questions raised by Frege's attempts to join logic and mathematics. "The mathematical logic of *Principia*," Russell wrote on the first page of that book, ". . . is specifically framed to solve the paradoxes which in recent years have troubled students of symbolic logic and aggregates." "The whole theory of definition, of identity, of classes, of symbolism, and of the variable is wrapped up in the theory of denoting," he had written in the *Principles of Mathematics* (§56), and this is the theme he pursued as he worked to solve the problems Frege's theory of denotation and identity poses for symbolic logic and the theory of classes.

§1. IDENTITY AND DENOTATION

Questions concerning identity and denotation played a determinant role in Russell's search for a way out of Frege's difficulties, for Basic Law V fails precisely because intensional phenomena exhibit different logical behavior as concerns identity than extensions do. Principles of extensionality like Leibniz's law, Basic Law V, and the Axiom of Reducibility are themselves theories of identity and denotation and are all harnessed with the same difficulties.[5]

It is now generally considered that Russell was confused as he wrote his famous article "On Denoting" (LK, pp. 39–56)[6] but his analyses become more comprehensible once they are studied in conjunction with Frege's analyses, analyses that do not take sufficient note of the diverse ways in which words relate to objects.

Frege left Russell with a defective formula for translating the statements of ordinary language into extensional language. Frege's theories do not account for the fact that certain very ordinary linguistic expressions relate to objects in a much more oblique way than other expressions do, and so, taken as they stand, Frege's analyses lead to what Russell called "certain curious difficulties which seem in themselves sufficient to prove that the theory which leads to such difficulties must be wrong" (LK, p. 48).

At the top of the list of problems Russell had to solve were problems involving a number of kinds of expressions that react in disconcerting ways when analyzed as Frege prescribed. Russell lumped these expressions under the heading "denoting phrases." An expression is denoting, Russell believed, by virtue of its form alone. He offered the following examples:

> . . . a man, some man, any man, all men, the present king of England, the present king of France, the centre of the mass of the solar system at the first instant of the twen-

tieth century, the revolution of the earth round the sun, the revolution of the sun round the earth. [LK, p. 41]

In the statements of everyday language these expressions can be found in either the subject or the predicate position; in Frege's symbolic language they could act as the saturated or unsaturated component. Any individual statement might contain several such expressions, and they clearly cannot be totally ignored since they often constitute the difference between a tautology and an informative statement. They do not, however, provide the clear access to objects that Frege and Russell needed, and that their successors need now (LK, pp. 47–55).

Russell had initially thought that all expressions denoted directly (MPD, pp. 62–63). He thought that this was what Meinong thought (LK, p. 45), and because Frege's logic allowed him to treat denoting phrases, concepts, functions, properties, and so on as objects, he thought that this is what Frege thought too (LK, p. 47). But Russell finally ceased to be worried by such problems, which, he says, "arose from the belief that, if a word means something, there must be something that it means" (MPD, p. 63). His 1905 theory of descriptions showed him that this was a mistake and "swept away a host of otherwise insoluble problems" (ibid.).

A look at how Russell thought identity functioned makes some of the difficulties apparent. George IV did not want to know if Scott was Scott (if $a=a$). Russell argued:

> No one outside a logic book ever wishes to say 'x is x,' and yet assertions of identity are often made in such forms as 'Scott was the author of *Waverley*' or 'thou art the man.' The meaning of such propositions cannot be stated without the notion of identity, although they are not simply statements that Scott is identical with another term, the author of *Waverley* or that thou art identical with another term, the man. [LK, p. 55]

Predicates exhibit a different logical behavior from objects. In particular, they differ as concerns identity. This is especially manifest in statements like the ones just cited that would equate a term standing for an object with a description. This being recognized, the trick is to make the properties of objects as expressed by predicates amenable to extensional treatment—that is, subject to the same formal rules of identity as those governing objects (PM, p. 180), which means liable to substitution. Russell's theory of definite descriptions represented a big step in that direction. According to the theory, "Scott was the author of *Waverley*" should be rendered: "Scott wrote *Waverley*; and it is always true of *y* that if *y* wrote *Waverly, y* is identical with Scott" (LK, p. 55). This analysis provides the needed one-to-one correspondence between an object and what is said of it. It yields a single well-defined object, eliminates all other contenders, and bars anything (linguistic, psychological, metaphysical, possible, necessary, or real) that might obscure access to it.

To mandate that there is no difference between identity and equality in the way Frege did is to eliminate all descriptions under which an object might be known other than the one description one has at hand. Basic Law V, if it could be true, would guarantee this. Any form of the principle of extensionality requires that, in some sense, the difference between equality and identity be overcome—or at least legitimately bypassed.[7] Russell's theory of definite descriptions represented a big step in accomplishing that too.

§2. OBTAINING OBJECTS FROM CONCEPTS VIA DEFINITE DESCRIPTIONS

No one outside certain logic books worries very much about securing a referent. Language is replete with nonreferring terms because they are useful and largely unproblematic.[8] It is just plain not true that, as Frege often said, words without referents are not of use in science (compare PW, pp. 122, 124; PMC, pp. 63–64; LI 1, §15). Frege and Russell, however, had to have referents, and the paradoxes showed them that they had to have a more effective way of coaxing them out of names and concepts than Frege was ever able to provide. The problem is serious. To be, some say, is to be the value of a variable.[9] Failure to secure a referent leads to difficulties in quite fundamental areas like existential quantification, identity, substitutivity of identicals, and inference.[10]

Frege had held, and with good reason, that by virtue of its predicative nature a concept could not play the role of a grammatical subject. The concept "must first be converted into an object, an object must go proxy for it" (GB, p. 46; FA, p. x). Frege's procedure for doing this, though, had the added but telling consequence that if an object is put on the same footing as a predicative expression, then from statements of the form "Socrates is wise" and "Tully is wise," one can draw the conclusion that Socrates is Tully.

Quine writes:

> Sometimes 'is' has the sense of '=' or 'is the same as'; such is its sense in 'Paris is the capital of France,' 'Tully is Cicero.' But in 'Paris is a city' or 'Tully is wise' or 'Socrates is wise' the word cannot be so construed; from 'Tully=wise' and 'Socrates=wise' indeed we could infer that Tully=Socrates. In such contexts 'is' expresses rather possession of a property, or membership in a class. . . . It is this sense of 'is' that is rendered symbolically by the connective 'ε'.

The fundamental differences between objects and predicates, and in particular the fact that there is no backward road from reference to sense because every object can be given by an infinite number of different predicates (see LK, p. 50), seems to afford some protection against invalid inference, so that when these differences are not respected problems with inference appear.

The trick is to juxtapose a name, one definitive description, and a referent in such a way that one description overshadows any others to such an extent that they seem not to be there. When there is a one-to-one relationship between a term and what it designates, the term appears to yield its referent directly, without intermediary. There is no longer any difference between the thing and the properties it enjoys at any given point in time. Then language, and the predicative element in particular, seems transparent. Substitution works because the bothersome intensional factor seems to have been neutralized. This is what a logic needs that is built on ambiguities concerning truth conditions about identity statements. This is what Frege needed and his successors need.

A logical sleight of hand was in order, and the theory of definite descriptions fit the bill. It set up a one-to-one relationship between a referent and a predicate that yielded it uniquely. Ambiguous reference was logically disambiguated, and empty reference was logically dismissed.

Modernizing Russell's Waverley example, let's say: The State of California wanted to know if Caryl Chessman was the red-light bandit (using "red-light bandit" as a description, not a proper name). According to Russell neither "Chessman" nor "the red-light bandit" refers to an entity in the simple direct way required by the logic Russell wanted (LK, p. 51), so Russell developed his famous theory by which all singular terms other than variables are short for natural or contrived descriptions. A name like Scott, Apollo, Socrates, Romulus, or Chessman is replaced by a description definite enough to pick out one and only one object (LK, p. 243). In this new analysis the name "Chessman" means "the object having such and such properties" (LK, p. 56). Formally: $(\iota x) (\phi x)$.

Out of any proposition Russell held that one could

> make a denoting phrase which denotes an entity if the proposition is true, but does not denote an entity if the proposition is false. E.g. it is true that the earth revolves round the sun and false that the sun revolves round the earth; hence 'the revolution of the earth round the sun' denotes an entity, while 'the revolution of the sun round the earth' does not denote an entity. [LK, pp. 53–54]

But denoting phrases are themselves incomplete and do not give direct access to the objects they help define (LK, p. 51). No constituent yet corresponds to them (LK, pp. 247–48). Taking ϕx to replace "x killed the red-light bandit's victims," Russell held:

> . . . it is plain that any statement apparently about (ιx) (ϕx) requires (1) that $\exists x. (\phi x)$ and (2) $\phi x . \phi y \supset_{x,y} . x=y$; here (1) states that *at least* one object satisfies ϕx, while (2) states that *at most* one object satisfies ϕx. The two together are equivalent to $(\exists c): \phi x \equiv_x .x=c$ which we define as E! $(\iota x) (\phi x)$. . . . The proposition "$a=(\iota x) (\phi x)$ is easily shown to be equivalent to $\phi x. \equiv_x .x=a$. [PM, p. 68]

The theory of definite descriptions apparently reduced most recalcitrant expressions to the logical form Frege's theories required. Subject-predicate statements could be rewritten to make them equivalent to a statement of the form $F(x)$ and then further dissolved into $x=y$. Such analyses afford what Russell called "a clean shaven picture of reality" (MPD, p. 63). Rewritten in Russell's way, a non-referring expression like "the king of France in 1905" becomes "there is no thing which is identical with the king of France in 1905" (assuming, of course, that one knows in advance whether or not there was a king of France in 1905). All talk of abstract entities can be dismissed as a circuitous way of getting to real things (LK, p. 243). Quine sums up the procedure:

> Instead of assuming a constant singular term or proper name, say "a," we can always assume or define a predicate "A" that is true only of the object a, and then take "a" itself as short for the eliminable description . . . "$(\iota x)\, Ax$". . . . An important thing about thus absorbing all singular terms other than variables is that the logic of quantification and identity need no longer to be conceived otherwise than in its simplest form, involving just predicate letters, variables, quantifiers, truth functions, and "$=$".[12]

Such analyses presuppose what Frege's analyses make plain—that is, some expressions that seem to denote an object in the way needed either do not denote any specific object at all, or do so obliquely. Thus the need for an additional procedure to strip away the conceptual veil to reveal that the expression referred to nothing at all, or, if there was indeed an object, could single it out and neutralize the mediating element that obscured access to it.

Confusions between use and mention aside, the fact that Russell insisted insisted that:

1. "Scott is the author of *Waverley*" is informative and not a tautology (LK, p. 55);

2. "Scott was the author of *Waverley* at a time when no one called him so, when no one knew whether he was or not. . . ." (LK, p. 245);

3. "Scott is the author of *Waverley*" is not the same as any proposition of the form "Scott is c" where "c" is a name (LK, p. 246);

4. "The truth or falsehood of a proposition is sometimes changed when you substitute a name of an object for a description of the object" (LK, p. 247), itself points up the problems with his conviction that "in 'Scott is the author of *Waverley*' the 'is,' of course expresses identity, i.e. the entity whose name is Scott is identical with the author of *Waverley*" (LK, p. 245). If that were the case, then the above four points would not obtain. His very reasons for developing the theory of definite descriptions indicate that names, descriptions, and objects are very different kinds of things.

Objects cannot be gotten from concepts. A lock is not a key. If you melt down your lock to make a key, then you have got to get another lock, because it is senseless to have a key without a lock. Via the theory of definite descriptions Russell managed to squeeze referents out of many expressions that would not normally yield them by reducing each expression to a description equivalent to a variable. This procedure presupposes that the logical form of an identity sentence flanked by a description can be transformed into a statement of the form "$x=y$."[13] It is only due to ambiguities inherent in ordinary language that when reference seems transparent an identity statement that equates an object with a name or a description can appear to be true. Only in opaque contexts do the differences come to the fore again.

§3. SUBSTITUTIVITY

If only in the case of objects can there be a question of identity, then one commits a logical sin when one identifies an object with anything that is not an object, or with anything that refers only indirectly to an object—that is, with a name, with what Russell called a denoting phrase, with a description, a property, attribute, or concept, and so forth. "Objects and concepts," Frege had warned, "are fundamentally different and cannot stand in for each other. And the same goes for the corresponding words and signs" (PW, p. 120). Russell's theory of definite descriptions represented his effort to neutralize the differences between words, things, and meanings-concepts—differences that, because of what Frege noted above, become particularly apparent when one makes the mistake of putting an expression belonging to one of those categories in the place of an expression designating something belonging to another category. When one makes the mistake of identifying one type of entity with an entity of an entirely different type (i.e., a concept with an object, a function with an object, an object with a name, a name with a concept, etc.), failure of substitutivity is the inevitable result. One ends up with the familiar aberrations: Socrates equals Tully; Barbarelli was so called because of his size; the loser of Waterloo was victorious; if Humphrey had been elected president in 1970, he would have been Nixon; and so on.[14] Through scrupulous use of quotation marks, confusions of name and object can be avoided, but for reasons deriving from the very nature of extensionality, confusions concerning objects and what can be predicated of them are more subtle and more resolutely defy eradication. Principles of extensionality need such confusions and thrive on their presence.

If, initially, Frege recognized the above-mentioned differences (GB, pp. 43–49), his technique for rewriting the sentences of ordinary language is a method for obscuring them once again. First, the difference between the "is" of identity and the "is" of predication is acknowledged. Identity concerns objects; predication concerns the relationship between an object and a concept. "An equation is reversible," Frege observed, "an object's falling under a concept is an irreversible relation" (GB, p. 44). Noting these differences, he set the cases of identity aside and proceeded to reduce statements involving predication (i.e., involving both concepts and objects) into statements involving objects only (see Chap. 4, §2; Chap. 6, §4).

Years later Quine would do it this way:

> What is ordinarily wanted to the right of 'ε' is a general term, eg. 'wise' or 'city,' rather than the name of some specific man or place. It is convenient to regard such general names as names on the same footing as 'Socrates' and 'Paris': names each of a single specific entity, though a less tangible entity than the man Socrates or the town Boston. The word 'wise' may be treated as the name of the *class* of wise beings, taken as a single object of an abstract kind. . . . The statement 'Socrates ε wise' now says something about two objects, a man and a class. . . . Once classes are freed thus of any deceptive hint of

> tangibility there is little reason to distinguish them from properties. It matters little whether we read 'xεy' as 'x is a member of the class y' or 'x has the property y.' If there is any difference between classes and properties, it is merely this: classes are the same when their members are the same, whereas it is not universally conceded that properties are the same when possessed by the same objects. . . . But classes may be thought of as properties if the latter notion is now qualified that properties become identical when their instances are identical. [15]

The reasoning seems to be that properties behave in an inconvenient way with respect to identity, so we postulate a realm of abstract entities where single specific entities that exhibit the desired behavior are introduced to correspond to unruly properties. For the ontologically parsimonious this would seem to be quite a concession.

Failure of substitution is one sign that you have not got a firm grasp on what your expression designates. Gross problems with substitution were among the first signs that something was seriously amiss in Frege's plans to transform concepts into objects. Russell provided a cosmetic remedy, but present-day problems with substitution (i.e., the questions raised by *oratio obliqua,* by propositional attitudes, by modality, by empty singular terms, by counterfactuals, by recent work on identity, etc.) serve as a reminder that these differences do not just go away; "intensional" phenomena strenuously resist being identified with the objects to which they are inextricably linked, or to any fictional objects like classes. The study of intensional contexts affords a glimpse of the logical world that lies cloaked behind the various forms of rigid designation. . . .

§4. THE INVERSE RELATION OF INTENSION AND EXTENSION

Russell's theory of definite descriptions plays on the logical illusion that intension and extension stand in inverse relation one to the other, and that when there is only one thing—and all the more so when there can be only one thing—the intension seems to disappear completely[16] (see chap. 6, §2.6).

This "law" seems to be grounded in the simple observations that:

1. the more detailed the definition, the less likely one is to find things that will fit the description;

2. when the field is narrowed to one, then, at any given point in time, that one thing itself embodies everything that is, or can be truthfully asserted of it. In the case of a proper name like Socrates, Russell noted in December 1904 that he could not distinguish between *Sinn* and *Bedeutung* at all (PMC, p. 169);

3. when there is no object, either we do not speak at all, or we only have descriptions of what the object would be if it existed;

4. only when we experience more than one instance of a thing, say a cat, do we begin to have a precise idea of what cathood might be as distinct from the single cat we have before us.

To anyone living in the wake of the Industrial Revolution, though, it must have been apparent that once one leaves the realm of definition and turns to the things themselves described the law fails. Mass production gives lie to the first point. A countless number of virtually identical things can be produced according to the same set of specifications. Opaque contexts calling for recourse to intensions invalidate the second point and are particularly lethal because they threaten principles of extensionality. Extensional logic has no place at all for points 3 and 4.

Although Frege seemed to accept uncritically the view that the intension diminishes as the extension increases and vice versa (FA, §29), he insisted repeatedly and vociferously that, in spite of all appearances and theories to the contrary, senses were never extinguished and that every expression retained both elements in meaning, even in cases of singular reference.

If the way things are in extralogical and extralinguistic reality counts at all, then the ultimate problem with Russell's theory of definite descriptions is that any expression that is short for an object is also short for all the descriptions (definite, possible, actualized, etc.) under which the object may be known. An expression is not an abbreviated description, but an abbreviation of multiple descriptions. No object is identical with any one description, no matter how definite. And each of those descriptions can be taken apart and dissected. If Caryl Chessman was the red-light bandit, then he was the sole killer of each of the red-light bandit's victims. To be executed as the red-light bandit, he need only to have been found guilty on one of the murder counts. Two names abbreviating the same object can contain disguised descriptions of that object—even disguised definite descriptions—that are incompatible one with the other; though both pick out the same object, no route obtains from one description to the other. Is everything that is true of Dr. Jekyll also true of Mr. Hyde? What of Clark Kent and Superman? Boney and Napoleon?

Proper names and definite descriptions are special cases because they seem to yield their referents directly. A symbol that represents an object uniquely, as Ruth Barcan Marcus has so aptly put it, "serves as a long finger of ostension over time and place . . . allows reference to an object despite the vicissitudes the objects undergo, and despite the absence of direct acquaintance."[17] A symbol that represents an object uniquely is a device for bypassing all the extra descriptions that might complicate things. Language appears transparent. This state of affairs has fostered a temptation to think that the names of definite descriptions themselves are the same as the objects they name or describe. Opaque contexts stand as a reminder that they are not and cannot be.

No expression is purely designative, and reference is always from at least one perspective which may be more or less encompassing. Though there are combinations of properties for which there can be no object (the round square for example), there are no propertyless objects, and though reference is always perspectival, there are no single-propertied, or partially propertied objects. Every object comes replete with the properties that make it what it is uniquely. No object of discourse coincides, or ever can coincide with everything that can be said of it.

By deft logical maneuvering one can eclipse intensions, but they do not evaporate into thin air. Frege was very conscious of this when he wrote in "On Sense and Meaning" that "comprehensive knowledge of the thing would require us to say immediately whether any given sense attaches to it. To such knowledge we never attain" (GB, p. 58). Toward the end of his life he frequently returned to this Kantian theme:

> An object can be determined in different ways; each way
> can give rise to a special name. . . . these names have dif-
> ferent senses. That it is the same object is not self-evident.
> [PMC, p. 80]

> . . . there is no reason why all the properties of the desig-
> natum should be capable of being known. Why could the
> loser of Waterloo not have properties which are not
> characteristic marks of the concept loser of Waterloo. . . .
> We can know this or that property of the designated ob-
> ject from the individual name; but there is no reason why
> all the properties of the designatum should be capable of
> being known in this way. [PMC, p. 97]

Talk of all functions was forbidden by the paradoxes. Truth value
finally depends not only on what is designated, but on what
is true or false of that object. What is true or false frequently
depends on the ways the object is given.

In cases of singular reference one cannot, of course, distinguish
between a thing and the properties it enjoys at any particular
instant in time, but it is illusory to think that either the particular piece of predicative knowledge that manages to secure
reference in a given context is informative enough, definitive
enough, or significant enough to play the philosophical roles
that it has been supposed it could in this century. That "Caryl
Chessman" (the proper name) designated the one and only person charged with committing certain specific capital crimes is
not in and of itself very interesting. That through his theory of
definite descriptions Russell managed artificially to establish the
one-to-one relationship between an object and a description
capable of singling it out in the way extensional logic requires is.

Frege blamed the introduction of extensions for the defeat of
his logical project. Russell wrote that mathematical logic requires
extensions, but philosophical logic refuses to provide anything
but intensions as he expounded theories by which he hoped
to make the nonextensional factor in logic amenable to extensional treatment. His theory of definite descriptions makes this
seem feasible. Through his theory he pared away at language
until objects, enjoying a new slim appearance, could slip unob-
trusively through most logical procedures as if unencumbered

by unwanted properties, concepts, attributes . . . intensions. But it is precisely the plethora of possible predicates that makes life interesting and identity statements informative . . . and that causes problems for extensionalist logicians.

§5. THE FINAL SOLUTION

Russell was aware that the measures he took to streamline logical statements were not entirely adequate to solve the problems they were designed to remedy. The theory of definite descriptions helped, and the theory of types went a long way in keeping functions in line by preventing untoward behavior on their part. More drastic measures proved necessary, however (PofM, §500; PMC, p. 147).

So Russell formulated his problematic axiom of reducibility to strike down any extra predicates that might obscure access to the referent. The axiom of reducibility, he wrote, "is equivalent to the assumption that any combination or disjunction of predicates is equivalent to a single predicate. . . ." (PM, pp. 58–59).

This axiom would effectively erase the difference between equality (coincidence from a given perspective), and identity (total coincidence). From it all the usual properties of identity and classes would follow. Two formally equivalent functions would determine the same class, and, conversely, two functions which determine the same class would be formally equivalent (PM, pp. 75–76). A coextensive attribute would exist every time.

Apart from it "or some axiom equivalent in this connection," Russell believed, "we should be compelled to regard identity as indefinable, and to admit (what seems impossible) that two objects may agree in all their predicates without being identical" (PM, p. 58; also pp. 167–68). From this axiom it also follows that: if x and y are the same and x satisfies F, where F is any function then y also satisfies Fy (PM, p. 168).

If valid, the Axiom of Reducibility would validate Leibniz's law, and so vitiate Husserl's complaints against it. But, despite the vital role it played in Russell's system, he could only justify it on pragmatic grounds (PM, pp. xiv, xxix, xliii–xlv, 49, 55–59, 75–80, 166–69): "The axiom of reducibility is introduced in order to legitimate a great mass of reasoning. . . ." (PM, p. xiv). "Many kinds of general statements become possible. . . . The fact that they are rendered possible . . . is an argument in favor of the axiom of reducibility" (PM, p. 76).

Such arguments are circular. If what this axiom would mandate could be true, then Leibniz's law or Basic Law V would have sufficed. Russell saw the difficulties: "That the axiom of reducibility is self-evident is a proposition that can hardly be maintained" (PM, p. 59), ". . . clearly it is not the sort of axiom with which we can rest content" (PM, p. xiv). But without it "many of the proofs of *Principia* become fallacious . . . and in some cases new proofs can only be obtained with considerable labor" (PM, p. xliii). The axiom of reducibility fell short of what was needed (LK, p. 325), but no satisfactory solution appeared to be attainable (PM, p. xiv).

"No particular philosophy is involved in the contradictions," Russell wrote as he tried to find a way to get out of them. "They spring from common sense and can only be solved by abandoning some common-sense assumption" (PofM, p. 105). Of all Russell's theories, the axiom of reducibility is the least compatible with common sense.[18]

CONCLUSION:
THE WAY THINGS ARE

The inscrutability of reference runs deep.

W. V. O. Quine[1]

FREGE'S PROJECT TO logicize mathematics came to a halt when in 1902 Russell informed him of the contradictions his logic generates. Mathematicians have drawn the consequences Russell's paradox has for them, but philosophers still working to further what Frege and Russell achieved have yet to work out the full implications that Russell's paradoxes have for their discipline. It has been generally thought that the logic that has girded analytic philosophy somehow survives Russell's paradox.

When in his *Philosophy of Arithmetic* Husserl studied the problems he found in Frege's theory of identity and denotation, his analyses pointed to difficulties that philosophers following in Frege's footsteps would eventually have to confront, and he provided clues we need to determine what the implications might be for philosophy now. Husserl's book is one of the few documents presently available that can give us an idea as to why Frege's contemporaries in Germany and Austria (not to mention Russell, Whitehead, Wittgenstein, and Frege himself) refused after a certain point to pursue Frege's logic any further. Frege had attempted a perspicuous amalgam of the logical doctrines of his time. The actual nature of his efforts has been hidden from us by the unusual vocabulary in which he clothed his insights, but that didn't waylay his contemporaries.

One way of approaching the problem is to study the question of identity. At each stage in the development of analytic thought philosophers have had to reposition themselves with respect to identity. Identity was at the heart of Frege's reflections on sense and reference (GB, p. 56), and it was identity statements that were to generate the logical concepts he needed for his analytical reconstruction of arithmetic (FA, p. x). "To obtain the concept of number we must fix the sense of a numerical identity" (FA, §62). Frege's doomed axiom of extensionality, Basic Law V, was designed to dictate the view of identity that Frege's logic required in order to work (BL, §§3, 9). Concepts would correspond to extensions of concepts, mutual subordination to equality (PW, pp. 181–82). But the many concepts that might conjoin with a given object makes the transformation of an identity into an identity of ranges of values impossible and leads to Russell's paradox (GB, p. 219).

Husserl's most pointed attacks on Frege's system were directed toward the role identity played in it (PA, pp. 104–5). But it was only Russell's later formulation of the famous paradox that brought the matter home to Frege (GB, p. 214). Then he located the error precisely where Husserl had indicated it would be (cf. PA, pp. 104–5; GB, p. 219). It was a matter of the identity of equivalent propositional functions (PofM, p. 527). As a remedy Frege appealed to a new criterion of identity for extensions (GB, p. 223), but his new reflections on identity finally proved inadequate.[2]

Russell's logic also derived from his reflections on identity and denoting. Idealism, the philosophy Russell wanted to ban, "leads to absolutely insoluble logical difficulties as regards identity," he complained in 1904.[3] "The whole theory of definition, of identity, of classes, of symbolism, and of the variable is wrapped up in the theory of denoting" (PofM, §56), he said as he struggled to overcome the paradoxes. His theory of descriptions and the axiom of reducibility, two of his principal remedies for Frege's failings, have identity considerations at their heart (LK, pp. 44–55, 85; PM, pp. 58, 75–76, 167). Through their employment Russell managed to guarantee the substitutivity of identicals for most expressions in most contexts.[4] Frege never understood how Russell's procedures could solve the problem (PMC, p. 81), but they did manage to obscure it. Russell abandoned philosophy forthwith. In his 1922 introduction to Wittgenstein's *Tractatus,* he conceded that Wittgenstein was probably right to banish identity in the way he did:

. . . the conception of identity is subjected by Wittgenstein
to a destructive criticism from which there seems to be no
escape. The definition of identity by means of the identity of indiscernibles appears to be not a logically necessary principle.[5]

In "On Sense and Meaning" Frege studied some of the cases
in which the holes in his extensionalist system showed through
to the intensional fabric beneath, and in mid-century Carnap,
Marcus, Church, Hintikka, Kripke, and others tried through new
reflections on sense, reference, and identity to develop intensional
logics that could neutralize the difficulties. By this time Frege's
ideas on meaning and intension had acquired a wholly different
cast. His senses had come to be seen as last minute imports
designed to patch certain logical holes.

Quine countered these efforts at the same time as he signaled
grave shortcomings in the key notion of analyticity as it had been
passed down from Kant. These shortcomings were also bound
in with questions of identity, meaning, and reference.[6] "The point
of this paper," Marcus writes in "Extensionality," is to show "that
opacity lies with Quine's use of such terms as 'identity,' 'true identity,' 'equality.' "[7] In recent years considerable effort has been ex-
pended to answer the questions Quine's inquiries have raised. All
the literature on the indeterminacy of translation, the inscrutability
of reference, essentialism, intensionality, modality, propositional
attitudes, possibilia, empty singular terms, and of course, identity, serves as a reminder that something remains amiss. Philosophers have fought to doctor these various symptoms of the ail-
ment as they surfaced until now there is a temptation to abandon Neurath's boat altogether. The problems will not go away
though because the logical errors that force the failure of Basic
Law V are grounded in the very insights into logic, language,
and epistemology that generated twentieth-century logic. The logic
itself is producing them.

"If a conqueror burns a city," Frege was prompted to write,
"he does not burn the name of the city; what happens to a thing
does not automatically happen to its sign" (GB, p. 177). So much
seems obvious, but, as Quine was prompted to write in *Word
and Object,* "Identity invites confusion between sign and object
in men who would not make the confusion in other contexts"

(§24). Though in ordinary discourse one rarely confuses a real thing with the set of letters that designates it, philosophers have managed to make the confusion between names and objects that leads to what Carnap has called the antinomies of name relation.[8] This error, though — as well as Russell's well-known confusion of meaning and naming[9] — is fairly easily detected and accounted for.

Although in ordinary discourse one rarely confuses a real thing with any one of its properties, no matter how determinant, Frege's logic, to work, requires a confusion of intension and object. Identity invites this confusion too, and it is this confusion that is finally decisive for extensional logic. It is decisive because, to work, Frege's logic must make intensions (i.e., meanings, properties, attributes, concepts) amenable to extensional treatment, and it is the ambiguity inherent in identity statements that makes it seem that this can be done. Using identity as he did, Frege managed to obscure the logical difference between intensions and objects. The "rather curious difficulties" Russell found in Frege's theory of denoting (LK, p. 48), and which he sought to remedy through his theory of descriptions, arise when object and sign or meaning are confused. Current difficulties with intensional contexts, possibilia, empty singular terms, and so forth arise because the fundamental differences between meanings and objects continue to be disregarded. These problems serve as a reminder that the necessary blur cannot be made with impunity.

Frege strove to uncover and define the differences between words, concepts, and things, and his innovative vocabulary was to a large extent developed to trace and display those differences. Though he was initially confident that his distinctions reflected facts about the central traits of reality and reality's relation to words and knowledge, his logic also played on confusions made possible by the fact that the same word, for example "tree," can designate a concept, an object, or the word itself. This promotes confusion between sign, object, and meaning. But a hard look at identity statements not only shows how, deftly employed, they can be used to blur the differences, it can also reveal the ontological gulf that separates signs, objects and meanings.

The differences between names and objects have been studied,[10] and those between meaning and naming,[11] but it is the differences between meanings and objects that are crucial for us here. The following interrelated observations illustrate some of the really intractable differences between meanings and objects.

1. The history of philosophy is replete with the false conclusions drawn through the artful manipulation of concepts where no attention was paid (nor in some cases could be) to the things themselves. It was Russell's ardent desire (and it has been that of his successors) to revolutionize logic in a way that would make philosophers less prone to make such errors. It has been thought that most of traditional metaphysics fell into this category.

2. As Hilary Putnam has noted, "Meaning may not fit the world, and meaning change can be forced by empirical discoveries."[12]

3. There is an apparently unbridgeable gap between the role objects play and the role concepts play in scientific theory. Kant's theory of the analytic and the synthetic represented one attempt to account for the difference.

4. There can be scientific theories of the world that are incompatible, yet empirically equivalent.

5. Incompatible translation manuals for any language may be set up among which there can be no objectively correct choice.

6. One cannot speak of the identity of concepts in the same sense as one speaks of the identity of objects, and every major philosopher in the analytic tradition has had to position himself with respect to this fact.[13] Husserl noted this in his *Philosophy of Arithmetic* (p. 104).

7. Two predicates may coincide in extension but differ in intension. "Creature with heart" and "creature with kidneys" is the classic example.

8. For any predicate one can construct an infinity of coextensional predicates that differ in intension. Hence neither the concept nor the intension that a predicate expresses can be determined from the extension of the predicate alone. One cannot determine whether a predicate expresses a given concept on the basis of extensional information alone.

9. Two terms can have the same extension and yet differ in intension; coincidence of properties does not ensure their identity.

10. It was Frege's attempts to make discourse concerning concepts equivalent to discourse concerning objects that led to the contradictions of set theory.

11. Hypotheses are conceptual constructs that posit states of affairs that may or may not obtain.

12. The concept atom managed to travel through time from Democritus to us, but it was only in this century that the word *"atom"* had an identifiable extension.

13. Wherever we have direct access to objects, extensional logic works. It can neither cope with empty singular terms nor with the numerous expressions mathematicians and scientists employ that do not have or cannot have any object.

14. "If I say 'I met a man' . . . what I met was a thing, not a concept, an actual man with a tailor and a bank account or a public house and a drunken wife" (Russell, PofM, p. 53).

15. Conceptual knives may be sharp, but they won't cut real wood.

16. The law of inverse relation of intension and extension may hold for extensions and intensions as logical entities, but it does not hold true for actual things and their properties, as the advent of the Industrial Revolution and mass production has shown.

17. One reason that concepts provide unity and continuity is that they generally survive both the people that use them and the individual things to which they apply. They can be transmitted across space and time and defy the barrier of subjectivity.

18. "Pencil" is not synonymous with any description.

19. ". . . the relation of a predicate to what it means is different from the relation of a name to what it means" (Russell, LK, p. 268).

Mathematical logic requires extensions, but philosophical logic supplies only intensions, Russell complained in *Principia* (p. 72). Frege wanted to revise Kant's definition of analyticity so as to maintain that there were analytic statements that were both true and informative. The ambiguity inherent in identity statements seemed to foster the union of intensional and extensional considerations and thus to make it seem that what Frege wanted could be so. A statement like "the morning star=the evening star" is true for extensional reasons; both terms refer to the same planet. It is informative because the two terms differ in sense (i.e., in intension).

To sustain his argument that statements of the form $a=b$ could be both true and informative, Frege had to blur the difference between identity and equality. Identity meant having all properties in common, being the same under all descriptions. Equality is being equivalent under a given description, as given in a particular way. The only way in which Frege could obtain the effect he desired was through the employment of an axiom that could neutralize officious intensions. The axiom Frege proposed did not work. Russell sought to mandate the removal of extra intensions through his axiom of reducibility, but that did not work either. When Frege dragged identity into logic in the way he did, he dragged intensions in too and fatally so. For, as Husserl observed, if the statements of Frege's extensional logic are to have scientific worth it is by virtue of intensions (PA, p. 134).

Another way of viewing the problem is to note that the notion of identity, understood as Frege would have it be understood (BS, §24; FA, §66; GB, pp. 56, 179; PMC, pp. 152, 164) is itself contradictory, and so leads to contradictions. The philosophical logic that admits "$a=b$" as a true statement in fact affirms both $a=b$ and $a \neq b$. Like the liar of the liar paradox (LK, p. 61) the statement "$a=b$," taken on the level of its signs or of the senses of its signs (and unless "a" and "b" designate the same object, on the level of objects too), would affirm something that is false. This opens the door to Russell's paradox, and that ultimately means that the mathematical logic and the philosophical logic deriving from Frege's efforts are fated to live out not separate, but analogous destinies.

The differences between a and b may be as trivial as the differences between "a" and "b" when both name the same object, but if identity statements are to have the import for science that Frege would have them have, then one has to assume that the differences would be consequential in enough cases to make his procedure worthwhile.

So, I contend that what has in recent years been called Frege's puzzle (i.e., How can identity statements be both true and informative?) is linked with Russell's paradoxes and is an illustration of the importance they have for philosophers now. Also puzzles about the ship of Theseus, and the pillar of salt that is both Lot's wife and not Lot's wife take the form of both $a=b$ and $a \neq b$, and are, I argue, the surfacings of Russell's paradox in its philosophical dress. Puzzles like these but ratify Kant's and Cantor's claims concerning indeterminacy. One cannot step into the same logical river twice, for fresh things can always be predicated of that river or of any other object of discourse. Identity statements provide the prime testing ground for referential inscrutability because the logical elusiveness of any object is most apparent when one tries to equate that object with another.

Focusing on identity problems is one way to make certain difficulties apparent. Another is to study the implications of Kant's observation that because one can never be sure of having exhaustively analyzed all the properties of a concept, all analytic definitions must remain indeterminate.

When Russell set out to remedy the logical ills that lead to the paradoxes of set theory, he found himself obliged to come to terms with problems generated by expressions containing the word "all." It is his study of expressions like "all functions" or "all properties" that tie in most directly with our concerns here.

". . . no statement can be made significantly about 'all a functions' where a is some given object. Thus such a notion as 'all properties of a' meaning 'all functions which are true with the argument a' will be illegitimate," he felt compelled to conclude (PM, p. 55). "It is impossible to obtain one variable which embraces among its values all possible functions of individuals" (PMP, xxxiv). Saying all values of ϕ is inadmissable (PM, p. 57). Use of such expressions, he found, leads directly to the paradoxes he wished to avoid (LK, pp. 61–80, 101).

They lead to the paradoxes because in certain cases (though not all, see LK, pp. 73, 79) in each of the paradoxes "something is said about all cases of some kind, and from what is said a new case seems to be generated, which is and is not of the same kind as the cases of which all were concerned in what was said" (LK, p. 61). We cannot talk about all properties of x because new properties would be thereby generated (LK, p. 68).

The source of the problem lies in the intensional fecundity noted by Kant. What appears verbally to be a single function is often really a conglomeration of many functions with different ranges of significance (LK, p. 74). A phrase expressing such a function may, because of this ambiguity, be significant throughout a set of values of the argument that exceeds the range of significance of any one function (LK, p. 73).

Russell encountered the problem paradoxes while studying Cantor, and in *Principles of Mathematics* he explicitly makes the link between them and Cantor's proof that if u be a class, the number of classes contained in u is greater than the number of terms of u (PofM, §344). Cantor's argument would show that there are more classes of objects than there are objects (PofM, §348). Applying Cantor's reasoning to the problems that concerned him, Russell saw that one could easily show that there were more propositional functions than objects (PofM, §348), that any attempt to establish a one-to-one or many-one correlation of all terms and all propositional functions must omit at least one propositional function (PofM, §102). From Cantor's proposition that any class contains more subclasses than objects, one could elicit constantly new contradictions of the kind Russell wished to avoid (PMC, p. 147). Because he found he could never be certain by any proof to have exhaustively analyzed all the properties of a given concept, Russell developed his theory of types to keep functions in line. The axiom of reducibility was his final solution to the problem of too many predicates.

When Russell wrote in "On Denoting" that "there is no backward road from denotations to meanings because every object can be denoted by an infinite number of denoting phrases" (LK, p. 50), he was drawing another consequence of Kant's thesis — that is, one cannot determine whether a given predicate is true of a given object on the basis of extensional information alone because, though a particular piece of information (say a definite description) may suffice to pick out a given object, the same class of objects has many determining functions, and so no one item of predicative knowledge, no matter how determinant, can suffice to determine the reference fully. If we could have comprehensive knowledge of a thing we could say immediately whether any given sense attaches to it, but, according to Frege, we never attain to such knowledge (GB, pp. 57–58). Individual predicates only determine objects piecemeal — we seem condemned to view our referents through a glass darkly.

The difficulty people are having nowadays fixing the reference of the expression "analytic philosophy" is a case in point. No single description, no matter how definite, seems adequate to fix its reference. Any characterization that is proposed is contested, and many argue (analytic philosophers in particular) that the expression doesn't designate anything specific at all.

Frege thought a statement could be both analytic and informative because for any predicate an infinite number of coextensional predicates could be generated. The logician could acquire new facts by carving up the *Inhalt* in new ways (FA, §64). It should never be a matter, Frege insisted, of simply taking out of our hat what we have put into it. The conclusions we draw should not have been evident in advance. "They are contained in the definition, but as plants are contained in their seeds" (FA, §88).

Frege's procedures would illuminate for scrutiny aspects of the reference that would not, upon initial inspection, be evident. They would bring what is hidden to light. But the problem is that once we begin carving away at *Inhalten,* we begin to acquire more new concepts than we can cope with. What we can know or say about any object can be refined, subdivided, and qualified ad infinitum. And intensional wealth ultimately means referential inscrutability. Chronically underdetermined, the references extensional logic needs will ever elude its grasp. Hilary Putnam joined Cantor when almost a hundred years later he wrote in reference to Quine's findings:

> I shall extend previous 'indeterminacy' results in a very strong way. I shall argue that even if we have constraints of whatever nature which determine the truth-value of every sentence in a language *in every possible world,* still the reference of individual terms remains indeterminate. In fact it is possible to interpret the entire language in violently different ways. . . . [14]

What makes analytic statements and identity statements informative makes them indeterminate. The indeterminacy that insures informativeness forces inscrutability.

The tendency intensions have to proliferate also means that identity is different for intensions than for extensions, and no adequate criterion for establishing the identity of intensions seems to exist. This fundamental difference between objects and what can be predicated of them forced the failure of Basic Law V.

A further consequence of Kant's thesis is that if we can't speak of all properties within this logic, then we can neither say of two things that they can always be substituted for each other *salva veritate.* Leibniz's law needs alteration. Russell modified it to read:

> . . . *x* and *y* are to be called identical when every predicative function satisfied by *x* is also satisfied by *y*. We cannot state that *every* function satisfied by *x* is to be satisfied by *y* because *x* satisfies functions of various orders, and these cannot all be covered by one apparent variable. [PM, p. 168]

But if what the axiom of reducibility would mandate could actually be the case, then there would have been no problem to begin with. Basic Law V would not have failed; Leibniz's law would suffice. The actual properties actual things actually enjoy cannot, however, be wiped away with the stroke of a pen.

I suggest, then, that Kant's thesis concerning analyticity, if true, would have the following important consequences for analytic thought: We could never speak of all properties or all functions of a given object. Reference would be underdetermined and inscrutable. There would be different identity conditions for intensions and extensions. One could not speak of equality of concepts. The sort of unqualified synonymy needed to free analytic statements from charges of triviality would be rare. Statements judged to be true by virtue of meanings would be plunged into uncertainty. Leibniz's law and its problematical offspring, Basic Law V and the axiom of reducibility, would fail. Substitutivity of identicals could not be guaranteed.

In 1918, realizing that he had accomplished something on the formal level to which nothing corresponded on the ontological plane (LK, pp. 267–68), Russell largely gave up his logical work. He would later say that it was only then that he had begun to be aware of the many problems concerned with the relations between words and things (MPD, p. 132). It was then, he would later claim, that he first became interested in the definition of meaning. Before that he "had regarded language as 'transparent'

and had never examined what makes its relation to the non-
linguistic world" (MPD, p. 145).

The realist in Russell apparently balked when he realized that
the modifications he had had to make in Frege's logic to make
it work offered a formally elegant solution to Frege's problems,
but one that could not be about "things themselves" (LK, p.
268). The theory of types he had conceived as a remedy for the
paradoxes, he told his audience in Gordon Square in 1918, "is
really a theory of symbols, not of things" (LK, p. 267). Frege's
logic led to contradictions that Russell's logic could not overcome and still respect the way things are. Later in his life Russell
would complain:

> The linguistic philosophy, which cares only about lan-
> guage, and not about the world is like the boy who pre-
> ferred the clock without the pendulum because, although
> it no longer told the time, it went more easily than before
> and at a more exhilarating pace.[15]

The point is not minor. The intellectual endeavors that brought
philosophy into the twentieth century, both on the Continent
and in England and America, grew out of work on the philosophy of mathematics inspired by realist thinkers like Brentano,
Bolzano, and Meinong. The main philosophers studied in this
work believed that they were exploring and describing something
objective, something that could not be altered by a masterful
manipulation of symbols and no product of the human mind
or imagination. What it was they were describing, though,
uttered a robust no to the extensional treatment some of them
were prescribing for it, so they abandoned their machinations.

The question of what exactly it was they encountered that
made their work seem feasible, that generated such enthusiasm
among their contemporaries, and that finally said no is a tantalizing one. I have argued that they came up against things
themselves, but did they also come up against the things-in-
themselves? Was it the objective order of the universe, or merely
deeply embedded linguistic conventions? The ancient philosophical paradigms that Western philosophers can hardly escape, or
the logical structure of the universe . . . ?

NOTES

INTRODUCTION

1. Allan Janik and Stephen Toulmin, *Wittgenstein's Vienna* (London: Weidenfeld and Nicholson, 1973).

2. In *Mind,* vols. 8, 13–16 (1899–1907). See Russell's *Essays in Analysis,* pp. 17–94.

3. Bernard Bolzano, *Paradoxes of the Infinite* (London, Routledge and Kegan Paul, 1950), p. 48. Also LI, p. 15.

4. Examined personally at the Husserl Library in Leuven, Belgium, in July 1985. Husserl underlined passages and wrote in the margins.

5. As Sheila Turcon of the Russell Archives at McMaster University informs in a letter of August 9, 1985.

6. Ibid.

7. Dallas Willard discusses Lotze's influence on Husserl in *Logic and Objectivity of Knowledge* (Athens: Ohio University Press, 1984), pp. 30–37, 152–55, 182–83, 189. Hans Sluga discusses Lotze's influence on Frege in *Gottlob Frege* (London: Routledge and Kegan Paul, 1980), pp. xi, 19, 40–41, 59–60, for example.

8. Bertrand Russell, *A Critical Exposition of the Philosophy of Leibniz* (London: Allen and Unwin, 1949 [1900]).

9. Besides *The Principles of Mathematics,* he had *The Analysis of Mind* and *Scientific Method in Philosophy* in English. He had a German translation of *Our Knowledge of the External World.*

10. Georg Cantor's review of *Foundations* in *Deutsche Literaturzeitung* 6 no. 20 (1885): 728–29.

11. Georg Cantor, "Grundlagen einer allgemeinen Mannigfaltigkeitslehre," in *Gesammelte Abhandlungen mathematischen und philosophischen Inhalts,* ed. E. Zermelo (Berlin: Springer, 1932), pp. 179–98. Article originally published in 1883. The review cited in note 10 is anthologized here (pp. 440–41).

12. Jean Cavaillès, "Avertissement à la Correspondance Cantor-Dedekind," *Philosophie Mathématique,* Paris: Hermann, 1962, p. 180.

13. Published in English in B. Rang and W. Thomas, "Zermelo's Discovery of the Russell Paradox," *Historia Mathematica* 8, 1 (February 1981): 16–17. Zermelo is referring to Husserl's RS (pages 84–85 of his *Early Writings*).

14. Gottlob Frege, *Gottlob Freges Briefwechsel mit D. Hilbert, E. Husserl, B. Russell* (Hamburg: Meiner, 1980), pp. 3, 47.

15. See the articles by Zermelo and Hilbert anthologized by Van Heijenoort in *From Frege to Gödel* (Cambridge, Mass.: Harvard University Press, 1967).

16. Karl Schuhmann, *Husserl-Chronik,* The Hague: Nijhoff, 1977, p. 158.

17. Frege, *Freges Briefwechsel* p. 44. The editors of the English edition fail to mention Husserl's reference to Bolzano.

18. Husserl's unpublished manuscript Ms A I 35. Roger Schmit, *Husserls Philosophie der Mathematik,* Bonn: Bouvier, 1981, p. 114. Guillermo Rosado Haddock, *Edmund Husserls Philosophie der Logik und Mathematik im Lichte der Gegenwärtigen Logik und Grundlagenforschung.* Dissertation Bonn, 1973, pp. 145–50.

19. Hao Wang, *Reflections on Kurt Gödel,* Cambridge, Mass: MIT, 1987. See the articles by Føllesdal and Tieszen listed in the bibliography.

20. Paul Schilpp, ed., *The Philosophy of Rudolf Carnap* (La Salle: Open Court, 1963).

21. Willard's *Logic and Objectivity of Knowledge* (note 7 above) is a notable exception.

CHAPTER I

1. Dagfinn Føllesdal, "Husserl's Notion of Noema," *Journal of Philosophy* 66 (1969): 680–87.

2. See Føllesdal's assessment of the situation before 1958 in his monograph *Husserl und Frege: ein Beitrag zur Beleuchtung der Entstehung des phänomenologischen Philosophie* (Oslo: Ascheloug, 1958), pp. 11–13. Translated in Haaparanta (ed.), pp. 3–50.

3. See Barry Smith's Husserl-Frege bibliography in "Frege and Husserl: The Ontology of Reference," *Journal of the British Society for Phenomenology* 9, no. 2 (May 1978): 125.

4. See the postface by J. Desanti in *Frege-Husserl Correspondance,* (Mauvezin: Trans-Europ-Repress, 1987), pp. 63–88.

5. A brief list of works where this view is defended can be found in D. W. Smith and R. McIntyre, *Husserl and Intentionality* (Dordrecht: Reidel, 1982), p. 22. See also Hubert Dreyfus, "Sinn and Intentional Object," *Phenomenology and Existentialism,* ed. Robert Solomon (New York: Harper and Row, 1972), pp. 196–210, where he concludes: "at each stage of his development Husserl tried a new way of combining Frege and Brentano. . . ." See also R. Solomon, "Sense and Essence in Frege and Husserl," *Analytic Philosophy and*

Phenomenology, ed. H. Durfee (The Hague: M. Nijhoff, 1976), pp. 31–54, esp. pp. 32 and 34; E. W. Beth, *Les fondements logiques des mathématiques,* 2 ed. (Paris: Louvain, 1955), p. 119; editor T. Bynum's comments in *Conceptual Notation* (Oxford: Clarendon Press, 1972), pp. 43–49.

6. See J. N. Mohanty, *Husserl and Frege* (Bloomington: Indiana University Press, 1982); Dallas Willard, *Logic and the Objectivity of Knowledge* (Athens: Ohio University Press, 1984); the exchange between Føllesdal and Mohanty in *Husserl, Intentionality and Cognitive Sciences* ed. H. Dreyfus (Cambridge, Mass. M.I.T. Press, 1982).

7. Michael Dummett, *The Interpretation of Frege's Philosophy* (Cambridge, Mass.: Harvard University Press, 1981), p. 56; see also p. 72.

8. Ibid., pp. 57–58.

9. Gottlob Frege, *Nachgelassene Schriften und wissentschaftlichen Briefwechsel,* vol. 2 (Hamburg: Meiner, 1976), p. 91.

10. Some of these are reproduced and commented on in Frege, *Begriffsschrift und andere Aufsätze,* 2d. ed. with comments by E. Husserl and H. Scholz ed. I. Angelelli (Hildesheim: Olms, 1964) and in Frege, *Kleine Schriften,* ed. I. Angelelli (Hildesheim: Olms, 1967).

11. Edmund Husserl, *Early Writings in the Philosophy of Logic and Mathematics,* Dordrecht: Kluwer, 1994, p. 247.

12. Alexius Meinong, *Philosophenbriefe aus der wissenschaftlichen Korrespondenz von Alexius Meinong,* ed. R. Kindinger (Graz: Akademische Druck—und Verlaganstalt, 1965), p. 100. Also cited Karl Schuhmann, *Husserl Chronik* (The Hague: M. Nijhoff, 1977), p. 43.

13. W. R. Boyce Gibson, "Excerpts from a 1928 Freiburg Diary," *Journal of the British Society of Phenomenology* 2, 1 (January 1971): 66.

14. Dreyfus, ed. *Husserl, Intentionality,* p. 55.

15. Føllesdal, "Husserl's Notion."

16. Mohanty, *Husserl and Frege;* Willard, pp. 118–24.

17. A. D. Osborn, *The Philosophy of Edmund Husserl in Its Development to His First Conception of Phenomenology in Logical Investigations* (Ph.D. Diss., Columbia University, 1934), p. 29.

18. Husserl defends himself against the charge that he borrowed unjustly from Bolzano in his "Review of Palagyi," *Zeitschrift für Psychologie und Physiologie der Sinnesorgane* 31 (1903): 287–94. Translated in Husserl, *Early Writings,* pp. 197–206. See E. Morscher's commentary in his article "Von Bolzano zu Meinong: zur Geschichte des logischen Realismus," in *Jenseits von Sein und Nichtsein* (Graz: Akademische Druck—und Verlagsanstalt, 1972), pp. 69–85.

19. Frege in "Über die Grundlagen der Geometrie," *Jahresbericht der deutscher Mathematikervereinung* 12, pt. 1 (1903): 319–24; pt. 2: 368–78; and Husserl in "The Origins of Geometry," appendix 3 to *Crisis* (The Hague: M. Nijhoff, 1954).

CHAPTER TWO

1. Føllesdal, *Husserl und Frege,* p. 48.

2. Roger Schmit, *Husserls Philosophie der Mathematik: platonische und konstructivische Moment in Husserl's Mathematik Begriff* (Bonn: Bouvier Verlag, 1981), pp. 14–15. Andrew Osborn, *The Philosophy of Edmund Husserl* (New York: International Press, 1934), pp. 49–51, 56.

3. Michael Dummett, *Frege: Philosophy of Language* (London: Duckworth, 1981), p. xlii.

4. Føllesdal, *Husserl und Frege,* pp. 23–25.

5. Føllesdal's reply to Mohanty in Dreyfus ed., *Husserl, Intentionality,* p. 56.

6. Schuhmann, *Husserl Chronik,* p. 18.

7. Edmund Husserl, "Persönliche Aufzeichnungen," *Philosophy and Phenomenological Research* 16 (1956): 294. (*Early Writings,* p. 490).

8. Meinong, *Philosophenbriefe,* p. 100. See also Schmit, p. 40.

9. Osborn, *Philosophy of Edmund Husserl,* p. 29.

10. Ibid., p. 27.

11. Ivor Grattan-Guinness, "How Bertrand Russell Discovered his Paradox, *Historia Mathematica* 5 (1978): 127.

12. Georg Cantor, "Review of Frege's *Grundlagen,*" *Deutsche Literaturzeitung* 6 (1885): 728–29.

13. Georg Cantor, "Gundlagen einer allgemeinen Mannigfaltigkeitslehre," in *Gesammelte Abhandlungen mathematischen und philosophischen Inhalts* (Berlin: Springer, 1932), pp. 179, 198. Cantor's review of Frege cited above is also anthologized here pp. 440-41.

14. J. N. Mohanty, *Readings on Edmund Husserl's Logical Investigations,* (The Hague: M. Nijhoff, 1977), pp. 22–23.

15. Føllesdal, *Husserl und Frege,* p. 24.

16. Husserl, "Persönliche Aufzeichnungen," p. 295. (*Early Writings,* p. 491). Willard, *Logic and the Objectivity of Knowledge,* pp. 5–6.

17. Osborn, *Philosophy of Edmund Husserl,* p. 13. Husserl's personal copy in his library at Leuven.

18. Schuhmann, *Husserl Chronik,* p. 463. Of interest are also Osborn, *Philosophy of Edmund Husserl,* pp. 15, 18, 20, 45 and Maria

Brück, *Über das Verhältnis Edmund Husserls zu Franz Brentano. Vornehmlich mit Rücksicht auf Brentanos Psychologie* (Würzburg: Tritsch, 1933), pp. 8–9.

19. Husserl, "Review of Palagyi," *Early Writings,* p. 201.

20. Franz Brentano, *Psychology from an Empirical Standpoint* (New York: Humanities Press, 1973). Originally published as *Psychologie vom empirischen Standpunkt,* (Leipzig, Duncher and Humbolt, 1874).

21. Ibid., p. 88.

22. Michael Dummett's lectures "The Origins of Analytical Philosophy" published in English in *Lingua e stile* 23 (1988): 3–49, 171–210 contain interesting discussions of the relationship between the ideas of Brentano, Husserl, and Frege as well as other material related to the present study. Barry Smith's review of these lectures has appeared in *Grazer philosophische Studien* 34 (1989).

23. These discussions are taken from the *Cartesian Meditations,* from sections 2 and 3 of *Ideas* I, and from section 2 of *Formal and Transcendental Logic* by Husserl.

24. Some very interesting discussions of these same matters are found in Barry Smith, "Logic and Formal Ontology," in *Husserl's Phenomenology: A Textbook,* ed. J. N. Mohanty and William R. McKenna (Washington, D.C.: University Press of America, 1989), pp. 29–67; and Karl Schuhmann and Barry Smith, "Against Idealism: Johannes Daubert vs. Husserl's *Ideas I,*" *Review of Metaphysics* 38, no. 4 (June 1985): 763–93.

CHAPTER THREE

1. Ignacio Angelelli, *Studies on Gottlob Frege and Traditional Philosophy* (Dordrecht: Reidel, 1967), chap. 2.

2. Dagfinn Føllesdal, "Husserl's Notion of Noema," *Journal of Philosophy* 66 (1969): 680–87. In "Husserl Fifty Years Later—The Noema Twenty Years Later," *Proceedings of the 18th World Congress of Philosophy,* Brighton, England, August 21–27, 1988, Føllesdal cites a 1983 English-language bibliography (104 entries) pertaining to his article: Ethel Kersey, "The Noema, Husserlian and Beyond: An Annotated Bibliography of English-Language Sources," *Philosophy Research Archives* 9 (1983). Microfiche supplement pp. 62–90, published March 1984.

3. J. N. Mohanty, *Husserl and Frege* (Bloomington, Indiana: University Press, 1982), pp. 63–64, 69–70.

4. Ronald McIntyre and David W. Smith, *Husserl and Intentionality* (Dordrecht: Reidel, 1982), p. 154. Barry Smith comments: "Husserl, Language and the Ontology of the Act," in *Speculative Grammar,*

Universal Grammar, and Philosophical Analysis of Language, ed. Dino Buzetti and Maurizio Ferriani (Amsterdam: John Benjamins, 1987), pp. 143–65.

5. Jaakko Hintikka, "Concept as Vision," in *The Intentions of Intentionality* (Dordrecht: Reidel, 1975), p. 228.

6. W. V. O. Quine, "Two Dogmas of Empiricism," in *From a Logical Point of View* (New York: Harper and Row, 1961 [1953]), p. 22; Hilary Putnam, "The Meaning of 'Meaning,'" *Philosophical Papers,* vol. 2 (Cambridge: Cambridge University Press, 1975), pp. 216–18; Rudolf Carnap, *Meaning and Necessity* (Chicago: University of Chicago Press, 1956 [1947]), p. 126; Alonzo Church, "Carnap's Introduction to Semantics," *Philosophical Review* 52 (1943): 301; Dagfinn Føllesdal's reply to Mohanty in Dreyfus, ed., *Husserl, Intentionality and Cognitive Science,* p. 53.

7. Morscher, "Von Bolzano zu Meinong," pp. 80–81.

8. Dreyfus, ed., *Husserl, Intentionality,* pp. 88–89.

9. Husserl, "Review of Palagyi," *Early Writings,* p. 197–203.

10. Compare LI §§3, 7, 12, 15, 17, 18, 29–31; Bernard Bolzano, *Theory of Science* (Dordrecht: Reidel, 1973), pp. 48–49, 78–80, 98; Frege's "On Sense and Meaning" and Føllesdal's "Husserl's Notion of Noema."

11. Angelelli, *Gottlob Frege, pp.* 39–42.

12. Ernst Tugendhat, "The Meaning of 'Bedeutung' in Frege," *Analysis* 30 (1970): 177. See also Hans Sluga, *Gottlob Frege* (London: Routledge and Kegan Paul, 1980), pp. 158–59.

13. Gareth Evans, *The Varieties of Reference* (Oxford: Clarendon Press, 1982), pp. 7–8 and note.

CHAPTER FOUR

1. An exception: Church's comments in his "Review of M. Farber, *The Foundations of Phenomenology," Journal of Symbolic Logic* 9 (1944): 64.

2. Jean-Toussaint Desanti, "Postface," *Frege-Husserl Correspondance,* (Mauvezin: Trans-Europ-Repress, 1987), pp. 67, 72. Willard's work is again exceptional here.

3. This fact has probably been somewhat obscured to readers of English by three faults in the English edition: (1) Although the statement of retraction and his statement of support of Frege's endeavors are included in a note on p. 179 of the text, they are not cited in the index either under Frege or under *Arithmetic, Philosophy of.* (2) The index fails to note five of the references to the *Philosophy of Arithmetic* (i.e., pp. 174, 179, 479, 480, 799). (3) The

pages cited as retracted are incorrect. All other editions cite pages 129–32, rather than 124–32, as the English edition reads.

4. Ludwig Wittgenstein, *Briefwechsel* (Frankfurt: Suhrkamp, 1980), pp. 241–43.

5. In his *Studies on Gottlob Frege and Traditional Philosophy* (Dordrecht: Reidel, 1967), pp. 50–52, Ignacio Angelelli discusses some other problems with Frege's notion of identity.

6. I have been obliged to alter Austin's translation of *"Gleichheit"* as "identity," and *"gleich"* as "the same" or "identical" to make this text agree with the translation of the same terms in other Frege texts and with common usage. Dictionaries define "identical" as "similar in every detail, exactly alike, the same." "Equal" means being the same in a given way (i.e., according to size, amount, value, status, etc.). For example, we say that all men are created equal (according to U.S. law), but we do not say that all men are created identical.

7. Ludwig Wittgenstein, *Tractatus* (London: Routledge and Kegan Paul, 1921), p. 17.

8. See, for example, Hilary Putnam, "The Meaning of Meaning," reprinted in *Philosophical Papers,* vol. 2 (*Mind, Language and Reality,* Cambridge: Cambridge University Press, 1975), pp. 215–72, esp. p. 227.

9. See, for example, Saul Kripke, *Naming and Necessity* (Oxford: Blackwell, 1980; rev. 1972), pp. 102–5. Or Peter Geach, "Russell on Meaning and Denoting," *Analysis* 19 (1958–59): 69–72. Or F. B. Fitch, "The Problem of the Morning Star and the Evening Star," *Philosophy of Science* 16 (1949): 137–41.

10. Immanuel Kant, *Logic* (New York: Dover, 1974), §104, p. 143. Originally published as *Logik*, ed. Gottlob Jäsche (Berlin: Heimann, 1800).

11. Nathan Salmon, *Frege's Puzzle* (Cambridge, Mass.: M.I.T. Press, 1986), p. 11.

12. Dummett, *Frege: Philosophy of Language* (2nd ed.), p. 544.

13. W. V. O. Quine, *Word and Object* (Cambridge, Mass.: M.I.T. Press, 1960), p. 117.

14. Friedrich Nietzsche, *Das Philosophenbuch* (Paris: Aubier, 1969), §150.

15. W. V. O. Quine, "Two Dogmas of Empiricism," in *From a Logical Point of View,* 2d ed. (New York: Harper and Row, 1961), pp. 20–47. Also his "On Frege's Way Out," *Mind* 64 (1955): 145–59.

16. Rudolf Carnap, *Meaning and Necessity* (Chicago: University of Chicago Press, 1956 [1947]), pp. 100, 105, 109, 154. See also Ruth Barcan Marcus, "Extensionality," *Mind* 69 (1960): 55–62; and Quine, "On Frege's Way Out."

17. W. V. O. Quine, "Ontological Relativity," *Journal of Philosophy* 65: 193.

18. Georg Cantor, "Review of Frege's *Grundlagen*," *Deutsche Literaturzeitung* 6 (1885): 728–29.

19. Dummett, *Frege: Philosophy of Language* (2d ed.), pp. 544–45.

20. Michael Byrd, "Part II of the *Principles of Mathematics*," *Russell* n.s. 7, 1 (Summer 1987): 61.

21. See B. Rang and W. Thomas, "Zermelo's Discovery of the Russell Paradox," *Historia Mathematica* 8, 1 (February 1981): 15–22, The Zermelo-Husserl exchange is translated on pp. 16–17.

22. Compare PA, pp. 104–5 with Dummett on identity in *Frege: Philosophy of Language*, pp. 543–45. See also Ruth Barcan Marcus, "Extensionality" and "Does the Principles of Substitutivity Rest on a Mistake," in *The Logical Enterprise*, ed. R. Marcus (New Haven: Yale, 1975); "Possibilia and Possible Words," *Grazer Philosophische Studien* 25–26, (1985–86): 107–33; and Russell on extensionality in *Inquiry into Meaning and Truth* (London: and Unwin, 1940), pp. 168, 260–61, 271.

CHAPTER FIVE

1. Edmund Husserl, "Psychological Studies in the Elements of Logic," *Early Writings*, p. 146. Also in *Husserl: Shorter Works*, ed. McCormick and Elliston (Notre Dame, Ind.: Notre Dame University Press, 1981), pp. 126–42.

2. A look at the articles on Russell's theory of descriptions anthologized in *Essays on Bertrand Russell*, ed. E. D. Klemke (Urbana: University of Illinois Press, 1971) shows the many difficulties in Russell's interpretation.

3. Bertrand Russell, "Meinong's Theory of Complexes and Assumptions," *Mind* 13 (1904): 204.

4. Ibid., p. 512.

5. Alexius Meinong, In *Zeitschrift für Psychologie und Physiologie der Sinnesorgane* 21 (1899): 182 n.

6. Bertrand Russell, *Problems in Philosophy* (Oxford: Oxford University Press, 1967 [1912]), p. 22.

7. Ibid., p. 26.

8. Ibid., p. 23.

9. Ibid., p. 26.

10. Ibid., p. 32. For another discussion of themes treated in this chapter see Dallas Willard, *Logic and the Objectivity of Knowledge* (Athens: Ohio University Press, 1984), pp. 118–24. Ironically, Hubert

Dreyfus's statement that "at each stage of his development Husserl tried a new way of combining Frege and Brentano" is more true of Russell in the early years of the century than it is of Husserl. See "*Sinn* and Intentional Object," in *Phenomenology and Existentialism,* ed. R. Solomon, (New York: Harper and Row,, 1972), pp. 196–210.

11. Føllesdal discusses this in "Brentano and Husserl on Intentional Objects and Perception," *Grazer Philosophische Studien* 5 (1978): 83-89. Anthologized in *Husserl, Intentionality and Cognitive Science,* ed. Dreyfus, pp. 31–41. See also Barry Smith, "The Soul and Its Parts: A Study in Aristotle and Brentano," *Brentano Studien* 1 (1989).

12. See Brentano's 1911 appendix to *Psychology from an Empirical Standpoint,* the section entitled "On Psychologism."

13. Kevin Mulligan and Barry Smith, "A Relational Theory of the Act," *Topoi* 5 (1986): 115–30.

14. Tyler Burge, "Frege on Extensions of Concepts from 1884 to 1903," *The Philosophical Review* 93, 1 (January 1984): 33–34; Jacques Bouveresse, "Frege critique de Kant," *Revue internationale de philosophie* 130 (1979): 739–60; Claude Imbert, introduction, *Les fondements de l'arithmétique* by Frege (Paris: Seuil, 1969), pp. 92–94.

15. See Russell's treatment of the subject twelve years later (PofM, p. 55): "Starting for example with *human,* we have man, men, all men, every man, any man, the human race, of which all except the first are two fold, a denoting concept and an object denoted."

16. Dummett, *Frege: Philosophy of Language,* 1981 ed. pp. 546–50.

17. Edmund Husserl, "Persönliche Aufzeichnungen," *Philosophy and Phenomenological Research* 16 (1956): 294.

18. See also: Farber, *Foundation of Phenomenology,* pp. 26–29; Osborn, *Philosophy of Edmund Husserl in Its Development,* p. 17; Schmit, *Husserls Philosophie der Mathematik,* pp. 30–33; Robert Sokolowski, *The Formation of Husserl's Concept of Constitution* (The Hague: M. Nijhoff, 1970), pp. 17–18; Miller, *Numbers in Presence and Absence,* p. 22.

19. Bernard Duquesne, "Les calculs dans le psychologisme du jeune Husserl," *Revue philosophique de Louvain* 82, 4th series no. 53, (February 1984): pp. 80–89.

20. Cited inWillard, *Logic and Objectivity,* pp. 115–16. Also in Husserl, *Early Writings,* 12–19.

21. Cited in Walter Biemel, ed., *Husserl* (Paris: Minuit, 1959), pp. 41–42. Also in Husserl, *Early Writings,* pp. 12–19.

22. Ibid.

23. Willard, *Logic and Objectivity,* p. 116. Also in Husserl, *Early Writings,* pp. 12–19.

24. See the introduction to the Husserliana edition of *Philosophie der Arithmetik,* p. xviii.

25. See the articles anthologized in Husserl's *Early Writings*.

26. Biemel, ed., *Husserl,* p. 49.

CONCLUSION: ANALYTICITY

1. Franz Brentano, §10 of the 1911 appendix to *Psychology from the Empirical Standpoint.*

2. Bernard Bolzano, *Theory of Science,* §148, 197, 305.

3. W. V. O. Quine, in *From a Logical Point of View* (New York: Harper Torchbooks, 1961), pp. 18–19 ("On What There Is") and pp. 70 & 77 ("Identity, Ostension, and Hypostasis"); "Ontological Relativity," *Ontological Relativity and Other Essays,* (New York: Columbia University Press, 1969), pp. 26–68; *Word and Object* (Cambridge, Mass.: M.I.T. Press, 1960), §12.

4. Quine, "Ontological Relativity," pp. 34–35.

5. On page 107 of his work *Husserl and Frege* Mohanty cites appendix 1, §1 of Husserl, *Formal and Transcendental Logic,* trans. D. Cairns (The Hague: M. Nijhoff, 1969), pp. 295–96.

6. Cited in J. N. Mohanty, "Intentionality and Possible Worlds: Husserl and Hintikka," in *Husserl, Intentionality and Cognitive Science,* eds. Dreyfus and Hall (Cambridge Mass.: M.I.T. Press, 1982), p. 235.

PART TWO INTRODUCTION

1. For example, Michael Dummett, *The Origins of Analytical Philosophy,* London: Duckworth, 1994.

2. See the exchange between Blackburn and Code, and Geach in *Analysis* 38, no. 4 (October 1978): 204–7.

3. In *Studies on Gottlob Frege and Traditional Philosophy* (Dordrecht: Reidel, 1967), Ignacio Angelelli provides complementary discussions of many of these terms in relation to traditional logic.

CHAPTER SIX

1. W. V. O. Quine, "Quantifiers and Propositional Attitudes," *Journal of Philosophy* 53 (1956): 185.

2. For English, see the relevant entries in the *Oxford English Dictionary:* for a more complete history, see Joseph Frisch, *Extension and Comprehension in Logic* (New York: Philosophical Library, 1969) or Paul Weingartner, "Die Fraglichkeit der Extensionalitätthese und die Probleme einer intensionalen Logik," in *Jenseits von Sein und Nichtsein,* ed. R. Haller (Graz: Akademische Druck, 1972), pp. 127,

163–69: "Denn seit Aristoteles, der die Extension und die Intension eingeführt hat, beschäftigt sich eine grosse Anzahl von Philosophen und Logikern mit beiden Begriffen und ihren Unterschiede."

3. Bernard Bosanquet, *Logic* (Oxford: Clarendon Press, 1911 [1888]), p. 44.

4. Edmund Husserl, "Review of Ernst Schröders *Vorlesungen über die Algebra der Logik,*" *Göttinger gelehrte Anzeigen,* no. 7 (1891): 243; in English in *The Personalist* 59 (April 1978): 115. "The Deductive Calculus and the Logic of Contents," *Vierteljahrsschrift für wissenschaftliche Philosophie* 15 (1891): p. 177; in English in *The Personalist* 60 (January 1979): 13. Both articles are anthologized in the *Aufsätze und Rezensionen,* vol. 22 of the Husserliana edition of Husserl's works and Husserl's *Early Writings.*

5. Stanley Jevons, *Elementary Lessons in Logic* (London: MacMillan, 1875), p. 37.

6. Stanley Jevons, *Principles of Science* (London: MacMillan, [1873], 1883), p. 47.

7. Bosanquet, *Logic,* p. 44.

8. Rudolf Carnap, *Meaning and Necessity* (Chicago: University of Chicago Press, [1947], 1956), p. 203.

9. Ibid., p. 125.

10. Bosanquet, *Logic,* p. 45.

11. Bernard Bolzano, *Theory of Science* (Dordrecht: Reidel, 1973), pp. 162–63.

12. Jevons, *Elementary Lessons,* p. 38.

13. Immanuel Kant, *Logik,* ed. Gottlob Jäsche (Berlin: Heimann, [1800], 1869), §7.

14. Michael Dummett, *Truth and Other Enigmas* (Cambridge, Mass.: Harvard University Press, 1978), p. 122.

15. F. H. Bradley, *Principles of Logic* (Oxford: Oxford University Press, (1883), 1922), p. 168.

16. Carnap, *Meaning and Necessity,* p. 246; also p. 234.

17. Ibid., p. 236.

18. Ibid., p. 199.

19. Bosanquet, *Logic,* p. 45.

20. Cited by Ivor Grattan-Guinness, "How Russell Discovered His Paradox," *Historia Mathematica* 5 (1978): 131.

21. Bradley, *Principles of Logic,* p. 168.

22. Bosanquet, *Logic,* p. 44.

23. Jevons, *Principles of Science,* p. 26.

24. Bolzano, *Theory of Science,* (Dordrecht: Reidel) p. 161.

25. Kant, *Logik,* §7.

26. Bradley, *Principles of Logic,* p. 170.

27. Gareth Evans, *Varieties of Reference* (Oxford: Clarendon Press, 1982), p. 8; also p. 30. In *Essays on Bertrand Russell,* ed. E. D. Klemke (Urbana: University of Illinois, 1971), p. 233 for Linsky's views and p. 211 for Geach's. For a view closer to my own see Tyler Burge, "Frege on Extensions of Concepts, from 1884–1903," *Philosophical Review* 93 no. 1 (January 1984); or Dummett, *Frege: Philosophy of Language,* p. 271; or Angelelli, *Studies on Gottlob Frege,* pp. 205–6.

28. Frege's contribution to Philip Jourdain's "The Development of the Theories of Mathematical Logic and the Principles of Mathematics," *Quarterly of Pure and Applied Mathematics* 43 (1912): 251. See also Dummett, *Frege: Philosophy of Language* (2d ed.), p. 662; PW, p. 269.

29. Reviews by Michaelis and Schröder are anthologized in Gottlob Frege, *Conceptual Notation and Related Articles,* ed. T. Bynum (Oxford: Clarendon Press, 1972), pp. 218, 220.

30. Boole's "Logical Calculus and the Concept-Script" and "Boole's Logical Formula Language and My Concept-Script" in PW, pp. 9–52. A third article was published later: *"Über die wissenschaftliche Berechtigung einer Begriffsschrift," Zeitschrift für Philosophie und philosophische Kritik* 81 (1882): 48–56. Burge cites additional texts in the article cited in note 27.

31. Compare to Evans, *Varieties of Reference* pp. 7–8.

32. For example, McIntyre and Smith, *Husserl and Intentionality,* p. 65.

33. See Dummett's reply to Sluga in *Interpretation,* p. 532.

34. Jourdain, "Mathematical Logic," Frege writes p. 239.

35. Ibid., p. 252.

36. Georg Cantor, "Rezension von Freges *Grundlagen,*" *Deutsche Literaturzeitung* 6 (1885): 728–29.

37. Jourdain, "Mathematical Logic," p. 251.

38. W. V. O. Quine, *Mathematical Logic,* rev. ed. (Cambridge: Harvard, 1951), §22. His *Methods of Logic* (London: Routledge and Kegan Paul, 1952), §§34, 38 and the 1982 edition (Cambridge, Mass.: Harvard University Press, 1982), §46. Frege, GB, pp. 42–55. Russell, LK, pp. 50–55, 268.

39. Ruth Barcan Marcus, "Extensionality," *Mind* (69), (1960): 55–62. Quite interesting on identity and extensionality.

40. Quine, *Mathematical Logic,* p. 120; *Methods of Logic,* §38 of 1952 ed.; §46 of 1982 ed.

41. The Quine-Carnap debate is well known.

42. Alonzo Church, *Journal of Symbolic Logic* 8 (1943): 45–47; his review of Quine's "Notes on Existence and Necessity," *Journal of Philosophy* 40 (1943): 113–27.

43. Dummett, *Frege: Philosophy of Language,* 2d ed. p. 271. Dummett's expression, his conviction, is quite the contrary.

Chapter Seven

1. Bertrand Russell, "Is Position in Space and Time Absolute or Relative?" *Mind,* n.s. 10 (1901): 312.

2. Immanuel Kant, *Logik,* ed. Jäsche (Berlin: Heimann, 1800), §3.

3. Ibid., p. 14. Compare with Husserl, LI, §55 of the *Prolegomena.*

4. Yehoshua Bar-Hillel, "Bolzano's Definition of Analytic Proposition," *Theoria* 16 (1950): 105. Published concurrently in *Methodos.*

5. For example, Michael Dummett, *The Interpretation of Frege's Philosophy* (Cambridge, Mass.: Harvard University Press, 1981), p. 72.

6. Franz Brentano, *Psychologie vom empirischen Standpunkt* (Leipzig: Meiner 1924–1928 (1874), p. 1.

7. See the 1911 appendix to the above-cited work by Brentano, section eleven ("Psychologism").

8. Russell, "Position in Space and Time," p. 315.

9. Jean Paul Sartre, "Intentionality: A Fundamental Idea of Husserl's Phenomenology," *Journal of the British Society of Phenomenology* 1, no. 2 (May 1970): 5.

10. Edmund Husserl, "Psychological Studies in the Elements of Logic," *Early Writings*: 146. Also anthologized in Husserliana, vol. XII.

11. See translator's introduction to LI, p. 38. For "imagination" see G. Frege, *Conceptual Notation and Related Articles* ed. T. Bynum (Oxford: Clarendon Press, 1972), p. 168. And PMC, pp. 159, 163.

12. Ivor Grattan-Guinness, "The Russell Archives: Some New Light on Russell's Logicism," *Annals of Science* 31, no. 5 (1974): 402–3.

13. Bertrand Russell, "Meinong's Theory of Complexes and Assumptions," *Mind* 14 (1905): 530.

14. Russell, "Meinong's Theory," *Mind* 13 (1904): 513.

15. Ibid., p. 516.

16. Ibid., p. 208.

17. Ibid., p. 522.

18. Russell, "Position in Time and Space," p. 312.

CHAPTER EIGHT

1. Michael Dummett, "Note: Frege on Functions," *Philosophical Review,* 65 (1956): pp. 229–30. Also in E. D. Klemke, ed., *Essays on Frege* (Urbana: University of Illinois Press, 1968), p. 296.

2. Klemke ed., *Essays on Frege,* p. 242.

3. Ibid., p. 224.

4. Ibid., p. 293.

5. See, for example, part 2 of the above-cited collection.

6. W. V. O. Quine, "On Frege's Way Out," p. 146. Also anthologized in Klemke, *Essays on Frege.*

7. Jaakko Hintikka, *Intentions of Intentionality* (Dordrecht: Reidel, 1975), pp. 206–7.

8. Rudolf Carnap, *Meaning and Necessity* (Chicago: University of Chicago Press, 1956), p. 233.

9. Quine, "Frege's Way Out," p. 147.

10. Carnap, *Meaning and Necessity,* p. 126.

11. Ibid., p. 125.

12. Gareth Evans, *Varieties of Reference* (Oxford: Clarendon Press, 1982), pp. 16–17.

13. See, for example, his review of Husserl or the preface to the *Basic Laws.*

14. W. V. O. Quine, "Russell's Ontological Development," in Klemke, *Essays on Russell,* pp. 9–10. Appeared for the first time in *Journal of Philosophy* 63 (1966): 657–67.

CHAPTER NINE

1. Ivor Grattan-Guinness, "Bertrand Russell on His Paradox and the Multiplicative Axiom: An Unpublished Letter to Philip Jourdain," *Journal of Philosophical Logic* 1: 106–7.

2. W. V. O. Quine, "Russell's Ontological Development," *Essays on Bertrand Russell,* ed. E. D. Klemke (Urbana: University of Illinois Press, 1968), p. 8. The article was originally published in the *Journal of Philosophy,* 63 (1966): 657–67.

3. Peter Strawson, "On Referring," *Mind* 59 (1950): 320–44. Also anthologized in Klemke, ed., *Essays on Russell.*

4. Tyler Burge, "Russell's Problem and Intentional Identity," in *Agent, Language, and the Structure of the World,* ed., Tomberlin (Hackett) (this is all the bibliographical information the author provided me), esp. pp. 81–83. Ruth Barcan Marcus, "Possibilia and Possible Worlds," *Grazer Philosophische Studien* 25–26 (1985–86): 107–33.

5. Ruth Barcan Marcus, "Extensionality," *Mind* 69 (1960): 55–62.

6. See Wilfred Sellars, "Acquaintance and Description Again," *Journal of Philosophy* 46 (1949): 496–504, or Quine in "Russell's Ontological Development," pp. 4, 9, 10; David Bell, *Frege's Theory of Judgment* (Oxford: Blackwell, 1979), pp. 60–61; Strawson in "On Referring" in Klemke, ed., *Essays on Russell,* p. 155; John R. Searle, "Russell's Objections to Frege's Theory of Sense and Reference," *Analysis* 18 (1957–58): 137–43.

7. Marcus, "Extensionality."

8. Burge, "Russell's Problem," esp. the opening pages.

9. W. V. O. Quine, "On What There Is," in *From a Logical Point of View* (New York: Harper and Row, 1961), pp. 12–17, for example.

10. Burge, "Russell's Problem," esp. pp. 80–81; and Alonzo Church, "A Review of Quine," *Journal of Symbolic Logic* 8 (1943): 45–47.

11. W. V. O. Quine, *Mathematical Logic,* rev. ed. (Cambridge: Harvard University Press, 1951) §22, p. 119.

12. W. V. O. Quine in *From Frege to Gödel,* ed. Jean van Heijenoort (Cambridge, Mass.: Harvard University Press, 1967), p. 217.

13. Ruth Barcan Marcus, "Does the Principle of Substitutivity Rest on a Mistake?" in *The Logical Enterprise,* ed. R. Marcus, A. Anderson, and R. Martin (New Haven: Yale University Press, 1975) p. 36. Also Marcus, "Possibilia," pp. 128–31.

14. Quine, *Mathematical Logic,* §4 and "Reference and Modality" in *From a Logical Point of View,* pp. 139–59. Saul Kripke, *Naming and Necessity,* rev ed. (Oxford: Blackwell, 1980) p. 75. PMC, p. 97.

15. Quine, *Mathematical Logic,* §22, pp. 119–20.

16. Bernard Bosanquet, *Logic* (Oxford: Clarendon Press, 1911 (1888), p. 45.

17. Marcus, "Possibilia," p. 122.

18. Wittgenstein, *Tractatus,* 6.1233. F. P. Ramsey, "Predicative Functions and the Axiom of Reducibility," in *The Foundations of Mathematics* (New York: Humanities Press, 1931 and London: Routledge and Kegan Paul, 1954), chap. 1, pp. 32–49. W. V. O. Quine, *Set Theory and Its Logic* (Cambridge, Mass.: Harvard University Press, 1963, 1969), pp. 241–58.

CONCLUSION: THE WAY THINGS ARE

1. W. V. O. Quine, "Ontological Relativity," in *Ontological Relativity and Other Essays* (New York: Columbia University Press, 1969), p. 41.

2. Michael Dummett, *Frege: Philosophy of Language,* 2d ed., pp. xli and 656–57; and Peter Geach, "On Frege's Way Out," *Mind* 65 (1956): 408–9.

3. Bertrand Russell, "Meinong's Theory of Complexes and Assumptions," *Mind* 13 (1904): 513.

4. Ivor Grattan-Guinness cites an unpublished letter from Russell to Philip Jourdain in "Bertrand Russell on His Paradox and the Multiplicative Axiom," *Journal of Philosophical Logic* 1: 106–7; and PM, pp. 56–59.

5. Wittgenstein, *Tractatus* (1922 ed.), pp. 16–17.

6. See the articles by Quine anthologized in *From a Logical Point of View* (New York: Harper, 1961 (1953).

7. Ruth Barcan Marcus, "Extensionality," *Mind* 69 (1960), p. 60.

8. Carnap, *Meaning and Necessity,* §31.

9. Peter Strawson, "On Referring," *Mind* 59 (1950): 320–44.

10. W. V. O. Quine, *Mathematical Logic* (Cambridge, Mass.: Harvard University Press, 1951 [1940]), §4; *Logical Point of View,* pp. 139–59.

11. Strawson, "On Referring."

12. Hilary Putnam, "The Meaning of 'Meaning,'" reprinted in *Philosophical Papers,* vol. 2, *Mind, Language and Reality* (Cambridge: Cambridge University Press, 1975), p. 256.

13. For example, PMC, p. 97; Carnap, *Meaning and Necessity,* p. 154; Quine in "On Frege's Way Out," *Mind* 64 (1955): 145–59.

14. Hilary Putnam, *Reason, Truth, and History* (Cambridge: Cambridge University Press, 1981), p. 33. Emphasis in the original.

15. Russell's introduction to Ernest Gellner's *Words and Things* (London: Gollancz, 1959), p. 15.

BIBLIOGRAPHY

Ajdukiewicz, Kazimierz. "Sprache und Sinn." *Erkenntnis* 4 (1934): 100–38.

Almeida, Guido. *Sinn und Inhalt in der genetischen Phänomenologie E. Husserls.* The Hague: Nijhoff, 1972.

Angelelli, Ignacio. "Friends and Opponents of the Substitutivity of Identicals in the History of Logic." In Schirn (ed.), Vol. 2: 141–66.

———. "Hans Sluga: *Gottlob Frege.*" *Journal of Philosophy* 80, 4 (1983): 232–39.

———. "Review of Bolzano *Tagebücher 1811–1817.*" *Journal of the History of Philosophy* 22, 2 (April 1984): 249–52.

———. *Studies on Gottlob Frege and Traditional Philosophy.* Dordrecht: Reidel, 1967.

———. "Die Zweideutigkeit von Frege's Sinn und Bedeutung." *Allgemeine Zeitschrift für Philosophie* 3 (1978): 62–66.

Arnauld, Antoine, and Pierre Nicole. *La logique ou l'art de penser.* Paris: Flammarion, 1978 (1662).

Ayer, Alfred Jules. *Central Questions of Philosophy.* London: Weidenfeld and Nicholson, 1973.

Bachmann, Friedrich. *Untersuchungen zur Grundlegung der Arithmetik mit besondere Beziehung auf Dedekind, Frege und Russell.* Leipzig: Felix Meiner, 1934.

Baker, Gordon, and P. M. S. Hacker. "Dummett's Frege; or, Through a Looking Glass Darkly." *Mind* 92 (1983): 239–46.

———. "Dummett's Purge: Frege without Functions." *The Philosophical Quarterly* 33, 131 (April 1983): 115–33.

———. *Frege: Logical Excavations.* Oxford: Blackwell, 1984.

Bar-Hillel, Yehoshua. "Bolzano's Definition of Analytic Propositions." *Theoria* 16 (1950): 91–117. Published concurrently in *Methodos.*

———. "Bolzano's Propositional Logic." *Archiv für mathematischen Logik und Grundlagenforschung* 1 (1952): 305–38.

Barwise, Jon, and John Etchemendy. *The Liar: An Essay on Truth and Circularity.* New York: Oxford University Press, 1987.

Becker, Oskar. "The Philosophy of E. Husserl." In Elveton (ed.): 40–72. Originally published as "Die Philosophie Edmund Husserls." *Kant-Studien* 35 (1930): 119–50.

Bell, David. *Frege's Theory of Judgement.* Oxford: Blackwell, 1979.

———. *Husserl.* London: Routledge, 1990.

Bergmann, Gustav. "Russell's Examination of Leibniz Examined." *Philosophy of Science* 23 (1956): 175–203.

Beth, Evert Willem. *The Foundations of Mathematics*. Amsterdam: North Holland, 2nd ed. rev. 1965 (1959).

Biemel, Walter. "The Decisive Phases in the Development of Husserl's Philosophy." In Elveton (ed.): 148–74.

_____, ed. *Husserl*. Paris: Minuit, 1959.

Black, Max. *The Nature of Mathematics*. London: Routledge and Kegan Paul, 1965.

Blackburn, Simon, and Alan Code. "The Power of Russell's Criticism of Frege: On Denoting pp. 48–50." *Analysis* 38 (October 1978): 65–77.

_____. "Reply to Geach." *Analysis* 38 (October 1978): 206–7.

Bôcher, Maxime. "The Fundamental Conceptions and Methods of Mathematics." *Bulletin of the American Mathematical Society* 11, 3 (December 1904).

Bodnar, Joanne. *Bolzano and Husserl: Logic and Phenomenology*. Ph.D. Dissertation, State University of New York, Buffalo, 1976.

Bolzano, Bernard. *Paradoxes of the Infinite*. London: Routledge and Kegan Paul, 1950. Originally published as *Paradoxien des Unendlichen* (1831).

_____. *Theory of Science*. Berkeley: University of California Press, 1972. Partial translation of his *Wissenschaftslehre* (1837) by R. George.

_____. *Theory of Science*. Dordrecht: Reidel, 1973. Partial translation of his *Wissenschaftslehre* (1837) by B. Terrell.

Boole, George. *An Investigation of the Laws of Thought*. London: Walton and Maherly, 1854.

Bosanquet, Bernard. *Logic*. Oxford: Clarendon Press, 1888.

Bouveresse, Jacques. "Frege critique de Kant." *Revue Internationale de Philosophie* 130 (1979): 739–61.

_____. *Le Pays des possibles: Wittgenstein et le monde réel*. Paris: Minuit, 1988.

Boyce Gibson, W. R. "From Husserl to Heidegger: Excerpts from a Freiburg Diary." *Journal of the British Society for Phenomenology* 2, 1 (January 1971): 58–83.

Bradley, F. H. *The Principles of Logic*. Oxford: Oxford University Press, 1922 (1883).

Brentano, Franz. *Psychology from an Empirical Standpoint*. New York: Humanities Press, 1973. Originally published as *Psychologie vom empirischen Standpunkt*. Leipzig: Meiner, 1924–28 (1874).

Brück, Maria. *Über das Verhältnis Edmund Husserls zu Franz Brentano. Vornehmlich mit Rücksicht auf Brentanos Psychologie*. Würzburg: K. Tritsch, 1933.

Burge, Tyler. "Frege and the Hierarchy." *Synthese* 40 (February 1979): 265–81.

_____. "Frege on Extensions of Concepts from 1884 to 1903." *Philosophical Review* 93, 1 (January 1984): 3–34.

_____. "Frege on Truth." In Haaparanta and Hintikka (eds.): 97–154.

_____. "The Liar Paradox Tangles and Chains." *Philosophical Studies* 41 (1982): 353–66.

_____. "Review of Hintikka, *The Intentions of Intentionality*." *Synthese* 27 (1979): 315–34.

_____. "Semantical Paradox." *Journal of Philosophy* 76 (1979): 169–98.

_____. "Sinning Against Frege." *Philosophical Review* 88 (1979): 398–432.

Byrd, Michael. "Part II of the *Principles of Mathematics*." *Russell* 7, 1 (Summer 1987): 59–67.

Cantor, Georg. *Contributions to the Founding of the Theory of Transfinite Numbers*. New York: Dover, 1955 (1915).

_____. *Georg Cantor Briefe*. H. Meschkowski and W. Nilson (eds.), New York: Springer, 1991.

_____. *Gesammelte Abhandlungen*. E. Zermelo (ed.), Berlin: Springer, 1932.

_____. "Rezension von Freges *Grundlagen der Arithmetik*." *Deutsche Literaturzeitung* 6 (1885): 728–29. Also in Cantor's *Gesammelte Abhandlungen*: 440–41.

Carnap, Rudolf. "Autobiography." In Schilpp (ed.), *The Philosophy of Rudolf Carnap*: 3–84.

_____. *The Logical Foundations of Probability*. Chicago: University of Chicago Press, 1950.

_____. *Logical Syntax of Language*. London: Routledge and Kegan Paul, expanded version 1937.

_____. "The Logicist Foundations of Mathematics." In Klemke (ed.), *Essays on Bertrand Russell*: 341–54.

_____. *Meaning and Necessity*. Chicago: University of Chicago Press, 1956 (1947).

Caton, Charles. "The Idea of Sameness Challenges Reflection." In Schirn (ed.), Vol. 2: 167–80.

Cavaillès, Jean. *Méthode axiomatique et formalisme*. Paris: Hermann, 1981 (1937).

_____. *Philosophie Mathématique*. Paris: Hermann, 1962.

_____. *Sur la logique et la théorie de la science*. Paris: P.U.F., 1947.

Church, Alonzo. "Carnap's Introduction to Semantics." *Philosophical Review* 52 (1943): 298–304.

_____. "Comparison of Russell's Resolution of the Semantical Antinomies with That of Tarski." *Journal of Symbolic Logic* 41 (1976): 747–60.

_____. "Ontological Commitment." *Journal of Philosophy* 55 (1958): 101–2.

_____. "Review of M. Farber, *The Foundations of Phenomenology.*" *Journal of Symbolic Logic* 9 (1944): 63–65.

Clavelin, Maurice. "Elucidation philosophique et 'écriture conceptuelle' dans le *Tractatus.*" *Wittgenstein et le problème d'une philosophie de la science.* Paris: CNRS, 1971: 104–12.

_____. "Quine contre Carnap: la polémique sur l'analyticité et sa portée." *Revue Internationale de Philosophie,* fasc. 162 (1983): 144–45.

Coffa, J. A. "The Humble Origins of Russell's Paradox." *Russell* 33–34 (1979): 31–37.

Couturat, Louis. *De l'infini mathématique.* Paris: Blanchard, 1973 (1896).

_____. "Kant et la mathématique moderne." *Bulletin de la Société Française de Philosophie* 20 (March 1904): 125–34.

_____. *Les Principes des mathématiques.* Paris: Alcan, 1905.

Couture, Jocelyne. "Une grammaire d'incomplétude référentielle: la logique intensionnelle des *Principia Mathematica.*" *Canadian Philosophical Review* 22, 1 (March 1983).

Cunningham, Suzanne. *Language and the Phenomenological Reduction of Edmund Husserl.* The Hague: Nijhoff, 1976.

Currie, Gregory. "Frege on Thoughts: A Reply." *Mind* 43 (1984): 256–58.

_____. "Interpreting Frege: A Reply to Michael Dummett." *Inquiry* 26, 2 (1983): 345–59.

da Silva, Jairo J. "Husserl's Conception of Logic." *Manuscrito* 22, 2 (October 1999): 367–97.

_____. "Husserl's Philosophy of Mathematics." *Manuscrito* 16, 2 (1993): 121–48.

Danik, Jaromir. *Les Projets de Leibniz et de Bolzano. Deux sources de la logique contemporaine.* Quebec: Presses de l'Université Laval, 1975.

Dauben, Joseph. *Georg Cantor: His Mathematics and Philosophy of the Infinite.* Princeton NJ: Princeton University Press, 1979.

Davidson, Donald, and G. Harman, eds., *Semantics of Natural Language.* Dordrecht: Reidel, 1972.

de Boer, Theodore. *The Development of Husserl's Thought.* The Hague: Nijhoff, 1978.

Dedekind, Richard. *Essays on the Theory of Numbers.* New York: Dover, 1963 (1887, 1893).

_____. "Letter to Keferstein." In van Heijenoort (ed.): 99–103.

Dejnožka, Jan. *The Ontology of the Analytic Tradition and Its Origins. Realism and Identity in Frege, Russell, Wittgenstein, and Quine.* Boston: Rowman & Littlefield, 1996.

Demopoulos, William, ed. *Frege's Philosophy of Mathematics.* Cambridge: Harvard University Press, 1995.

de Rouilhan, Philippe. *Frege: les paradoxes de la représentation.* Paris: Minuit, 1988.

Desanti, Jean-Toussaint. *Les idéalités mathématiques*. Paris: Seuil, 1968.
_____. "Postface." In *Frege-Husserl Correspondance*. Mauvezin: Trans-Europ-Repress, 1987: 63–88.
Donnellan, K. S. "Reference and Definite Descriptions." *Philosophical Review* 75 (July1966): 281–304.
Dreyfus, Herbert. "*Sinn* and Intentional Object." In *Phenomenology and Existentialism*. R. Solomon (ed.). New York: Harper and Row, 1972: 196–210.
_____, and Harrison Hall, eds. *Husserl, Intentionality and Cognitive Science*. Cambridge MA: M.I.T. Press, 1982.
Dugac, Pierre. *Richard Dedekind et les fondements des mathématiques*. Paris: Vrin, 1976.
Dummett, Michael. "Frege on Functions: A Reply." *Philosophical Review* 64 (1955): 96–107. Also in Klemke (ed.), *Essays on Frege*: 268–83.
_____. *Frege, Philosophy of Language*. London: Duckworth, 2nd ed. rev. 1981 (1973).
_____. *Frege, Philosophy of Mathematics*. London: Duckworth, 1991.
_____. *The Interpretation of Frege's Philosophy*. London: Duckworth, 1981.
_____. "Note: Frege on Functions." *The Philosophical Review* 65 (1956): 229–30. Also in Klemke (ed.), *Essays on Frege*: 295–97.
_____. "The Origins of Analytical Philosophy." *Lingua e stile* 23 (1983): 3–49; 171–210.
_____. *Origins of Analytic Philosophy*. London: Duckworth, 1993.
_____. *Truth and Other Enigmas*. Cambridge: Harvard University Press, 1978.
_____. "An Unsuccessful Dig." Wright (ed.): 194–226.
Duquesne, Bernard. "Les calculs dans le psychologisme du jeune Husserl." *Revue philosophique de Louvain* 82 (4th series), 53 (February 1984): 80–99.
Edie, James M. "The Concept of Intentionality." *Southwestern Journal of Philosophy* 5 (Spring 1974): 205–17.
Eley, Lothar. Editor's introduction to the Husserliana edition of Husserl's *Philosophie der Arithmetik*: XIII–XXVIX.
Elliston, Frederick A., and Peter McCormick, eds. *Husserl: Expositions and Appraisals*. Notre Dame IN: Notre Dame University Press, 1981.
Elsas, A. "A Review of Husserl *Philosophie der Arithmetik*." *Philosophische Monatshefte* 30 (1894): 437–40.
Elveton, R. O., ed. *The Phenomenology of Husserl: Selected Critical Readings*. Chicago: Quadrangle Books, 1970.
English, Jacques. "Sur la traduction de certains termes de Husserl." In the French edition of Husserl's *Philosophie de l'arithmétique*: 385–418.

Evans, Gareth. *The Varieties of Reference*. Oxford: Clarendon Press, 1982.

Farber, Marvin. *The Foundations of Phenomenology*. Cambridge: Harvard University Press, 1943.

Fels, H. "Bolzano und Husserl." *Philosophisches Jahrbuch der Görresgesellschaft* 39 (1926): 410–18.

Findlay, J. N. Translator's Introduction to Husserl's *Logical Investigations*.

Føllesdal, Dagfinn. "Brentano and Husserl on Intentional Objects and Perception." *Grazer Philosophische Studien* 5 (1978): 83–94.

_____. "Husserl and Frege: A Contribution to Elucidating the Origins of Phenomenological Philosophy." In Haaparanta (ed.): 3–47. A translation of his Norwegian Master's Thesis: *Husserl und Frege: Ein Beitrag zur Beleuchtung der Enstehung des phänomenologische Philosophie*. Oslo: Ascheloug, 1958.

_____. "Husserl: fifty years later . . . the Noema twenty years later." *Proceedings of the Eighteenth World Congress of Philosophy* held in Brighton, England, in August 1988.

_____. "Husserl's Notion of Noema." *Journal of Philosophy* 66 (1969): 680–87.

_____. "An Introduction to Phenomenology for Analytic Philosophers." In Olson and Paul (eds.): 417–29.

_____. "Introductory Note." In Gödel's *Collected Works*, Vol. 3: 364–73.

Fraenkel, A. A. "Georg Cantor." *Jahresbericht der deutschen Mathematiker Vereinigung* 39, 1930: 189–266. Abridged in Cantor's *Gesammelte Abhandlungen*: 452–83.

Frege, Gottlob. *The Basic Laws of Arithmetic*. Berkeley: University of California Press, 1964.

_____. *Begriffsschrift, a formal language, modeled upon that of arithmetic, for pure thought*. In van Heijenoort (ed.): 5–82.

_____. *Begriffsschrift und andere Aufsätze*. I. Angelelli (ed.), 2nd German ed., Hildesheim: Olms, 1964 (1879). Includes E. Husserl's and H. Scholz's markings.

_____. *Conceptual Notation and Related Articles*. T. Bynum (ed.). Oxford: Clarendon Press, 1972.

_____. *Collected Papers on Mathematics, Logic and Philosophy*. Oxford: Blackwell, 1984. Translation of his *Kleine Schriften*.

_____. *Foundations of Arithmetic*. Oxford: Blackwell (2nd rev. ed.), 1986 (1884).

_____. *Gottlob Freges Briefwechsel mit D. Hilbert, E. Husserl und B. Russell*. G. Gabriel (ed.). Hamburg: Meiner, 1980.

_____. *Grundgesetze der Arithmetik I, II*. Hildesheim: Olms, 1966 (1893, 1903).

_____. *Kleine Schriften*. I. Angelelli (ed.), 2nd ed., Hildesheim: Olms, 1990 (1967).

_____. *Philosophical and Mathematical Correspondence*. Abridged by B. McGuinness. Oxford: Blackwell, 1980.

_____. *Posthumous Writings*. Oxford: Blackwell, 1979.

_____. "Reply to Cantor's Review of *Grundlagen der Arithmetik*." In his *Collected Papers*: 122. Originally published as "Erwiderung auf Cantors Rezension der *Grundlagen der Arithmetik*." *Deutsche Literaturzeitung* 6, 28 (1885): 1030.

_____. "Review of Dr. E. Husserls *Philosophy of Arithmetic*." *Mind* 81, 323 (July 1894): 321–37. Also in his *Collected Papers*: 195–209.

_____. "Rezension von Georg Cantor, *Zur Lehre vom Transfiniten. Gesammelte Abhandlungen aus der Zeitschrift für Philosophie und philosophische Kritik*." *Zeitschrift für Philosophie und philosophische Kritik* 100 (1892): 269–72. Translated in his *Collected Papers*: 178–81 and his *Conceptual Notation*.

_____. *Translations from the Philosophical Writings*. P. Geach and M. Black (eds.). Oxford: Blackwell (3rd ed.), 1980 (1952).

_____. "Über die Grundlagen der Geometrie." *Jahresbericht der deutscher Mathematiker Vereinigung* 12 (1903): 319–24; 369–78. Translated in his *Collected Papers*: 273–84.

_____. "Über formale Theorien der Arithmetik." *Jenaische Zeitschrift für Naturwissenschaft* 19 (1886): 95–104. Translated in his *Collected Papers*: 112–21.

Frisch, Joseph C. *Extension and Comprehension in Logic*. New York: Philosophical Library, 1969.

Garciadiego, Alejandro. *Bertrand Russell and the Origins of the Set-theoretic 'Paradoxes.'* Basel: Birkhäuser, 1992.

Geach, Peter. *Logic Matters*. Berkeley: University of California Press, 1972.

_____. "On Frege's Way Out." *Mind* 65 (1965): 408–9.

_____. "Russell on Denoting." *Analysis* 38 (1978): 204–5.

_____. "Russell on Meaning and Denoting." *Analysis* 19 (1959): 69–72.

Gellner, Ernst. *Words and Things*. London: Gollancz, 1959.

Gerlach, H. and Sepp, H., eds. *Husserl in Halle*. Bern: Peter Lang, 1994.

Gier, N. F. *Wittgenstein and Phenomenology*. Albany: State University of New York Press, 1981.

Gilson, Lucienne. *Méthode et métaphysique selon Franz Brentano*. Paris: Vrin, 1955.

_____. *La Psychologie descriptive selon Franz Brentano*. Paris: Vrin, 1955.

Gödel, Kurt. *Collected Works*. 3 vols. New York: Oxford University Press, 1990–95.

Grattan-Guinness, Ivor. "Achilles Is Still Running." *Transactions of the Charles S. Peirce Society* 10, 1 (Winter 1974): 8–16.

_____. "Bertrand Russell on His Paradox and the Multiplicative Axiom: An Unpublished Letter to Philip Jourdain." *Journal of Philosophical Logic* 1 (1972): 103–10.

_____. "Bertrand Russell's Logical Manuscripts: An Apprehensive Brief." *History and Philosophy of Logic* 6 (1985): 53–74.

_____. "The Correspondence between Georg Cantor and Philip Jourdain." *Jahresbericht der deutscher Mathematiker Vereinigung* 73 (1971): 111–30.

_____. *Dear Russell-Dear Jourdain, a commentary on Russell's logic based on his correspondence with Philip Jourdain.* London: Duckworth, 1977.

_____. "Georg Cantor's Influence on Bertrand Russell." *History and Philosophy of Logic* 1 (1980): 61–93.

_____. "How Russell Discovered His Paradox." *Historia Mathematica* 5 (1978): 127–37.

_____. "Notes on the Fate of Logicism from *Principia Mathematica* to Gödel's Incompletability Theorem." *History and Philosophy of Logic* 5 (1984): 67–78.

_____. "Psychology in the Foundations of Logic and Mathematics: The Cases of Boole, Cantor and Brouwer." *History and Philosophy of Logic* 3 (1982): 33–53.

_____. "The Russell Archives: Some New Light on Russell's Logicism." *The Annals of Science* 31, 5 (1974): 387–406.

_____. "Russell's Logicism versus Oxbridge Logics 1890–1925: A Contribution to the Real History of the Twentieth Century." *Russell* 5 (1985–86): 101–31.

_____. "Towards a Biography of Georg Cantor." *Annals of Science* 27, 4 (1971): 345–91.

Griffin, N. "Russell on the Nature of Logic." *Synthese* 45: 117–88.

Guenther, Franz. "Comments on Hintikka's 'A Hundred Years Later." *Synthese* 59 (1984): 51–58.

Haaparanta, Leila, ed. *Mind, Meaning and Mathematics, Essays on the Philosophical Views of Husserl and Frege.* Dordrecht: Kluwer, 1994.

_____, and Jaakko Hintikka, eds. *Frege Synthesized.* Dordrecht: Reidel, 1986.

Hahn, Lewis, and Schilpp, Paul, eds. *The Philosophy of W. V. Quine.* La Salle IL: Open Court, 1986.

Hale, Bob, *Abstract Objects.* Oxford: Blackwell, 1987.

Haller, Rudolf, ed. *Jenseits von Sein und Nichtsein: Beiträge zur Meinong Forschung.* Graz: Akademische Druck- und Verlagsanstalt, 1972.

Hallett, Michael. *Cantorian Set Theory and Limitation of Size.* Oxford: Clarendon Press, 1984.

Helme, Mark. "Frege's Beurtheilbarer Inhalt." *Analysis* 43, 2 (March 1983): 70–72.

Hilbert, David. *Die Hilbertischen Probleme: Vortrag "Mathematische Probleme 1900."* Leipzig: Akademische Verlagsgesellschaft, 1983.
_____. "On the Foundations of Logic and Arithmetic." In van Heijenoort (ed.): 129–38.
_____. "On the Infinite." In van Heijenoort (ed.): 367–92.
Hildebrand, Franz. "Rezension von *Philosophie der Arithmetik.*" *Göttingische gelehrte Anzeigen* 17 (1893): 175–80.
Hill, Claire Ortiz. "Circling Gottlob Frege, Review of *Frege Importance and Legacy*, M. Schirn (ed.)." *Diálogos* (January 1999): 203–13.
_____. "De-intensionalization and Radical Information Loss." *Proceedings of the Third International Symposium on Logic and its Applications*. Sofia, 1994: 140–50.
_____. "Frege's Letters." In Hintikka (ed.): 97–118.
_____. "From Empirical Psychology to Phenomenology: Husserl on the Brentano Puzzle." In Poli (ed.): 151–67.
_____. "Husserl, Frege and 'the Paradox'." *Manuscrito*, October 2000.
_____. *La logique des expressions intentionnelles.* Mémoire de Maîtrise, Université de Paris-Sorbonne, April 1, 1979.
_____. *Rethinking Identity and Metaphysics.* New Haven CT: Yale University Press, 1997.
_____. "Review of Edmund Husserl's *Logik und allgemeine Wissenschaftslehre*, Husserliana Vol. 30." *History and Philosophy of Logic* 19 (1998): 115–17.
_____, and Guillermo E. Rosado Haddock. *Husserl or Frege? Meaning, Objectivity, and Mathematics.* La Salle IL: Open Court, 2000.
Hintikka, Jaakko. "A Hundred Years Later: The Rise and Fall of Frege's Influence in Language Theory." *Synthese* 59 (1984): 27–49.
_____. "The Idea of Phenomenology in Wittgenstein and Husserl." *Austrian Philosophy Past and Present*. K. Lehrer and J. C. Marek (eds.). Dordrecht: Kluwer, 1997: 101–23.
_____. "Identity, Variables and Impredicative Definitions." *Journal of Symbolic Logic* 21 (1956): 225–45.
_____. *The Intentions of Intentionality and Other New Models for Modalities.* Dordrecht: Reidel, 1975.
_____. *Knowledge and Belief.* Ithaca NY: Cornell University Press, 1962.
_____. *Models for Modalities.* Dordrecht: Reidel, 1969.
_____. "On the Development of the Model-Theoretic Viewpoint in Logical Theory." *Synthese* 77 (1988): 1–36.
_____, ed. *From Dedekind to Gödel, Essays on the Development of the Foundations of Mathematics.* Kluwer: Dordrecht, 1995.
_____, and G. Sandu. "The Skeleton in Frege's Cupboard: The

Standard vs. Non-Standard Distinction." *The Journal of Philosophy* 89 (1992): 290–315.

_____, and D. Davidson, eds. *Words and Objections, Essays on the Work of W. O. Quine.* Boston: Reidel, 1969.

Holenstein, Elmar. Editor's introduction to the Husserliana edition of Husserl's *Logische Untersuchungen:* VI–LIV.

Hülsmann, Heinz. *Zur Theorie der Sprache bei Edmund Husserl.* Munich: Anton Pustet Verlag, 1964.

Husserl, Edmund. "A. Voigt's 'Elemental Logic' in Relation to My Statements on the Logic of the Logical Calculus." *The Personalist* 60 (July 1979): 26–35. In his *Early Writings:* 121–30.

_____. *Aufsätze und Rezensionen 1890–1910.* Husserliana Vol. XXII. The Hague: Nijhoff, 1979. These papers are translated in his *Early Writings.*

_____. *Briefwechsel, Die Brentanoschule.* Vol. I. Dordrecht: Kluwer, 1994.

_____. *Cartesian Meditations: An Introduction to Phenomenology.* The Hague: Nijhoff, 1973. Translation of *Cartesianische Meditationen* in Husserliana Vol. I.

_____. "The Deductive Calculus and the Logic of Contents." In his *Early Writings:* 92–114, and *The Personalist* 60 (January 1979): 7–25.

_____. *Early Writings in the Philosophy of Logic and Mathematics.* Translator D. Willard. Dordrecht: Kluwer, 1994.

_____. *Einleitung in die Logik und Erkenntnistheorie, Vorlesungen 1906/07.* Husserliana Vol. XXIV. Dordrecht: Nijhoff, 1984.

_____. *Formal and Transcendental Logic.* The Hague: Nijhoff, 1969.

_____. *Ideas: General Introduction to Pure Phenomenology.* New York: Colliers, 1962.

_____. *Ideas Pertaining to a Pure Phenomenology and to Phenomenological Philosophy. Second Book. Studies in the Phenomenology of Constitution.* Dordrecht: Kluwer, 1989.

_____. *Introduction to the Logical Investigations: A Draft of a Preface to the Logical Investigations (1913).* The Hague: Nijhoff, 1975.

_____. "Letter from Edmund Husserl to Carl Stumpf." In his *Early Writings:* 12–19.

_____. *Logical Investigations.* New York: Humanities Press, 1970.

_____. *Logik und allgemeine Wissenschaftstheorie, Vorlesungen 1917/18, mit ergänzenden Texten aus der ersten Fassung 1910/11.* Husserliana Vol. XXX. Dordrecht: Kluwer, 1996.

_____. *Logische Untersuchungen.* Halle: Niemeyer, 1900–01 (2nd ed. rev., 1913). Also published as Husserliana Vols. XVIII, XIX/I–II. The Hague: Nijhoff, 1975, 1984.

_____. Ms A I 35. Unpublished, untitled, undated manuscript on set theory available at the Husserl Archives in Cologne, Leuven, and Paris.

_____. "On the Concept of Number. Psychological Analyses." *Philosophica Mathematica* 9 (Summer 1972): 44–51; (Summer 1973): 37–87. Also in McCormick and Elliston (eds.): 92–120.

_____. "The Origins of Geometry." Appendix to his *Krisis der europäischen Wissenschaften und die transzendentale Phänomenologie*. The Hague: Nijhoff, 1954.

_____. "Personal Notes." In his *Early Writings*: 490–500. Translation of his "Persönliche Aufzeichnungen." *Philosophy and Phenomenological Research* 16 (1956): 293–302.

_____. *Philosophie de l'arithmétique*. Paris: PUF, 1972.

_____. *Philosophie der Arithmetik*. Halle: Pfeffer, 1891.

_____. *Philosophie der Arithmetik, mit ergänzenden Texten (1890–1901)*. Husserliana Vol. XII. The Hague: Nijhoff, 1970.

_____. "Psychological Studies in the Elements of Logic." In his *Early Writings*: 139–70, and McCormick and Elliston (eds.): 126–42.

_____. "Recollections of Franz Brentano." In McCormick and Elliston (eds.): 342–49 and Mc Alister: 47–55.

_____. "Review of Ernst Schröder's *Vorlesungen über die Algebra der Logik*." In his *Early Writings*: 52–91 and in *The Personalist* 59 (April 1978): 115–43.

_____. "Review of Melchior Palaygi's *Der Streit der Psychologisten und Formalisten in der modernen Logik*." In his *Early Writings*: 197–206, and *The Personalist* 53 (Winter 1972): 5–13.

_____. *Studien zur Arithmetik und Geometrie, Texte aus dem Nachlass (1886–1901)*. Husserliana Vol. XXI. The Hague: Nijhoff, 1983.

_____. *Vorlesungen über Bedeutungslehre, Sommersemester 1908*. Husserlian Vol. XXVI. Dordrecht: Nijhoff, 1987.

Husserl, Malvine. "Skizze eines Lebensbildes von E. Husserl." *Husserl Studies* 5 (1988): 105–25.

Illemann, Werner. *Husserls vorphänomenologische Philosophie*. Leipzig: Hirzel, 1932.

Imbert, Claude. "L'héritage frégéen du *Tractatus*." *Wittgenstein et le problème d'une philosophie de la science*. Paris: CNRS, 1971: 59–76.

_____. Introduction to Frege's *Fondements de l'arithmétique*. Paris: Seuil, 1969: 13–94.

Ishiguro, Hidé. *Leibniz's Philosophy of Logic and Language*. Cambridge UK: Cambridge University Press, 1990.

Jackson, Howard. "Frege on Sense-Functions." *Analysis* 23, 4 (March 1963): 84–87.

Jacques, Francis. *Référence et description: Russell, lecteur de Meinong*. Nanterre: Thèse d'Etat, 1975.

Janik, Allan, and Stephen Toulmin. *Wittgenstein's Vienna*. London: Weidenfeld and Nicholson, 1973.

Jevons, Stanley. *Elementary Lessons in Logic: Deductive and Inductive*. London: Macmillan, 5th ed. 1875.

_____. *Principles of Science*. London: Macmillan, 1973 (1883).

Jones, Constance. "Mr. Russell's Objections to Frege's Analysis of Propositions." *Mind* 19 (1910): 379–87.

Jourdain, Philip. "The Development of the Theories of Mathematical Logic and the Principles of Mathematics." *The Quarterly of Pure and Applied Mathematics* 48 (1912): 219–315. Includes Frege's comments.

_____. "The Development of the Theory of Transfinite Numbers." *Archiv der Mathematik und Physik* 14 (1908–09): 289–311; 16 (1910): 21–43; 22 (1913–14): 1–21. In his *Selected Essays on the History of Set Theory and Logic*: 33–99.

_____. "The Philosophy of Mr. Bertrand Russell." *Monist* 21 (1911): 483–508; 26 (1916): 24–63.

_____. *Selected Essays on the History of Set Theory and Logic*. I. Grattan-Guinness (ed.). Bologna: CLUEB, 1991.

Kant, Immanuel. *Logic*. New York: Dover, 1974. A translation of his *Logik*, G. Jäsche (ed.). Berlin: Heimann, 1800.

Kaplan, David. "How to Russell a Frege-Church." *Journal of Philosophy* 72: 716–29.

_____. "Opacity." In Hahn and Schilpp (eds.): 229–94.

_____. "What Is Russell's Theory of Descriptions." *Bertrand Russell*. D. Pears (ed.). Garden City NY: Doubleday Anchor, 1972.

_____, and Richard Montague. "A Paradox Regained." *Notre Dame Journal of Formal Logic* 1, 3 (July 1960): 79–90.

Kerry, Benno. "Über Anschauung und ihre psychische Verarbeitung." *Vierteljahrsschrift für wissenschaftliche Philosophie* 9–16, 1885–1891. Eight articles discussing Frege and Bolzano.

_____. "Über Georg Cantors Mannichfaltigkeitsuntersuchungen." *Vierteljahrsschrift für wissentschaftliche Philosophie* 9, 1885: 191–232.

Kersey, Ethel. "The Noema, Husserlian and Beyond: An Annotated Bibliography of English Language Sources." *Philosophy Research Archives* 9, Microfiche supplement, 1984 (1983): 62–90

Keyser, C. J. "Concerning the Axiom of Infinity and Mathematical Induction." *Bulletin of the American Mathematical Society* 9: 424–35.

Kilminster, C.W. *Russell*. Brighton: The Harvester Press, 1984.

Klemke, E. D., ed. *Essays on Bertrand Russell*. Urbana: University of Illinois Press, 1971.

_____, ed. *Essays on Gottlob Frege*. Urbana: University of Illinois Press, 1968.

Kline, Morris. *Mathematical Thought from Ancient to Modern Times*. Vol. 3. New York: Oxford University Press, 1972.

Kraus, Oskar, ed. *Franz Brentano: Zur Kenntnis seines Lebens und seiner Lehre*. Munich: Beck'sche, 1919.

Kreiser, Lothar. "Bemerkungen zu einer Paradoxie Freges." *Teorie a metoda* 4, 1 (1972).

_____. "Review of Frege's *Nachgelassene Schriften*, vol. 1." *Deutsche Zeitschrift für Philosophie* 21 (1973): 519–24.

_____. "Zur Geschichte des wissenschaftlichen Nachlasses Gottlob Freges." *Ruch filozoficznej* 33, 1 (1974): 42–47.

Kripke, Saul. *Naming and Necessity.* Oxford: Blackwell, 1980 (1972).

_____. "An Outline of a Theory of Truth." *The Journal of Philosophy* 72 (1975): 690–716. Also in Martin (ed.), *Recent Essays on Truth and the Liar Paradox:* 53–82.

Küng, Guido. "Husserl on Pictures and Intentional Objects." *Review of Metaphysics* 26 (1973): 670–80.

_____. "Zur Erkenntnistheorie von Franz Brentano." *Grazer Philosophische Studien* 5 (1978): 169–81.

Kusch, Martin. *Language as Calculus vs. Language as Universal Medium.* Dordrecht: Kluwer, 1989.

Landgrebe, Ludwig, and Jan Patocka. *Edmund Husserl: Zum Gedächtnis.* New York: Garland, 1980.

Linke, Paul. "Gottlob Frege as Philosopher." In Poli (ed.): 49–72.

Linsky, Leonard. *Names and Descriptions.* Chicago: University of Chicago Press, 1977.

_____. *Oblique Contexts.* Chicago: University of Chicago Press, 1983.

_____. "Reference and Referents." In Klemke (ed.), *Essays on Russell:* 220–35.

_____, ed. *Reference and Modality.* Oxford: Oxford University Press, 1971.

Lipps, Hans. *Die Verbindlichkeit der Sprache.* Frankfurt: Klostermann, 1958.

Löwenheim, Leopold. "Über das Auflösungsproblem im Logischen Klassenkalkuls." *Sitzungsberichte der berliner mathematischen Gesellschaft* 63 (24 June 1908): 89–94.

Lohmar, Hans. *Husserls Phänomenologie als Philosophie der Mathematik.* Dissertation, Cologne, 1987.

Lotze, Hermann. *Logic.* New York: Garland, 1980 (1843).

Lotze, Hermann. *Metaphysik.* Leipzig: Hirzel, 1879.

McAlister, Linda Lopez. *The Philosophy of Franz Brentano.* London: Duckworth, 1976.

McCormick, Peter, and Frederick A. Elliston, eds. *Husserl Shorter Works.* Notre Dame IN: Notre Dame University Press, 1981.

McDowell, John. "On the Sense and Reference of a Proper Name." *Mind* 86 (1977): 159–85.

McIntyre, Ronald, and David Smith. *Husserl and Intentionality.* Dordrecht: Reidel, 1982.

_____. "Husserl's Identification of Meaning and Noema." *The Monist* 59 (1975): 111–32.

Mahnke, Dietrich. "From Hilbert to Husserl: First Introduction to Phenomenology, especially that of formal mathematics." *Studies in the History and Philosophy of Science* 8 (1966): 71–84.

Mancosu, Paolo. *From Brouwer to Hilbert, the Debate on the Foundations of Mathematics in the 1920s.* New York: Oxford University Press, 1998.

Marcus, Ruth Barcan. "A Backward Look at Quine's Animadversions on Modality." In her *Modalities*: 215–32.

_____. "Critical Review of Linsky." *Philosophical Review* (July 1978): 497–504.

_____. "Does the Principle of Substitutivity Rest on a Mistake?" In her *Modalities*: 101–110, and Marcus (ed.): 31–38.

_____. "Essential Attribution." *Journal of Philosophy* 67, 7 (1971): 187–202. In her *Modalities*: 53–70.

_____. "Essentialism in Modal Logic." *Noûs* 1 (March 1967): 91–96. In her *Modalities*: 45–52.

_____. "Extensionality." *Mind* 69 (1960): 55–62.

_____. "The Identity of Individuals in a Strict Functional Calculus of First Order." *Journal of Symbolic Logic* 12 (1947): 12–15.

_____. "Interpreting Quantification." *Inquiry* 5, 3 (1962): 252–59.

_____. *Modalities*. New York: Oxford University Press, 1993.

_____. "Modalities and Intentional Languages." *Synthese* 13, 4 (1961): 303–22. In her *Modalities*: 3–38.

_____. "Possibilia and Possible Worlds." *Grazer Philosophische Studien* 25–26 (1985–86): 107–33. In her *Modalities*: 189–214.

_____, ed. *The Logical Enterprise*. New Haven CT: Yale University Press, 1975.

Martin, Robert, ed. *The Paradox of the Liar.* New Haven CT: Yale University Press, 1970.

_____, ed. *Recent Essays on Truth and the Liar Paradox.* Oxford: Oxford University Press, 1984.

Martinez, Bonan Felix. *La concepción del lenguaje en la filosofía de Husserl.* Santiago: Anales, 1960.

Maxsein, Agnes. "Die Entwicklung des Begriffs 'A priori' von Bolzano über Lotze zu Husserl." Ph.D. dissertation, Giessen, 1933.

Meinong, Alexius. *Philosophenbriefe aus der wissenschaftlichen Korrespondenz von Alexius Meinong.* R. Kindinger (ed.). Graz: Akademische Druck- und Verlagsanstalt, 1965.

Miller, J. Philip. *Numbers in Presence and Absence.* The Hague: Nijhoff, 1982.

Mohanty, J. N. *Edmund Husserl's Theory of Meaning.* The Hague: Nijhoff, 3rd ed. 1976 (1964).

_____. *Husserl and Frege.* Bloomington: Indiana University Press, 1982.

_____. "Husserl and Frege: a New Look at Their Relationship." *Research in Phenomenology* 4 (1974): 51–62.

_____. "Intentionality and Possible Worlds: Husserl and Hintikka." In Dreyfus and Hall (eds.): 233–55.

_____. "On the Roots of Reference: Quine, Piaget and Husserl." *Southwestern Journal of Philosophy* 9, 2: 21–43.

_____. *Transcendental Phenomenology*. Oxford: Blackwell, 1989.

_____, ed. *Readings on Husserl's Logical Investigations*. The Hague: Nijhoff, 1977.

_____, and W. Mc Kenna, eds. *Husserl: A Textbook*. Lanham MD: University Press of America, 1988.

Morscher, Edgar. *Das logische An-sich bei Bernard Bolzano*. Salzburg: Anton Pustet, 1973.

_____. "Von Bolzano zu Meinong: Zur Geschichte des logischen Realismus." In Haller (ed.): 69–85.

Mulligan, Kevin, and Barry Smith. "A Relational Theory of Act." *Topoi* 5 (1986): 115–30.

_____, Peter Simons, and Barry Smith. "Truth-makers." *Philosophy and Phenomenological Research* 44, 3 (March 1984): 287–319.

Natorp, Paul. "Zur Frage der logischen Methode mit Beziehung auf Edmund Husserls Prolegomena zur reinen Logik." *Kant Studien* 6 (1901): 270–83.

Neemann, U. "Husserl und Bolzano." *Allgemeine Zeitschrift für Philosophie* 2 (1977): 52–66.

Nidditch, Paul. "Peano and the Recognition of Frege." *Mind* 72 (1963): 103–10.

Nietzsche, Friedrich. *Das Philosophenbuch*. Paris: Aubier, 1969.

Null, Gilbert. "Review of *Aufsätze und Rezensionen*. Husserliana XXII." *Southwestern Journal of Philosophy* 11, 3: 155–64.

O'Briant, W. "Russell on Leibniz." *Studia Leibnitiana* 11 (1979): 159–222.

Orth, Ernst. *Bedeutung, Sinn, Gegenstand: Studien zur Sprachphilosophie Husserls und Richard Hönigwalds*. Bonn: Bouvier, 1967.

Olson, R. E., and A. M. Paul, eds. *Contemporary Philosophy in Scandinavia*. Baltimore: Johns Hopkins Press, 1972.

Osborn, Andrew. *The Philosophy of E. Husserl in Its Development to His First Conception of Phenomenology in the Logical Investigations*. New York: International Press, 1934. Reprinted in 1949.

Palacios, Leopoldus-Eulogius. "De habitudine inversa inter comprehensionem et extensionem conceptuum." *Laval Théologique Philosophique* (February 1971): 81–87.

Parsons, Charles. "The Liar Paradox." *Journal of Philosophical Logic* 3 (1974): 381–412.

Patton, Thomas. "On a Persistent Fallacy Regarding *de re*." *Analysis* 47, 2 (March 1987): 65–71.

Peano, Giuseppe. "The Principles of Arithmetic Presented by a New Method." In van Heijenoort (ed.): 83–97.

Peckhaus, Volker. *Hilbertsprogramm und kritische Philosophie, das Göttinger Modellinterdiziplinärer Zusammenarbeit zwischen Mathematik und Philosophie.* Göttingen: Vandenhoeck & Ruprecht, 1990.

Picker, Bernold. "Die Bedeutung der Mathematik für die Philosophie Edmund Husserls." *Philosophia Naturalis* 7 (1962): 266–355. His 1955 Münster dissertation.

Plessner, Helmuth. *Husserl in Göttingen.* New York: Garland, 1980.

Poli, Roberto, ed. *The Brentano Puzzle.* Ashgate UK: Aldershot, 1998.

Proust, Joëlle. *Questions of Form.* Minneapolis: University of Minnesota Press, 1989.

Purkert, Walter, and Hans Ilgauds. *Georg Cantor 1845–1918.* Basel: Birkhäuser, 1991.

Putnam, Hilary. *Philosophical Papers.* 2 vols. Cambridge UK: Cambridge University Press, 1975. Especially "On Properties," "The Analytic and Synthetic," "Is Semantics Possible," and "The Meaning of 'Meaning.'"

———. *Reason, Truth and History.* Cambridge UK: Cambridge University Press, 1981.

Quine, Willard. "Designation and Existence." *Journal of Philosophy* 36 (1939): 701–9.

———. *From a Logical Point of View.* New York: Harper and Row, 2nd ed. 1961 (1953).

———. *Mathematical Logic.* Cambridge: Harvard University Press, rev. ed. 1951.

———. *Methods of Logic.* London: Routledge and Kegan Paul, 1952.

———. "Notes on Existence and Necessity." *The Journal of Philosophy* 40 (1943): 113–27.

———. "On Cantor's Theorem." *Journal of Symbolic Logic* 2 (1937): 120–24.

———. "On Frege's Way Out." *Mind* 64 (1955): 145–59.

———. *Ontological Relativity and Other Essays.* New York: Columbia University Press, 1969.

———. *Philosophy of Logic.* Englewood Cliffs NJ: Prentice Hall, 1970.

———. "The Problem of Interpreting Modal Logic." *Journal of Symbolic Logic* 12 (June 1947): 43–48.

———. "Promoting Extensionality." *Synthese* 98 (1994): 143–51.

———. "Quantifiers and Propositional Attitudes." *Journal of Philosophy* 53 (1956): 177–87.

———. *Set Theory and Its Logic.* Cambridge: Harvard University Press, 1969.

———. *Ways of Paradox.* Cambridge: Harvard University Press, 1976.

_____. *Word and Object.* Cambridge MA: M.I.T. Press, 1960.

Ramsey, Frank. *The Foundations of Mathematics.* London: Routledge and Kegan Paul, 1931. Especially chapter 1: "Predicative Functions and the Axiom of Reducibility."

Rang, Bernard, and W. Thomas. "Zermelo's Discovery of the Russell Paradox." *Historia Mathematica* 8, 1 (February 1981): 15–22.

Reid, Constance. *Hilbert.* New York: Springer, 1970.

_____. *Courant in Göttingen and New York.* New York: Springer, 1979.

Resnik, Michael. *Frege and the Philosophy of Mathematics.* Ithaca NY: Cornell University Press, 1980.

Richards, J. "Pre- 'On Denoting' Manuscripts in the Russell Archives." *Russell* 21–22 (1976): 28–34.

Ricketts, Thomas. "Frege, the *Tractatus* and the Logocentric Predicament." *Noûs* 19, 1 (March 1985): 3–17.

Rodriguez-Consuerga, Francisco. *The Mathematical Philosophy of Bertrand Russell: Origins and Development.* Basel: Birkhäuser, 1991.

Rorty, Richard, ed. *The Linguistic Turn.* Chicago: University of Chicago Press, 1967.

Rosado-Haddock, Guillermo E. *Edmund Husserls Philosophie der Logik und Mathematik im Lichte der gegenwärtigen Logik und Grundlagenforschung.* Bonn: Dissertation, Rheinische Friedrich-Wilhelms-Universität, 1973.

_____. *Exposición Crítica de la Filosofía de Gottlob Frege.* Privately printed, 1985.

_____. "On the Semantics of Mathematical Statements." *Manuscrito* 11, 1 (1996): 149–75.

Russell, Bertrand. *The Analysis of the Mind.* London: Allen and Unwin, 1921.

_____. *Collected Papers.* London: Allen and Unwin, 1983.

_____. *A Critical Exposition of the Philosophy of Leibniz.* London: Allen and Unwin, 1949 (1900).

_____. "Descriptions." In Linsky (ed.), *Semantics and the Philosophy of Language*: 95–108.

_____. *Essays in Analysis.* D. Lackey (ed.). New York: Braziller, 1973.

_____. *Inquiry into Meaning and Truth.* London: Allen and Unwin, 1940.

_____. His introduction to Gellner.

_____. *Introduction to Mathematical Philosophy.* London: Allen and Unwin, 1919.

_____. "Is Position in Time and Space Absolute or Relative?" *Mind* 10 (1901): 293–317.

_____. *Logic and Knowledge.* London: Allen and Unwin, 1956.

_____. "Meinong's Theory of Complexes and Assumptions." *Mind* 13 (1904). In his *Essays on Analysis*: 21–76.

_____. "Mr. Strawson on Referring." *Mind* 66 (1957): 385–89.

_____. "My Mental Development." In Schilpp (ed.): 3–20.

_____. *My Philosophical Development*. London: Allen and Unwin, 1959.

_____. *Mysticism and Logic*. London: Allen and Unwin, 1950.

_____. "On Some Difficulties in the Theory of Transfinite Numbers and Order Types." *Proceedings of the London Mathematical Society* 4, series 2 (1906): 29–53. In his *Essays in Analysis*: 135–64.

_____. "On the Distinction Between the Psychological and Metaphysical Points of View." (1894). In his *Collected Papers*: 195–98.

_____. *Our Knowledge of the External World*. London: Allen and Unwin, 1926.

_____. "Les Paradoxes de Logique." *Revue de métaphysique et de morale* 14 (1906): 627–50. English version: "On 'Insolubilia' and Their Solution by Symbolic Logic" in his *Essays in Analysis*: 190–214.

_____. *Principles of Mathematics*. London: Norton, 1903.

_____. *Problems of Philosophy*. Oxford: Oxford University Press, 1967 (1912).

_____. "Recent Work on the Philosophy of Leibniz." *Mind* 12 (1903): 177–201.

_____. "Recent Work on the Principles of Mathematics." *The International Monthly* (July 1901): 83.

_____. "Review of A. Meinong's *Über die Bedeutung des Weberschen Gesetzes*." *Mind* 8 (1899): 251–56.

_____. "Review of A. Meinong's *Über die Erfahrungsgrundlagen unseres Wissens*." *Mind* 15 (1906): 412–15.

_____. "Review of A. Meinong's *Untersuchungen zur Gegenstandstheorie im System der Wissenschaften*." *Mind* 16 (1907): 436–39. In his *Essays on Analysis*: 89–93.

_____. "Review of A. Meinong's *Untersuchungen zur Gegenstandstheorie und Psychologie (1905)*." In his *Essays in Analysis*: 77–88.

_____. *Skeptical Essays*. New York: Norton, 1928.

_____. *Scientific Method in Philosophy*. Oxford: Clarendon Press, 1914.

_____. "Whitehead and *Principia Mathematica*." *Mind* 57 (April 1948): 137–38.

_____ , and Alfred N. Whitehead. *Principia Mathematica to *56*. Cambridge UK: Cambridge University Press, 2nd ed., 1964 (1927–28, 1910).

Salmon, Nathan. *Frege's Puzzle*. Cambridge: MIT Press, 1986.

_____. *Reference and Essence*. Princeton: Princeton University Press, 1981.

Sartre, Jean Paul. "Intentionality: A Fundamental Idea of Husserl's Phenomenology." *Journal of the British Society of Phenomenology* 1, 2 (May 1970): 4–5.

Schilpp, Paul, ed. *The Philosophy of Bertrand Russell*. La Salle IL: Open Court, 1944.

————. *The Philosophy of Rudolf Carnap*. La Salle IL: Open Court, 1963.

Schirn, Matthias. "Axiom V and Hume's Principle in Frege's Foundational Project." *Diálogos* 66 (1995): 7–20.

————, ed. *Frege: Importance and Legacy*. Berlin: de Gruyter, 1996.

————, ed. *Studies on Frege (Studien zu Frege)*. 3 vols. Stuttgart-Bad Cannstatt: Frommann-Holzboog, 1976.

Schmit, Roger. *Husserls Philosophie der Mathematik: Platonische und konstruktivische Momente in Husserls Mathematik Begriff*. Bonn: Bouvier, 1981.

Schoen, Henri. *La Métaphysique de Herman Lotze ou la philosophie des actions et des réactions réciproques*. Paris: Fischbacher, 1902.

Schoenflies, Arthur. "Über logischen Paradoxien der Mengenlehre." *Jahresbericht der deutschen Mathematiker Vereinigung* 15 (January 1906): 19–26.

Scholz, Heinrich. *Concise History of Logic*. New York: Philosophical Library, 1961.

————. "Review of Quine's *Mathematical Logic*." *Zentralblatt für Mathematik* 44 (1952): 247–48.

————. "Verzeichnis des wissenschaftlichen Nachlasses von Gottlob Frege." In Schirn (ed.), Vol. 1: 86–103.

————, and Friedrich Bachmann. "Der wissenschaftliche Nachlass von Gottlob Frege." *Actes du Congrès International de Philosophie Scientifique, Paris 1935*. In *Histoire de la logique et de la philosophie scientifique*. Paris: Hermann: 24–30.

Schröder, Ernst. *Vorlesungen über die Algebra der Logik*. Leipzig: Teubner, 1890–1895.

Schuhmann, Karl. "Forschungennotizen über Husserls Entwurf einer Vorrede zu den logischen Untersuchungen." *Tijdschrift voor Filosofie* 34 (1972): 513–24.

————. *Husserl-Chronik*. The Hague: Nijhoff, 1977.

————, and Barry Smith. "Against Idealism: Johannes Daubert vs. Husserl's *Ideas I*." *Review of Metaphysics* 38, 4 (June 1985): 763–93.

Searle, John R. "Russell's Objections to Frege's Theory of Sense and Reference." *Analysis* 18 (1957): 137–43.

Sebestik, Jan. "Bolzano et Brentano: Deux sources autrichiennes du Cercle de Vienne." *Fundamenta Scientiae* 5, 3–4 (1984): 219–35.

————. *Logique et mathématique chez Bernard Bolzano*. Paris: Vrin, 1992.

————. "Nicht-existierende Gegenstände und Strukturale Ontologie bei Twardowski." *Grazer Philosophische Studien* 35 (1989): 175–88.

_____. "Premiers paradoxes bolzaniens de l'infini." *Archives de Philosophie* 50, 3 (July–September 1987): 403–11.

Seebohm, Thomas et al., eds. *Phenomenology and the Formal Sciences*. Dordrecht: Kluwer, 1991.

Sellars, Wilfred. "Acquaintance and Description Again." *Journal of Philosophy* 46 (1949): 496–504.

_____. *Science and Metaphysics*. New York: Humanities, 1968.

Sepp, Hans Rainer, ed. *Edmund Husserl und die phänomenologische Bewegung*. Freiburg: Alber, 1988.

Skyrms, Brian. "Intensional Aspects of Semantical Self-Reference." In Martin (ed.): 119–32.

Sluga, Hans. "Frege and the Rise of Analytic Philosophy." *Inquiry* 18 (1975): 471–87.

_____. "Frege und die Typentheorie." *Logik und Logikkalkül*. Freiburg: Käsbauer and von Kutschera (eds.), 1962: 195–209.

_____. *Gottlob Frege*. London: Routledge, 1980.

Sluga, Hans. "Semantic Content and Cognitive Sense." In Haaparanta and Hintikka (eds.): 47–64.

Smith, Barry. "Acta cum fundamentis in re." *Dialecta* 38 (1984): 157–78.

_____. *Austrian Philosophy, the Legacy of Franz Brentano*. La Salle IL: Open Court, 1994.

_____. "Frege and Husserl: The Ontology of Reference." *Journal of the British Society for Phenomenology* 9, 2 (May 1978): 111–25.

_____. "Husserl, Language and the Ontology of Act." *Speculative Grammar, Universal Grammar and Philosophical Analysis of Language*. D. Buzzetti and M. Ferriani (eds.), Amsterdam: John Benjamins, 1987: 143–65.

_____. "Logic and the *Sachverhalt*." *Monist* 72, 1 (January 1989): 52–69.

_____. "Logic and Formal Ontology." In J. N. Mohanty and W. McKenna (eds.): 31–68.

_____. "Logic, Form and Matter." *Proceedings of the Aristotelian Society*, sup. Vol. 55 (1981): 47–63.

_____. "On the Cognition of States of Affairs." *Speech Act and Sachverhalt: Reinach and the Foundations of Realist Phenomenology*. Dordrecht: Nijhoff, 1987: 189–225.

_____. "On the Origins of Analytic Philosophy." *Grazer Philosophische Studien* 34 (1989): 153–73.

_____. "Phänomenologie und angelsächsische Philosophie." *Philosophischer Studien* 34 (1989): 153–73.

_____. "The Soul and Its Parts: A Study in Aristotle and Brentano." *Brentano Studien* 1 (1989): 75–88.

_____, ed. *Parts and Moments, Studies in Logic and Formal Ontology*. Munich: Philosophia, 1982.

_____, and Kevin Mulligan. "Mach and Ehrenfels: The Founda-
tions of Gestalt Theory." *Foundations of Gestalt Theory*, B. Smith
(ed.). Munich: Philosophia, 1988: 124–57.

_____, and David W. Smith, eds. *The Cambridge Companion to
Husserl*. Cambridge UK: Cambridge University Press, 1995.

Smith, David W., and Ronald McIntyre. *Husserl on Intentionality*.
Dordrecht: Reidel, 1982.

_____. "Intentionality via Intensions." *Journal of Philosophy* 68:
541–61.

Smullyan, Arthur. "Modality and Description." *Journal of Symbolic
Logic* 13: 31–37.

Sobocinski, B. "L'analyse de l'antinomie russellienne par Lesniewski.
iv: La correction de Frege." *Methodos* 1 (1949): 94–107, 220–28,
308–16.

Sokolowski, Robert. "Displacement and Identity in Husserl's Phenomenology." Paper given at the Husserl Archives in Leuven Belgium, September 1988.

_____. "Exorcising Concepts." *Review of Metaphysics* 40, 3
(March 1987): 451–63.

_____. *The Formation of Husserl's Concept of Constitution*. The
Hague: Nijhoff, 1970.

_____. "Husserl and Frege." *Journal of Philosophy* 84, 10 (Octo-
ber 1987): 524–28.

Solomon, Robert. "Sense and Essence in Frege and Husserl." *Analytic Philosophy and Phenomenology*. H. Durfee (ed.). The Hague:
Nijhoff, 1976: 31–54.

Spiegelberg, Herbert. *The Context of the Phenomenological Movement*. The Hague: Nijhoff, 1981.

_____. "Remarks on Findlay's Translation of Husserl's *Logical In-
vestigations*." *Journal of the British Society for Phenomenology* 3,
2 (May 1972): 195–96.

_____. *The Phenomenological Movement*. The Hague: Nijhoff, 3rd
ed., 1982 (1960, 1965).

Strawson, Peter. "Concepts and Properties in Predication and Copu-
lation." *The Philosophical Quarterly* 37, 149: 402–6.

_____. "On Referring." *Mind* 59 (1950): 320–44.

Stroud, Barry. "The Physical World." *The Aristotelian Society* 87, 15
(1986–1987): 263–77.

_____. "Quine's Physicalism." *Logic, Words and Objects: Perspec-
tives on the Philosophy of W. Quine*. Gibson and Barret (eds.).
Oxford: Blackwell, 1989.

Sylvan, Richard Routley. "Radical Pluralism: An Alternative to Realism, Anti-Realism and Relativism." *Relativism and Realism in Science*. Nola (ed.). Dordrecht: Kluwer, 1998: 253–91.

_____, and G. G. Priest. "On Paraconsistency." Privately circulated.

Thiel, Christian. *Sense and Reference in Frege's Logic*. Dordrecht: Reidel, 1968.

Tieszen, Richard. "Frege and Husserl on Number." Paper given at the APA Central Division Meeting, March 1989.

————. "Gödel's Philosophical Remarks on Logic and Mathematics." *Mind* 107, 425 (January 1998): 219–32.

————. "Kurt Gödel and Phenomenology." *Philosophy of Science* 59 (1992): 176–94.

————. *Mathematical Intuition: Phenomenology and Mathematical Knowledge*. Dordrecht: Kluwer, 1989.

Tragresser, Robert. *Husserl and Realism in Logic and Mathematics*. Cambridge: Cambridge University Press, 1984.

————. *Phenomenology and Logic*. Ithaca NY: Cornell University Press, 1977.

Treder, Hans Jürgen. "Zum Kontinuumsbegriff bei Bolzano." *Sitzungsberichte der Akademie der Wissenschaften der DDR Gesellschaftswissenschaften* 6/G (1982): 24–27.

Trendelenburg, Adolf. "Über Leibnizs Entwurf einer allgemeinen Charakteristik." *Historische Beiträge zur Philosophie*. Vol. 3. Berlin: Bettge, 1867: 1–48.

Tugendhat, Ernst. "The Meaning of 'Bedeutung' in Frege." *Analysis* 30 (1970): 177–89.

Twardowski, Kasimir. *Zur Lehre vom Inhalt und Gegenstand der Vorstellungen*. Munich: Philosophia, 1982 (1894).

van Heijenoort, Jan, ed. *From Frege to Gödel: A Source Book in Mathematical Logic, 1879–1931*. Cambridge: Harvard University Press, 1967.

Vuillemin, Jules. "L'élimination des définitions par abstraction chez Frege." *Revue Philosophique* 156 (1966): 19–40.

————. *Leçons sur la première philosophie de Russell*. Paris: Colin, 1968.

Wang, Hao. *Beyond Analytic Philosophy*. Cambridge: M.I.T. Press, 1986.

————. *From Mathematics to Philosophy*. London: Routledge and Kegan Paul, 1974.

————. *A Logical Journey, From Gödel to Philosophy*. Cambridge: M.I.T. Press, 1996.

————. *Reflections on Kurt Gödel*. Cambridge: M.I.T. Press, 1987.

Weingartner, Paul. "Die Fraglichkeit der Extensionalitätsthese und die Probleme einer intensionalen Logik. In Haller (ed.).

Welton, Don. *The Origins of Meaning*. The Hague: Nijhoff: 1983.

Whitehead, Alfred North. *An Introduction to Mathematics*. Oxford: Oxford University Press, 1958 (1911).

Wiggins, David. "Frege's Problem of the Morning Star and the Evening Star." In Schirn (ed.), Vol. 2: 221–55.

_____. "The Sense and Reference of Predicates: A Running Repair to Frege's Doctrine and a Pleas for the Copula." In Wright (ed.): 126–43.

Willard, Dallas. "The Absurdity of Thinking in Language." *Southwestern Journal of Philosophy* 4, 1: 125–32.

_____. "Concerning Husserl's View of Number." *Southwestern Journal of Philosophy* 5, 3 (Fall 1974): 97–109.

_____. "Crucial Error in Epistemology." *Mind* 76 (October 1967): 513–23.

_____. "Expression and Assertions." *Journal of Philosophy* 66 (April 1969): 238–47.

_____. "Husserl on a Logic That Failed." *The Philosophical Review* 89, 1 (1980): 46–64.

_____. *Logic and the Objectivity of Knowledge*. Athens: Ohio University Press, 1984.

_____. "Perceptual Realism." *Southwestern Journal of Philosophy* 1, 3 (Fall 1970): 75–84.

_____. "Review of *Aufsätze und Rezensionen (1890–1910)*." *Journal of the British Society for Phenomenology* 12, 3 (October 1981): 275–77.

_____. "Why Semantic Ascent Fails." *Metaphilosophy* 14, 3–4 (July, October 1983): 276–90.

Wittgenstein, Ludwig. *Briefwechsel*. Frankfurt: Suhrkamp, 1980.

_____. *Letters to C. K. Ogden*. Oxford: Blackwell, 1973.

_____. *Tractatus Logico-Philosophicus*. London: Routledge and Kegan Paul, 1981 (1922).

Wright, Crispin. *Frege's Conception of Numbers as Objects*. Aberdeen: Aberdeen University Press, 1983.

_____, ed. *Gottlob Frege: Tradition and Influence*. Oxford: Blackwell, 1984.

Wußing, Hans. "Bernard Bolzano und die Grundlegung der Analysis." *Sitzungsberichte der Akademie der Wissenschaften der DDR Gesellschaftswissenschaften* 6/G (1982): 28–33.

Zalta, Edward. *Intensional Logic and the Metaphysics of Intentionality*. Cambridge: M.I.T. Press, 1988.

Zermelo, Ernst. "A New Proof of the Possibility of a Well-ordering." In van Heijenoort (ed.): 183–98.

_____. "Memorandum of a Verbal Communication from Zermelo to Husserl." In Husserl's *Early Writings*: 442.

INDEX